Wig Making and Styling

Wig Making and Styling

A Complete Guide for Theatre & Film

Martha Ruskai

Allison Lowery

ELSEVIER

AMSTERDAM • BOSTON • HEIDELBERG • LONDON

NEW YORK • OXFORD • PARIS • SAN DIEGO

SAN FRANCISCO • SINGAPORE • SYDNEY • TOKYO

Focal Press is an imprint of Elsevier

Focal Press is an imprint of Elsevier
30 Corporate Drive, Suite 400, Burlington, MA 01803, USA
The Boulevard, Langford Lane, Kidlington, Oxford, OX5 1GB, UK

Main cover photograph by Akin Abayomi, Dreadheadphoto.com. Model: Kelly Jackson

Notices
Knowledge and best practice in this field are constantly changing. As new research and experience broaden our understanding, changes in research methods, professional practices, or medical treatment may become necessary.

Practitioners and researchers must always rely on their own experience and knowledge in evaluating and using any information, methods, compounds, or experiments described herein. In using such information or methods they should be mindful of their own safety and the safety of others, including parties for whom they have a professional responsibility.

To the fullest extent of the law, neither the Publisher nor the authors, contributors, or editors, assume any liability for any injury and/or damage to persons or property as a matter of products liability, negligence or otherwise, or from any use or operation of any methods, products, instructions, or ideas contained in the material herein.

Library of Congress Cataloging-in-Publication Data
Ruskai, Martha.
  Wig making and styling: a complete guide for theatre and film / Martha Ruskai, Allison Lowery.
     p. cm.
  Includes index.
  ISBN 978-0-240-81320-2
  1. Theatrical wigs. I. Lowery, Allison. II. Title.
  PN2069.R97 2010
  792.02'6—dc22   2009042441

British Library Cataloguing-in-Publication Data
A catalogue record for this book is available from the British Library.

ISBN: 978-0-240-81320-2

For information on all Focal Press publications
visit our website at *www.elsevierdirect.com*

10   11   12   13   14   5   4   3   2   1

Printed in China

This book is dedicated with gratitude to Lenna Kaleva

Table of Contents

Acknowledgments   ix

Chapter 1 Wig-Making Terms, Tools, and Techniques   1

Glossary of Wig and Hair Terms   1
Wig-Making Tool Kit   8
Wig Styling Tool Kit   10
Hairpins and Clips   11
Rollers/Curlers   12
A Well-Equipped Wig Area   12
Handling a Wig   15
   Blocking a Wig   15
   Blocking Hard-Front Wigs   15
   Blocking Lace-Front Wigs   16
Basic Hand Sewing Stitches   17

Chapter 2 Wig-Making Basics: Learning to Ventilate   19

Ventilating Needles and Holders   19
Loading Your Needle   20
Wig-Making Laces and Nets   20
   Fronting Laces   20
   Back/Foundation Laces   21
   Other Wig-Making Materials   22
The Direction and Stretch of the Lace   23
Types of Hair   23
Basic Wig-Knotting/Ventilating Technique   24
   Double Knotting   27
   Ventilating Positions   28
   Hair Density and Ventilating Patterns   29
   Ventilating Direction   30
   Untying Knots   30
Color Blending   31
Sewing with Invisible Thread   32

Chapter 3 Taking Accurate Measurements   35

Proper Head Measurements   35
   Transferring Head Measurements to a Block   39
Plastic-Wrap Head Tracings   41
Padding Out a Block with a Plastic Tracing   44

Chapter 4 Facial Hair   47

Creating the Pattern for the Facial Hair Piece   47
Adding Texture to the Hair   49
Individual Hairpiece Characteristics   53
   Eyebrows   53
   Mustaches   54
   Sideburns   55
   Beards and Goatees   56
   Cutting and Styling the Facial Hair   58
   Applying the Facial Hair   61
   Removing the Facial Hair   62

Chapter 5 Fronting and Other Adaptations of Commercial Wigs   63

Types of Fronts   63
The Human Hairline   65
Changing the Hairline   68
Building the Fronts   68
   Variation 1   69
   Variation 2   69
   Variation 3   69
Truing the Hairline   69
Lace Direction and Hair Growth Direction   70
Quick Front: A Step-by-Step Example   74
Standard Front   75
Deep Fronts   78
   Deep Front Variation 1   78

Variation 2   78
Variation 3   78
Mini Fronts   79
Silk Blenders   79
Nape Lace   81
Piecing Together Wigs   83

Chapter 6 Building a Wig from Scratch   87

Types of Foundations   88
Building a Circumference-Band Foundation   89
   Vegetable Net & Caul Net/Circumference Band/Right-Side-Out/Hand Sewn   89
   Variations on Circumference Band Foundations   93
   Variations on Nape-Piece Foundations   98
Variations on One-Piece Foundations   102
   Notes About Adding Hair   102
Parts, Crown Swirls, and Cowlicks   103
Miscellaneous Foundations   104
   Balding Wigs   105
   Fringes   107
Summary   108

Chapter 7 Partial Wigs, Toupees, and Hairpieces   109

Toupee   109
Graying Temple Pieces   110
Pull-Throughs   110
Falls   111
   Type 1   111
   Type 2   112
   Type 3   112
   Type 4   113
Switches   113
Kabuki-Inspired Lion Wig   114

Full-Bottom Wigs 115
Making Custom Weft 115

Chapter 8 Wig Application and Removal 119

Hair Prep 119
Long Hair 119
Short Hair 121
How to Hold and Put on a Lace-Front Wig 123
Applying Hard-Front Wigs and Falls 125
Removing Wigs After a Performance 126
A Word About Quick Changes and Tap
Dancing 127

Chapter 9 Wig Styling Techniques 129

Elements of a Hairstyle 129
Straight Hair 130
   Wetting and Drying 130
   Flat-Ironing and Roller Setting 130
   Steaming the Hair 131
Wavy Hair 132
   Finger Waves/Water Waves 132
   Marcel Waves 134
   Pin curls 136
   Waving and Crimping Irons 138
Curly Hair 139
   Roller Setting 139
   Roller Setting: Ringlets/Sausage Curls 142
   Roller Setting: Spiral Rolling
   Techniques 143
   Medusa Set 145
Braids 146
   The Standard Basic Braid 147
   French Braids 148
   Reverse French Braid 148
   Rope Braids 148
   Herringbone Braids 149
Dreadlocks 149

Chapter 10 Creating a Hairstyle 151

Break the Hairstyle Down into Sections 151
Understand the Hairstyle 152
Interpreting Research 152
Draw Your Setting Pattern 154
Set Your Wig 155
   Comb Out the Set 155
Teasing and Stuffing 156
Wire Frames 157
Styling Men's Wigs 159
Wig Setting and Styling Tips 160
From Set to Style: Examples 162
   Example 1: Cosette in *Les Miserables* 163
   Example 2: 1930s Hollywood Movie-Star
   Look 164

Chapter 11 Choosing, Cutting, Coloring, and Perming the Hair 165

Dyeing Wigs and Wig Fibers 167
   Universal Hair Color Systems 167
   American Cosmetology Hair Level
   System 167
   Types of Hair Color Products 167
   Dyeing Protein Fibers 169
   Using Fabric Dyes 169
   Preparing Hair Bundles for Dye 170
   Dyeing Synthetic Fibers 171
Perming Wigs and Wig Fibers 172
Cutting Wigs 173

Chapter 12 Hair that Isn't Hair: Wigs Made from Other Materials 175

Bases and Foundations 176
Fosshape™ Bases 178
Other Types of Bases 179
Covering the Cap 180
Building a Structural Support Frame 180

Combining Hair and Non-Hair Materials 182
Example of the Step-by-Step Process of
Creating an Unusually Shaped Wig 183
Gallery of Non-Hair/Fantasy Wigs 186

Chapter 13 How to Get a Show into Production 189

Analyzing and Understanding the Play 189
   Forms of Drama 190
   Basic Plot Structure 190
   Scene Breakdowns 191
Organizing Your Show Notebook 193
Character Design 194
Group Relationships 195
Designing an Overall Look for a
Production 196
Budgeting for a Production 197
Wig Jobs and How to Get Them 198
Charging for Your Work 200

Chapter 14 Care and Maintenance of Wigs 201

Cleaning Wig Laces 201
Cleaning Facial Hair 203
Touching up a Wig 204
Washing Wigs 205
   Washing the Wig off the Block 206
   Washing the Wig on the Block 208
Storing Your Wigs 209
   Storage Systems 210

Subject Index 213

Acknowledgments

Acknowledgments go out to:

Stephanie Williams Caillabet; the University of Texas Department of Theatre and Dance; Texas Performing Arts, especially the costume shop; Fletcher Opera Institute; the University of North Carolina School of the Arts, especially the Dance Costume Department; the Blanton Museum of Art; the Alabama Shakespeare Festival; Pennsylvania Shakespeare Festival and deSales University; Parkway United Church of Christ; Wake Forest University Baptist Medical Center; Linda Pisano, Lara Southerland Berich, Robbie Stanton, Mark Rampmeyer, Jennifer Mooney Bullock, Caitlyn Thomson, Kevin McCullom, and the Producing Office for *West Side Story*; Opera Carolina; Bradley M. Look; Amanda French; photographers Mark Rutkowski, Will Willner, Amitava Sarkar, Lee A. Butz, Ken Grant, and Akin Abayomi; Susan Mickey; James Glavan; Kelly Yurko; Christina Tollefson; Frederic Burleigh; Bill Brewer; Cheryl Thomas; Rita Freimanis; James Allbritten; Sam Flemming; Patricia Mueller; Casey Gallagher; Lisa Higgins, Nancy Dickson; Laura Horowitz; Patricia Wesp; Darren Jinks; all of the performers and models who generously allowed us to use their images and wore their wigs with such panache; Ray, Martha, and Scott Lowery; Lois Melina; Beth Ruskai; the Wednesday Whistling Women; and most importantly, the students and alumni who continue to inspire us and teach us, especially Tammy Potts-Merritt, Tera Willis, Kara Meche, Christina Grant, Anna Fugate, Kaylan Paisley, Scott Darby, Sarah Baloche Redding, Sarah Lankenau, Jessica Gambardella, Elisa Solomon, Jessica Mills, Chelsea Bunn, Jenny Valentine, Beauty Thibodeau, Nichole Annis, Sarah Shade, Adam Ulrich, Heather Koslov, Tiffany Knight, Carrie Lynn Rohm, Amanda Ramirez, Ming-yen Ho, Joshua Conyers, Natalie Maynard, Michael Ferguson, and Renee Horner.

CHAPTER 1

Wig-Making Terms, Tools, and Techniques

Before you can begin your quest to become a wig expert, you must learn some of the basic lingo and assemble the proper tools. In this chapter, we have provided an extensive glossary of hair wig terms. Familiarize yourself with these definitions before beginning to work on your wig-making and wig-styling skills. We will also discuss what tools are essential for wig making and styling and the different types of tools used. We will also go over different types of hairpins and brushes and when to use each, as well as a few basic techniques for handling a wig.

GLOSSARY OF WIG AND HAIR TERMS

There are many different terms used in wig making and styling. It is really helpful to know these terms before beginning work on your wig. Reading through these terms will help you understand many of the explanations in the rest of this book.

3/4 Wig

A type of wig that is meant to sit a few inches back from the wearer's hairline. The front of the wearer's own hair is then brushed back over the front of the wig in order to conceal the edge and make the wig look natural. 3/4 wigs are usually best if they are a very good color match to the wearer's own hair color.

Afro

A hairstyle popularized in the 1960s and 1970s. Many African-Americans let their hair grow out in its natural, tightly curled texture. The hair was then picked out with a comb to form a round shape or silhouette.

Alopecia

A medical condition that causes the patient to lose their hair; the hair loss can be partial or total.

"Amazon" Pins

Large, heavy hairpins that are used to pin wigs onto the wearer's head. They are often sold as "three-inch hairpins." These pins are best used for pinning heavy wigs that require extra support or for pinning on heavy hats.

Angora/Mohair

The fine silky hair from either an angora goat or rabbit. This hair ties into very small knots and is often used for the fronts of film wigs.

Backcombing

Another term for teasing hair. The hair is combed down towards the scalp in order to create more volume.

Beehive

A hairstyle that became popular in the 1960s. The hair was teased, sprayed, and smoothed into a cone shape that resembled a beehive.

Blocking A Wig

The act of securing a wig to a wig block so that wig is ready to be worked on.

Blocking Pins

Round-headed pins, usually called quilter's pins, that are used to secure the wig to the wig block.

Blocking Tape

A strip of ribbon, bias tape, hem tape, or twill tape that is used to hold the lace edge down flat when blocking a lace-front wig.

Blunt Cut

A haircut in which all of the hair is cut to one equal length.

Boardwork

The European term for the art of wig making.

Bob

A haircut in which all of the hair is cut to chin length. This hairstyle became very popular in the 1920s.

Cascade

A type of hairpiece, usually rectangular in shape, that consists of rows of curls that "cascade" down.

Caul Net

A type of wig-making net that is characterized by its large, open, diamond-shaped holes. It is often used in wig foundations when the wig needs to have a little stretch or where the wig needs to be easily pinned through. Also called *cawl net, cowl net.*

Chignon

A roll of hair worn at the nape of the neck.

Chin Block

A type of wig block that is specially made for building, styling, and cutting on facial hair. They are shaped like a chin and are made of either wood or canvas stuffed with sawdust (Figure 1-1).

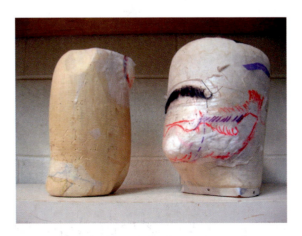

Figure 1-1 Examples of two different kinds of chin blocks.

Chin Tuft

A name for the small, usually triangular patch of hair that grows just beneath the lower lip. Also called a *soul patch* or *French dot.*

Cleaning the Lace

The act of cleaning the glue and makeup residue off of a lace-front wig or facial hair piece.

Clippies

A term for small, hinged hair clips that are used as a styling aid. They can have either one or two prongs. Also called *roller clips.*

Cornrows

A style of hair where the hair is divided into sections and braided into small braids that sit very close to the scalp.

Crepeing Hair

The act of weaving hair through a set of strings and then boiling it so that it has a permanently frizzed texture.

Crepe Wool

Wool that has been through the crepeing process. It is often used for creating facial hair directly on the face.

Drawing Cards

A pair of cards used for organizing hair that is being used on a wig project. These cards keep the roots and tips of the hair organized and make it easy to transport the hair for a wig-making project (Figures 1-2, 1-3).

Dreadlock

A natural hairstyle that is formed when hair becomes matted and eventually twists itself into a column or "lock".

Duckbill Clip

A type of clip, used in styling, that is about three inches long and opens like a duck's bill to clamp onto the hair. Also known as an *alligator clip*.

End Papers

Also sometimes referred to as *end wraps*. They are precut pieces of tissue paper that are sold for wrapping the ends of hair when you are setting it on rollers. They keep the ends nice and smooth.

Fall

Any hairpiece with long, hanging hair.

Finger Shield

A type of metal thimble, worn on the middle finger of the nondominant hand, that is used when sewing materials on top of a wig block.

Finger Wave/Water Wave

A method of hairstyling where the hair is styled into waves using only wet hair, the fingers, and a comb.

Flat Iron

A type of curling iron that has two flat plates that the hair is pulled through in order to straighten it.

Fontange

A hairstyle that is made of curls that are piled high over the forehead. The term also refers to a tall headpiece that sits over the forehead. Named after the Duchess of Fontanges.

Foundation

A head-shaped base made of wig nets and laces that hair is attached to in order to make a wig (Figure 1-4).

Figure 1-2 A drawing card.

Figure 1-3 The drawing card opened so that the teeth are visible.

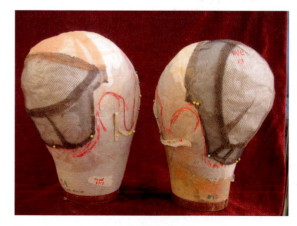

Figure 1-4 Two examples of a wig foundation.

Frontal Bone

The bone that makes up the forehead of the skull.

Fronting Lace

Any type of wig lace that is suitable for using at the hairline of a wig. The more closely the wig is going to be viewed, the finer and more delicate the fronting lace needs to be.

Galloon

A tightly woven silk ribbon that is used to reinforce the edges and interior structure of a wig foundation (Figure 1-5).

Goatee

A type of facial hair that consists of the hair in the chin area only, not a full beard.

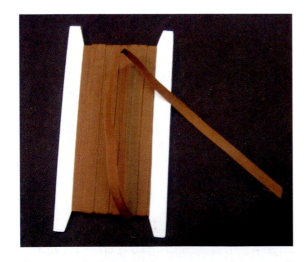

Figure 1-5 A card of galloon.

Growth Pattern

The unique set of directions that the hair grows in on an individual's head. They are specific and unique to each individual person.

Hackle

An extremely sharp metal comb that is used for detangling extra long hair and for blending several colors of hair to create a new color. A hackle usually resembles a bed of nails (Figure 1-6).

Haircutting Shears

Scissors made for cutting hair.

Hair Extentions

False hair that is attached directly to the wearer's head. This is done by gluing the hair directly to the wearer's hair, braiding the hair into the wearer's hair, or by sewing the hair onto cornrows braided from the wearer's own hair.

Figure 1-6 A hackle.

Hairpiece

Any piece of artificial hair that does not cover the entire head.

Hank of Hair

A bundle of loose hair.

Hard-Front Wig

A type of wig where the front edge is finished with rows of hair or material, resulting in a heavy, blunt edge. Most commercially purchased wigs are hard-front wigs.

Horse Hair

Either hair from the tail of a horse, used in wig making, or plastic fibers that are woven into a fabric braid, of which small pieces are sewn onto hats and headpieces to aid in pinning them on securely.

Human Hair

Hair from the head of a human.

Invisible Thread

A clear nylon thread that is used for sewing together wig foundations.

Lace-Front Wig

A wig that has had the original hard front cut off, replaced with fronting lace, and had its hairline knotted onto the lace. This term can also refer to a wig that has been custom made from scratch with a tied lace front.

Marcel Iron

A type of curling iron that is heated up in an oven, allowing it to get very hot (Figure 1-7).

Marcel Oven

An oven used to heat up metal curling tongs or irons. Prior to the invention of this oven, curling irons were heated in fires.

Marcel Wave

A type of wave styling method, introduced by French hairdresser Marcel Grateau, in which a curling iron is used to clamp waves in alternating directions into the hair, instead of wrapping the hair around the curling iron.

Figure 1-7 A selection of Marcel irons.

Medical Adhesive

A clear adhesive that is used to glue down wig lace when spirit gum is not a strong enough option.

Mohawk

A hairstyle in which the hair is shaved on both sides, leaving a strip of hair that runs down the center of the head from the forehead to the nape. The hair is often spiked up.

Monofilament Top

A type of wig made with a translucent, monofilament material on the top that the hair is knotted into. This fabric gives the appearance of a scalp underneath the hair. Also called *mono-top wigs*.

Mullet

A hairstyle in which the hair is cut short in the front and left longer in the back.

Nature Lace

A very fine and delicate type of fronting lace, made of clear nylon fibers with hexagonal holes. It is suitable for use on film wig fronts.

Net Lace

A type of wig-making lace that is made of opaque cotton fibers with hexagonal holes. It is used for either fronting lace (very large venues only) or as the lightest-weight foundation lace.

Occiputal Bone

The bone that makes up the back and base of the skull.

Parietal Bones

The pair of bones that form the top and sides of the skull.

Periwig

A British term for a wig, used especially in the seventeenth and eighteenth centuries. This term often refers to a men's wig that it pulled back into a queue.

Peruke

A French term for a wig, used especially in the seventeenth and eighteenth centuries. This term also often refers to a men's wig that is pulled back into a queue.

Pin Curl

A type of curl where the hair is rolled flat into a circle and secured with bobby pins or styling clips. Pin curls are used both as a styling technique and also as a way to prepare the hair for a wig to be put on over it.

Pompadour

A hairstyle where the hair is combed up high off of the forehead. It was named for the Marquise de Pompadour.

Postiche

Any piece of false hair.

Queue

A ponytail on a man's wig, especially in seventeenth- and eighteenth-century hairstyles. This style is also sometimes called a *tieback wig*.

Rat

A pad of hair that is used to stuff a hairstyle in order to add volume. These can be made by collecting hair and forming it into a pad. There are also premade rats available commercially for purchase.

Ringlet

A long, spirally curled section of hair.

Roots

The part of the hair that is attached to the scalp.

Shag

A haircut that is choppy and layered all over.

Skin-Top Wig

A type of wig that has a plastic top that has hair mechanically punched into it. This plastic gives the appearance of a scalp underneath the hair.

Spirit Gum

A type of adhesive, derived from tree sap, that is used to glue down the lace edges of a lace-front wig or facial hair piece.

Steaming A Wig

The act of applying steam to a synthetic wig in order to either straighten the hair fibers or set the curl into the hair fibers.

Stock Wig

A wig that is built to be used over and over again by a company or person or a wig that is already owned by a company.

Super Lace

A type of fronting lace, often used for theatrical wigs, and made of clear nylon fibers with hexagonal holes.

Switch

A false ponytail, often made with a loop on one end for easy attachment.

Synthetic Hair

Plastic fibers that are made to resemble hair. It is the cheapest and most versatile material that wigs are made of. Some other names for synthetic wig fibers include modacrylic, kanekelon, and elura.

Tendril

A small, thin, curling wisp of hair, often located around the face.

Thinning Shears

A special type of haircutting scissors in which one of the blades is notched, so that all of the hair is not cut (Figure 1-8).

Tips

The part of the hair shaft that is farthest away from the scalp; the ends of the hair.

Tonsure

The shaved crown of a monk's or priest's head.

Tracks

Small sections of hair that have been braided or cornrowed close to the scalp so that *wefts* of hair can be sewn onto them.

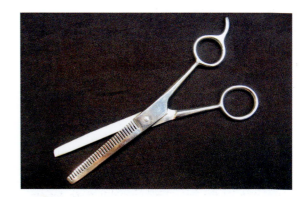

Figure 1-8 Thinning shears.

Toupee

A hairpiece meant to fill in the top section of a balding head.

Toupee Clips

Small rubberized snap clips that grab onto very small amounts of hair; often used to secure toupees.

Toupee Tape

Double-sided, skin-safe tape that is used to either hold on toupees or to hold down lace edges of hairpieces. Toupee tape is very shiny, so it should be used only to hold on lace-front wigs when there is no other choice.

Trichotillomania

A nervous condition that causes the sufferer to compulsively pull the hair out of their face and off of their head. Sometimes this condition also causes the sufferer to ingest the hair.

Ventilating

The act of knotting hair to wig lace in order to give the appearance that the hair is growing directly out of the head. Also called *knotting* or *tying* hair.

Ventilating Hook/Needle

A specially made hook that is shaped like a crochet hook and is used to grab the hair to be knotted onto a wig. Ventilating hooks come in sizes that refer to approximately how many hairs the needled will grab at one time (for example, a size 3 hook picks up three hairs).

Vegetable Net

A type of wig lace, made of cotton fibers, that is very heavy and has hexagonal holes. It is the best choice for building very sturdy foundations.

Virgin Hair

Hair that has never undergone any type of processing (perming, dyeing, etc.).

Waving Iron

A type of curling iron that sandwiches the hair between shaped plates in order to create a wave.

Weft

Hair that has been woven together on strings to form strips of hair. Weft is used to make hairpieces or to quickly fill in full wigs (Figure 1-9).

Wefting

The act of weaving the hair onto strings in order to form strips of hair that are used to create wigs and hairpieces.

Wig Bag

A bag, often made of black velvet or silk, that men in the seventeenth and eighteenth centuries wore over their powdered ponytails at the napes of their necks and secured with a bow. These came into fashion as a means of keeping the hair powder off of their expensive coats (Figure 1-10).

Figure 1-9 A piece of weft.

Figure 1-10 An example of a wig bag.

Wig Block

A head-shaped block, made of either wood or canvas stuffed with sawdust, that is used to mount wigs onto for styling or construction.

Wig Cap

A thin nylon cap that is used to flatten down, contain, and secure the hair underneath a wig.

Wig Clamp

A device that clamps to a table edge and has a post that a wig block sits on; it allows the wig to be worked on without having to worry about it falling off of the table.

Wig Dryer

A device used to dry wigs. These are usually large wooden boxes with a current of warm air flowing through them.

Wiglet

A type of hairpiece that consists of a small circle of hair mounted on a round base. They are used to fill in thin places in a hairstyle or to add a little extra volume in the style (Figure 1-11).

Wig Pins

Large hairpins that are used to pin through a wig in order to secure it to the wearer's head.

Figure 1-11 A wiglet.

Wig Points

Tiny headless nails that are used to hold a wig or wig-making materials to a wooden wig block (Figure 1-12).

Wig Prep

The act of preparing a person's hair as flat as possible to their head so that a wig may be put on over it.

Wig Stays

Small pieces of metal, plastic, or springs that give extra support to a wig in high-stress places. Common places to find wig stays in a wig are over each ear, on either side of the nape of the neck, and at the center front of the wig.

Wonder Lace

A type of wig lace that is made of clear nylon fibers with hexagonal holes. It is

Figure 1-12 Wig points.

heavier and shinier than super lace and can be used either for fronting lace or for making wig foundations.

Yak Hair

Hair from a yak that is used for wig making. It is slightly coarser than human hair. It is the most readily available source of white hair. The softest yak hair comes from the belly of the yak.

WIG-MAKING TOOL KIT

Wig making is the art of adapting existing wigs or making wigs from scratch. Because a lot of the work is similar to sewing, many sewing tools are used. Other tools are specific to building wigs, and must be purchased from wig suppliers. Many kinds of containers can be used to keep all of these supplies in—plastic tackle boxes are ideal, but

Figure 1-13 A wig maker's tool kit.

other options are lunchboxes, cosmetics cases, pencil cases, or shoeboxes. The most important thing is that your kit be lightweight and portable.

Items to include in your kit:

- **Ventilating needles.** The art of tying hair onto wig bases is called ventilating. This is done with tiny needles that have small barb on the end, like a fish hook or a crochet hook. Ventilating needles come in different sizes. The size refers to the number of average hairs that the needle will easily grab. Thus, a size three needle should pick up three average hairs.

- **Ventilating needle holders.** When ventilating, you hold your tool much like holding a pencil. Because of this, the needle must be inserted into some kind of holder. Holders are available in plastic, metal, and wood—what you choose is a matter of personal preference.
- **Something to keep your ventilating needles and holders in.** When you find a needle that you like, keep it stored with the holder. As the needles will snag or catch on everything else in your kit, you want to store them in something hard.
- **A drawing card.** This is for organizing and holding loose hair while you are working. These must be specially ordered from wig supply stores. If you are unable to find

Figure 1-14 Examples of ventilating needle holders.

Figure 1-15 Finger shield.

one, you can substitute two wire brushes sandwiched on top of each other.
- **Finger shield.** A finger shield is a special type of metal thimble used by wigmakers.
- **Small sharply pointed scissors.** You will need your scissors to have very sharp points so that you can carefully cut into tiny areas.
- **Seam ripper.**
- **Slant-tipped tweezers.**
- **Hand sewing needles in a variety of sizes.** It is good to have a mix of heavier needles and delicate needles.
- **Curved needle.**
- **Soft tape measure.**
- **Several different colors of thread.** Keep gray, beige, brown, and a bright color. It is good to have sturdy cotton thread for sewing on wig foundations. The bright color can be cotton or embroidery floss, as it will be used only for marking on wig foundations.
- **Invisible thread.** Clear nylon thread in a light to medium gauge that will be used to sew on fine laces.
- **Small needle-nosed pliers.** The kind that have built in wire cutters are the most useful; these can usually be found in the

Figure 1-16 Needle nosed pliers.

artificial flower department. Beading pliers are also a good choice, because they are small and can get into delicate areas of the wig easily.

- **Thimble.** You can use either a metal or leather thimble. Go with your personal preference.
- **Haircutting shears.** These do not have to be the expensive ones. You will want to have a pair of shears in your kit that are used only for cutting hair. Cutting other materials will dull your scissors, so keep a pair for hair only. Thinning shears are also nice to have in your kit.
- For craftier wig projects, it is useful to have a supply of **millinery wire** (fabric-covered wire that is sold by hat-making suppliers), **floral tape**, **buckram**, **Fosshape**, **felt hoods**, **sturdy thread**, and sturdy **craft scissors**. These materials will be further discussed in Chapter 12.

These items will give you a good start to building a wig-making kit. As you develop more skills, you may discover other tools that you would find useful. By all means, add them to your kit!

WIG STYLING TOOL KIT

A huge variety of different kinds of combs and brushes is available for purchase. There are a few basic kinds of tools are essential to wig styling that you should have on hand:

- **Rat-tail combs.** Useful for making clean separations in the sections of hair you are working on. They are also useful for fine detail work.

- **Large wooden brush with wire bristles.** Useful for brushing out large, thick sections of hair. Dog brushes are a good source for these.
- **Wide-toothed comb or pick.** Good for combing through hair when you want to keep a lot of texture, but still untangle the hair. Wide-toothed combs are also essential for gently combing out wet hair.

Figure 1-17 Rat-tail comb.

Figure 1-18 Large wooden brush.

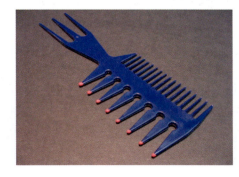

Figure 1-19 Wide toothed comb/pick.

- **Teasing/smoothing brush.** We often refer to this as the "magic brush," because it is good for so many jobs. Like the name indicates, it is good for teasing hair. It is also good for smoothing over sections of hair that have been teased and for smoothing curls around your finger.
- **Lifting/teasing pick.** This tool has a teasing comb on one end and a wire pick at the other. If you look closely, the comb end has little ridges on the teeth to allow you to pack the hair tightly when teasing. The other end allows you to lift more volume into already styled hair.

Figure 1-20 Teasing/smoothing brush.

Figure 1-21 Lifting/teasing pick.

HAIRPINS AND CLIPS

When working, you will need a wide variety of hairpins. Each hairpin has a different name and purpose:

- **Bobby pins.** This type of pin can be distinguished by its shape—one side is usually straight and one side is crimped. The sides almost meet at the open end, giving them a strong grip. These pins are used when you want a lot of hold—they hold pin curls tightly and add stability to hairstyles.
- **Hair pins.** A more open, U-shaped pin. They are used to hold small sections of hair or curls in place; these pins do not hold the structure of the style together. They hold better when they are holding together a coil or twist of hair.

- **Roller pin.** A large version of a pin that is similar to a bobby pin shape. They do not usually have the crimped side that a bobby pin has. They are designed to hold a curler in place once it has been rolled. They are also good for holding large sections of hair in place when styling.
- **Wig pin.** A large version of the hairpin. These pins are used to pin a wig onto the head of someone with pin curls underneath.
- **Amazon pin.** An extra large version of the hairpin. They are used to hold heavy wigs and hats on the head. Ballerinas also like these pins to hold their hair buns in place while dancing.

- **T-pin.** A T-shaped pin that is used when roller setting a wig on a wig block. They are long enough and strong enough to pin through a curler all the way into the wig block. Be careful with these pins—they snag on everything.
- **Duckbill clip.** These clips can be used for holding divided sections of hair. They can also be used to create finger waves in a hairstyle.
- **Clippies.** These are small clips that are used to hold small sections of hair while styling. These can also be used to hold styling-pin curls.

Figure 1-22 Bobby pin.

Figure 1-23 Hair pin.

Figure 1-24 Roller pin.

Figure 1-25 A hair pin, a wig pin, and an Amazon pin.

Figure 1-26 T-pin.

Figure 1-27 Duckbill or alligator clip.

Figure 1-28 Clippies.

Figure 1-29 Toupee clip.

- **Toupee clips.** These are small comb clips designed to grab very short or thin sections of hair. They can be used to attach wigs to people with very small amounts of hair. They come in a variety of sizes and colors. They are often rubberized.

ROLLERS/CURLERS

Simply put: you can never have too many rollers. There are many rollers with different purposes out there—it is good to buy new varieties when you see them. There are some basic rollers you want to have around. The plastic mesh rollers that have a metal spring inside are great—they are easy to pin through and it is easy to steam synthetic wigs through them. These rollers are available at most beauty supply stores. They often come with a little round brush inside; we usually remove these brushes before using the rollers. Plastic rollers work perfectly fine as well. We do not like to use Velcro® rollers on wigs— they tangle in the hair easily and also often create static electricity problems. For ease of reference, we often refer to

Figure 1-30 A selection of rollers.

rollers by size names, using the size of the opening at the end as the guide. You will need at least one dozen each of pencil-sized, dime-sized, nickel-sized, quarter-sized, and silver dollar-sized rollers. It is also very helpful to have very tiny rollers and perm rods on hand. Very large rollers (anything larger than silver dollar–sized) are good for adding just a little body and lift to straight wigs. You can also use things like straws and chopsticks as very tiny rollers in order to create a tight curl.

A WELL-EQUIPPED WIG AREA

There are a few other supplies and tools you will need to begin setting up your work area:

- **Work table.** Your work table must be a good height for you to work at, both when sitting and when standing. It also needs to have an edge that a wig clamp can be screwed onto.
- **Good lighting.** Natural light is preferable. If you do not have a space with windows, use a mix of fluorescent and incandescent light bulbs to provide a good balance of

Figure 1-31 The wig making and styling area at the University of Texas-Austin.

Figure 1-32 A selection of canvas and wooden head blocks.

Figure 1-33 Wig clamp.

light. It is also a good idea to have some swing arm lamps so that you can direct light exactly where you need it.

- **Adequate ventilation.** You will need ventilation when you are cleaning wigs with solvents.
- **Safety equipment.** Chemical-resistant gloves, a properly fitted respirator, a protective apron, and eye goggles are a must have when cleaning wig laces in order to be safe.

- **Head forms/blocks.** Wig making and styling both require some sort of sturdy head form to work on. Canvas wig blocks are the most versatile, but there are also blocks available in wood and foam. Styrofoam head blocks are really good only for storage once the wig is made and styled.
- **Wig clamp.** This is a special type of device that clamps onto the edge of the table; it has a post that fits the hole in the bottom of your head form. This way, you do not

have to worry about knocking the wig and wig block off the table every time you try to do something to it.

- **Blocking tape.** Whenever you are working on a wig, it should be properly blocked on the head form (see the end of this chapter). This is so that the delicate materials wigs are made from do not get damaged while you are working. For blocking tape, you can use bias tape, hem tape, or twill tape from a sewing store. Narrow ribbon or cloth shoelaces also work. Blocking tape should be between {1/4}″ and {1/2}″ wide.

- **Blocking pins.** Round-headed pins used to hold the blocking tape in place. Quilter's pins are ideal, because they are longer.

- **Corsage pins.** Longer, sturdier pins with round heads that are sold for pinning on corsages. These are great for holding a wig on a styrofoam block after it has been styled, especially when the wig has a lot of volume and a shorter pin would otherwise get lost.

- **Straight pins.** These are used whenever round head pins get in the way.

- **Magnetic pin cushions.** For all those pins.

- **End papers.** Papers that are sold in beauty supply stores that are used when rolling hair to help keep the ends of the hair neat.

- **Steamer.** Small hand-held steamers that are sold for steaming out clothes when traveling are great. If you buy a small steamer from a wig supply company, you can get one with a plastic tube attached that will allow you to get in to steam each individual curler. Larger industrial steamers also work.

- **Wig dryer.** There are wooden cabinets that are specifically sold for drying wigs. If you do not have access to a wig dryer, you can also use an old-fashioned bonnet hairdryer or make your own by cutting a hole for the nozzle of a hairdryer in a large box. If you use the homemade box method, please make sure you keep an eye on the materials as the drying is happening. Sometimes the hairdryer or the wig can overheat!

Figure 1-36 A commercially made wig dryer.

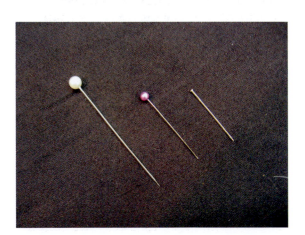

Figure 1-34 Corsage pin, blocking pin, straight pin.

Figure 1-35 A steamer sold specifically for working on wigs.

Figure 1-37 An example of a "homemade" wig dryer.

- **A variety of spray bottles filled with water.** Make sure your spray bottles have a spray setting—one with a stream only setting is not useful. You can also use your spray bottles to hold diluted styling products.
- **Styling products.** Especially setting lotion, gel, hairspray (both pump and aerosol), and pomade. Setting lotion is a thin lotion that is combed through hair before setting in order to help a style hold shape. Pomade is a thicker styling product that is used for more control in the hair, especially on short hairstyles.
- **Shampoo and conditioner.** It is nice to have shampoo and conditioner made especially for wigs, but it is absolutely not essential. Cheap drugstore shampoos and conditioners work just fine.
- **Towels.**
- **Tiny rubber bands.**
- **Hair elastics.**
- **Spirit gum.**
- **Chamois cloth or powder puffs for blotting wig glue.**
- **Spirit gum remover.**
- **Rubbing alcohol (99 percent).**
- **Cotton swabs.**
- **Wig caps in a variety of colors.**
- **Natural-bristle and wooden-handled stencil brushes or toothbrushes (used for cleaning laces).** Wig glue solvents will melt plastic stencil or tooth brushes.
- Multiple colors of **permanent markers and colored pencils**.
- **Crepeing and wefting sticks.** These sticks come in kits with weaving strings. These sticks are used to make both creped hair and wefted hair. Crepeing hair will be discussed in Chapter 4; wefting hair will be covered in Chapter 7.

HANDLING A WIG

Whenever you are handling a wig, make sure you do so carefully. Never grab a lace-front wig by the front lace—the lace is fragile and can tear pretty easily. Instead, always support any wig by holding it from the inside of the strongest part of the foundation. Do not grab, tug, pull on, or twist a wig.

BLOCKING A WIG

No matter what you are doing to a wig, make sure that it is securely pinned to the block. This process is called *blocking* a wig. Improper blocking will cause irreparable damage to your wig, so always be careful and vigilant about this!

BLOCKING HARD-FRONT WIGS

A *hard-front wig* is a wig that is in the condition that it came from a manufacturer. It is called a "hard front" because the front hairline of the wig is a thick, solid material that is bound. Its appearance is very dense. Because hard-front wigs are less delicate than lace-front wigs, they do not have to be blocked as carefully as lace-front wigs. Here's how to do it:

1. Position the wig on the block. Make sure that it is far back enough to look like it is sitting on the block the way it would sit on the wearer's head. Also check the position of the sideburn pieces and make sure they are even.
2. Place one blocking pin in the center front of the wig.

3. Place one blocking pin at the bottom of each sideburn piece.
4. Place one blocking pin at the bottom corner of each side of the nape of the neck.

BLOCKING LACE-FRONT WIGS

A *lace-front wig* is a wig that has either had the commercial front cut off and replaced with wig-making lace or a wig that has been made from scratch with wig-making lace in front. This lace is delicate, so it must be handled carefully in order to prevent the wig lace from stretching out of shape or ripping at the holes:

1. Position the wig on the block. Make sure that it is far back enough to look like it is sitting on the block the way it would sit on the wearer's head. Also check the position of the sideburn pieces and make sure they are even.
2. Place one blocking pin about an inch behind the front hairline of the wig.
3. Place one blocking pin just in front of each ear on the wig.
4. Place one blocking pin at the bottom corner of each side of the nape of the neck (Figure 1-38).
5. Get a piece of blocking tape and a blocking pin. Begin at the center front of the wig. Place the tape about a half-inch above the edge of the

Figure 1-38 Pinning the wig at the corner of the nape of the neck.

Figure 1-39 The blocking tape should cover the edge of the wig lace. The pins should be placed about a half an inch apart.

8. Continue working your way around the front lace, alternating from right to left. This will keep the tension evenly balanced on your lace. Continue pinning every half-inch, all the way around the sideburn area

lace. Slide it down until the edge of the lace is covered. Pin it squarely in the center of the blocking tape. Make sure you have actually pinned through not only the blocking tape, but also through the wig lace itself. (Figure 1-39)
6. Move a half-inch to the right of the center pin and repeat the process.
7. Move a half-inch to the left of the center pin and repeat the process.

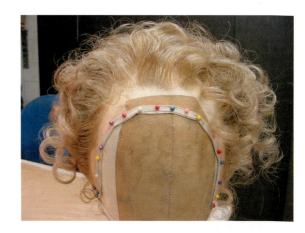

Figure 1-40 Properly blocked wig.

Figure 1-41 The wig lace, pinned all around the sideburn area.

and back up toward the ears (Figure 1-41). If there is excess blocking tape, pin it down so that you don't catch it with a brush, comb, or ventilating needle.

BASIC HAND SEWING STITCHES

When you are working with wigs, it is good to be familiar with a couple of basic sewing stitches. The two most useful are the whip stitch and the cross stitch hem stitch.

The whip stitch is used to join two pieces of fabric together. It is a diagonal stitch that can be done with either a single thread or a doubled thread. Follow these steps:

1. Thread your needle and knot it at the end.
2. Insert the needle diagonally through both layers of the fabrics you are joining together. Pull it through until it is tight.
3. Again, insert the needle diagonally through both layers of fabric. Pull it through tightly. Repeat until you reach the end of what you are sewing.
4. Securely knot off your thread and trim away the excess.

The whip stitch can be used to join pieces of a wig foundation together, to attach a piece of lace to a wig for fronting, or for sewing weft to a wig or hairpiece.

The cross stitch is traditionally used as a hemming stitch. In wig making, it is used to form a sort of casing to hold elastic in place and still allow the wig to stretch as it needs to. The steps are:

1. Thread your needle and knot the end of your thread.
2. The cross stitch is unusual in that although the stitches will move from left to right, your needle will actually be going into the fabric from right to left. Insert your needle in the fabric from right to left. Make a stitch {1/4}-inch in length. Pull your thread through.
3. Bring your needle over the top of whatever you are sewing and move left about an inch. Again, insert the needle into the fabric from right to left and make a stitch that is {1/4}-inch long. Pull your thread through.
4. Return to the bottom of whatever you are stitching over and move about an inch to the left. Make another right to left stitch and pull it through.
5. Continue to alternate top and bottom stitches while moving left along what you are sewing. When you reach the end, securely knot off your thread and trim away the excess.

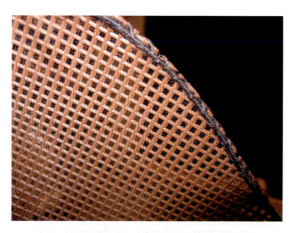

Figure 1-42 An example of millinery wire whip-stitched to plastic canvas.

Figure 1-43 An example of elastic held in place with a cross stitch.

CHAPTER 2 Wig-Making Basics: Learning to Ventilate

The most essential basic skill used to make a wig is *ventilating*—tying the knots of hair that will make up your hairline, wig, or facial hair piece. These knots will allow any wig or hair piece to look as though it is growing out of the wearer's skin. Before beginning to ventilate, you need to become a little more familiar with your tools.

VENTILATING NEEDLES AND HOLDERS

Ventilating needles/hooks come in a range of sizes. The size refers to the number of average hairs the hook will pick up. A size four ventilating hook will pick up approximately four hairs. The very small sizes of hook are labeled with zeros. This represents the very finest hook you can use. A double-zero (00) is a finer hook than a single-zero (0). There are different shapes to the curves and bends of needles as well.

It is impossible to tell by looking at the needle what size it is, so it is very important that you store them labeled by their size.

Once you develop more control with your hands and tools, you personally (not the needle size) will be better able to determine how many hairs you pick up. When you are first learning, it is better to let the hook help you pick up the correct number of hairs. Ventilating

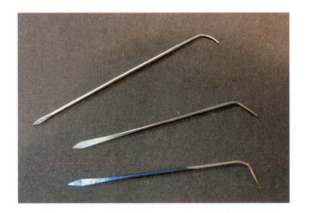

Figure 2-1 Notice the different curves and bends in the shape of different brands of needles.

holders are also available in a variety of sizes and materials. Plastic ones and metal ones are commercially available. It is possible to make wooden ones out of dowel rods about the size of a pencil. However, in order to do this, you will need the metal end that holds the needle off of a premade holder. What material you choose depends on what you like the feel of in your hand.

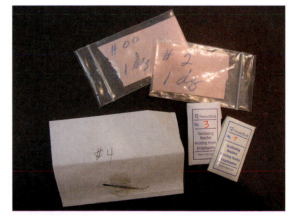

Figure 2-2 Different methods of storing ventilating needles by their size.

LOADING YOUR NEEDLE

1. Unscrew the metal end of your needle holder. The cross at the end will get wider as you do this. Do not unscrew the metal end so far that it comes off. If it does come off, however, simply screw it part way back on.

Figure 2-3 The cross at the end of the needle holder gets wider as it is unscrewed.

2. Once you have the metal end open wide enough, slide your needle down into the middle of the cross. It may take a couple of tries before you feel the needle slide all the way in. How far in you want your needle to be is a matter of personal preference. About three-quarters of an inch sticking out above the metal is a good length to start with.
3. Tighten the metal end until it is firmly gripping your needle.

Your needle is now ready for use!

Figure 2-4 Loading the ventilating needle.

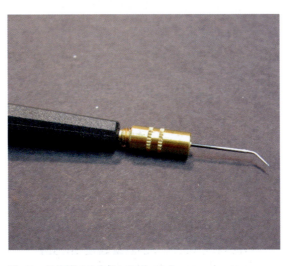

Figure 2-5 Properly loaded needle.

WIG-MAKING LACES AND NETS

There are several types of wig laces, and each has a specific purpose. The following nets and laces are shown with grain running from top to bottom of the page. Each square shown is 2 inches with a ruler guide for scale.

FRONTING LACES

1. **Fronting laces for stage.** Super lace (Figure 2-6) is DeMeo brothers brand name for fronting lace—a very fine lace used for the fronts of wigs. This lace is woven out of nylon. It is translucent and blends in with many skin tones; it can also be tinted with union dye (Rit or Tintex) or Design marker to match any skin tone or fantasy foundation colors perfectly. There are other brands of stage fronting laces made by other companies. Super lace is the most readily available in the United States.

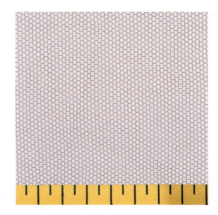

Figure 2-6 Super lace.

Figure 2-7 Film lace.

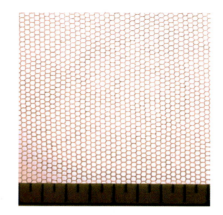

Figure 2-8 Back lace (Wonder Lace).

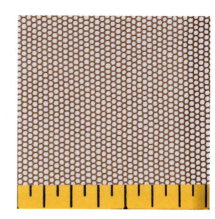

Figure 2-9 Vegetable net.

2. **Film lace (Figure 2-7).** The finest lace available used for the fronts of wigs. It is very similar to super lace, but it is more delicate and does not hold up as well to wear and tear. It is sometimes called nature lace and it is suitable for the fronts of film wigs.

BACK/FOUNDATION LACES

3. **Back lace.** (formerly known as opera lace). "Wonder Lace" (Figure 2-8) is the brand name used by DeMeo Brothers—it is a heavier translucent lace. This lace is used for the nape and crown sections of lightweight or light colored wigs. It can be easily identified by its high shine.

4. **Vegetable net (Figure 2-9).** A sturdy cotton lace. This lace is the heaviest used in wig making. It is used to make the backs and crowns of strong heavy wigs that will need to last for a long time. It is called "vegetable net"

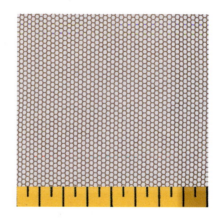

Figure 2-10 Net lace.

Figure 2-11 Caul net.

because it is made out of cotton, a vegetable fiber.

5. **Net lace (Figure 2-10).** Another variety of cotton lace. This lace is lighter in weight than vegetable net. It is a softer, more flexible alternative to vegetable net.

6. **Caul net (Figure 2-11).** An open-weave cotton/elasticized-blend lace. The lace is the easiest one to pin through, so it is most often used on

the crowns of wigs. The lace is easily identified by its large, diamond-shaped holes. This lace is not particularly strong and can be torn somewhat easily. Companies sometimes sell this lace under the name of *cawl net* or *cowl net*.

7. **Bobbinette (Figure 2-12).** The European version of caul net. It is less stretchy than the caul net sold by DeMeo Brothers. The spellings

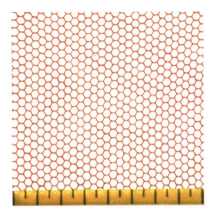

Figure 2-12 Bobbinet.

Figure 2-13 Silk gauze.

Figure 2-14 Galloon used on the nape edge of a foundation.

"bobbinette" and "bobbinet" are both used when referring to this product.

OTHER WIG-MAKING MATERIALS

1. **Silk gauze (Figure 2-13).** A specially made silk that is very tightly woven. It comes in white and must be dyed to match the skin of the wearer. After being dyed, it is still translucent and must be covered with makeup (crème makeup is recommended) in order for it to become opaque. Silk gauze can be used under other wig laces when the wearer's hair or pin curls would otherwise show through. It is used under parts, balding areas, and under hairlines where the wearer's hair shows through too much (usually when the performer has dark hair and the wig is much lighter). From stage distances, it blends in with the wearer's skin. Silk is not suitable for film use. Silk can

also be ventilated into directly, although this often results in bulkier knots.

2. **Galloon/silk ribbon (Figure 2-14).** Galloon is a tightly woven silk ribbon that is used for finishing the edges of a wig foundation. It can also be used to smooth out a seam between two joined pieces of lace.

3. **Monofilament ribbon (Figure 2-15).** This ribbon is used in the same manner as galloon to finish off the edges of a foundation. Instead of being opaque, it is a translucent ribbon that is more suitable for use in lighter-weight foundations with thinner hair.

4. **Stays (Figure 2-16).** Stays are small lengths of wire or springs that are used to give a wig extra support. They are flexible enough to be bent in order to make a wig conform to the shape of the wearer's head. You can buy specially made stays from a

Figure 2-15 Monofilament ribbon.

Figure 2-16 An assortment of stays.

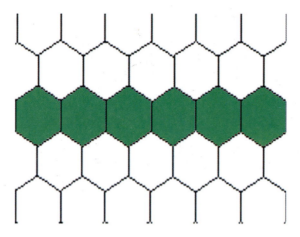

Figure 2-17 The "grain" of the lace running from side to side (horizontal grain).

wig supplier, or you can use commercially available collar stays. You can also make you own stays by folding a length of wire (floral wire and millinery wire are two good choices) over at each end and binding the middle with floral tape. Make sure there are no blunt ends of the wire exposed—you don't want to stab the person wearing the wig!

The net and lace manufactured specifically for wig making have the best combination of stretch, fineness, and durability. Whenever possible, use the real thing.

THE DIRECTION AND STRETCH OF THE LACE

Most wig laces are a form of a weave called *bobbinette*. Bobbinette is also found in theatrical scrim fabrics. Bobbinette is characterized by a hexagonal pattern. In plain fabric, the word "grain" is used to describe the lengthwise direction of the fabric. *Cross grain* is the term for the width of the fabric running from side to side and the term *bias* is used for the 45-degree diagonal. In a fabric with true grain, the lengthwise direction, or grain, has little or no stretch; the cross grain some stretch; and the bias significant stretch. In any bobbinette or wig lace, the term "cross grain" is not really accurate; however, the directions of bobbinette and wig lace do possess the same relative stretch characteristics and so the term "grain" is used when describing wig laces as well. (We hope that textile purists will forgive us for choosing to use "grain" over the more cumbersome phrase "lengthwise of the fabric.") To determine the "grain" of your lace, look for the direction where the holes of the lace line up in a row—that is the grain.

You can use the lace with the grain running either up and down (vertical grain) or side to side (horizontal grain). The diagonal/bias grain is much stretchier than the other two directions—if you use the bias grain, your piece will always bubble, gape, and generally not lay flat.

TYPES OF HAIR

There are five basic types of hair used in wig making:

1. **Human hair.** This refers to hair that is grown by a human being and cut off. Virgin human hair is hair that has never been processed in any way—no dyeing or perming ever. Human hair comes in many qualities, from top-of-the-line, very expensive cuticle hair to cheaper, coarser hair that has gone through more processing. Cuticle hair is hair in which the cuticle remains intact after the hair is processed. It is more expensive because it is finer, shinier, and it moves very realistically. The reason why finer hair is more desired, and thus more expensive, is because finer hair will make tinier knots when tied. This will make the hairline look more real. Strangely enough, many people think that hair in human hair wigs comes from dead people. This is not true! Human hair is also the best choice for making facial hair and short haired

wigs. The solvents used to clean wig glue out of facial hair will dissolve synthetic hair. It is a good choice for short-haired wigs because it will move more realistically than synthetic hair when it is cut short. Human hair comes in straight, curly, and wavy. There are ethnic differences in the shape of the hair shaft, resulting in the differences in hair texture. Most human hair that is commercially available has gone through some sort of processing. A lot of human hair is purchased from Asia. Because this hair is usually very dark in color, it must be processed into lighter colors. The pigment is stripped out and the hair is overdyed with the new color. This process damages the cuticle of the hair and makes each strand a little larger and coarser. It makes slightly larger knots than virgin hair.

2. **Synthetic hair.** This hair is made of plastic and is extruded through a machine to make the strands. There are many different brand names for synthetic hair: elura, kanekalon, and modacrylic are a few examples. Because synthetic hair will melt under high heat, it must be handled differently than human hair when it is being styled. Though synthetic hair used to be extremely fake-looking, the quality of synthetics is getting better every day. The hair now moves much more realistically and also comes in a wide range of both realistic and fantasy colors. It is much cheaper than human hair. Synthetic hair is an especially good choice for hairstyles that need to hold up under strenuous dancing or high humidity (outdoor theatres and musicals, for example). Synthetics are also an excellent choice for fantasy looks, due to the wide selection of colors and lengths available.

3. **Yak hair.** Hair from a yak. Yaks grow hair that is reasonably long in length. It is coarser than human hair. It is widely available in pure white; this is handy, because pure white human hair is rare. Hair from the belly of the yak is the finest and softest. Yak hair is a good choice for making wigs that have the powdered look of the eighteenth century. It can also be dyed nearly any color and is a good choice for short spiky looks. Yak hair is commonly used to make clown wigs.

4. **Mohair/angora.** Very soft fine hair from an Angora rabbit, or more likely, Angora goat. The hair shaft of angora hair is much thinner than that of human hair. It makes the most undetectable knots. Mohair/angora is most often used at the hairlines of the finest wigs, especially in film.

5. **Protein hair.** A man-made material that is manufactured from collagen and/or keratin, depending on the manufacturer. This hair can be heat-intolerant, but it dyes well and takes curl with a low-temperature iron. This type of hair is a relatively new development in the wig industry.

BASIC WIG-KNOTTING/ VENTILATING TECHNIQUE

You will begin practicing the art of ventilating on a small piece of lace (2 inches by 2 inches is a good place to start). Net lace is an excellent lace for learning to ventilate on, because it is sturdy and easily visible:

1. Securely pin down a piece of wig lace on top of a canvas block with straight pins. Pin every quarter of an inch around the edges so that the lace will be stable as you are knotting onto it.
2. Hold the ventilating hook and holder in your dominant hand (the hand you write with). Hold it as though it were a pencil (Figure 2-18).

Figure 2-18 Proper hand position for holding a ventilating hook.

3. Fold a small section of hair (twelve to fifteen hairs in your hand is a good number to start with) over at the root end so that you have a little less than two inches folded over (this is referred to as your "amount of turnaround") (Figure 2-19). Pinch the loop you have made tightly between the thumb and index finger of your other hand (Figure 2-20).

4. Slide the ventilating hook under a bar of your lace (Figure 2-21).

5. Bring the loop of hair close enough to the hook to catch a couple of hairs (Figure 2-22). Do not try to bring the hook to the hair—this will cause your lace to stretch or tear.

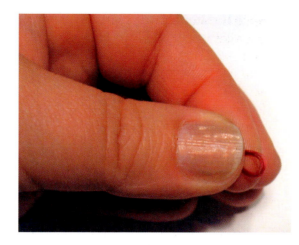

Figure 2-20 The loop of hair being held securely by the thumb. Note how little of the loop of hair sticks out past the finger.

6. After catching the hairs, pull the hair back under the bar (Figure 2-23). Make sure you keep enough tension in the hand holding the hair. Also, do not pull so far that the turned-over end of the loop of hair pulls free.

7. Slide the hairs off the barb of the hook. Slide the hook forward so that

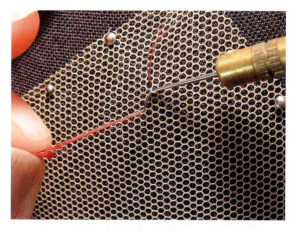

Figure 2-22 Catch a couple of hairs with the barb on the end of your ventilating hook.

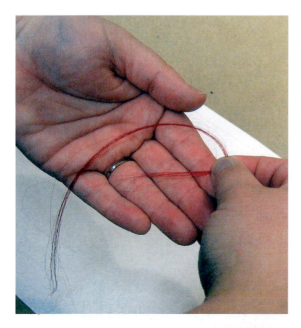

Figure 2-19 Folding over the top inch or two of the hair in order to create turnaround.

Figure 2-21 Slide the ventilating hook under a bar of the lace.

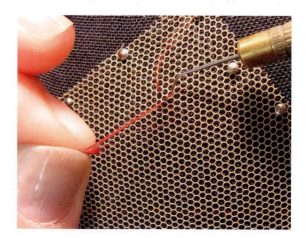

Figure 2-23 Pull the hairs you have caught with the hook back under the bar on the lace.

the loop of the hair rests in the curve of the needle (Figure 2-24).

8. Pull the hook, with the hair, back towards the hair in your hand. Wrap the hair in your hand over the top of the needle (Figure 2-25).

9. Turn the hook away from you so that it rests against the hair you just wrapped (Figure 2-26).

10. Pull the hair you just wrapped around the needle through the loop you made when you first began the knot (Figure 2-27).

11. Pull the hair partway through the loop and then tighten the knot (Figure 2-28). Pull the hair the rest of the way through.

Congratulations! You have made your first knot! Do not be discouraged if the knot is not tied properly the first few dozen times you try it. You will need to keep trying until you find the set of hand motions that is right for you. Pay careful attention to the amount of tension you are using to hold the hair. If there is not enough tension, your knot will be difficult to tie and probably end up loose. If you are using too much tension, your hand will start to cramp. Another thing to be aware of is getting all of the hairs through the loop in step 10. Sometimes, a hair or two may slip off of the ventilating needle as you are trying to pull it through the loop. This will result in a messy, spiky knot that is

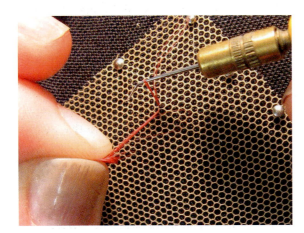

Figure 2-24 Slide the hair off of the bard on your needle and push the needle slightly forward so that the loop of hair rests in the curve of the needle.

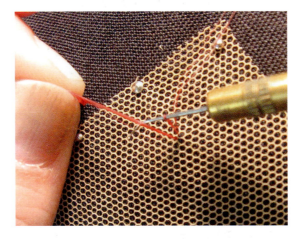

Figure 2-25 Wrap the hair in your hand over the top of the needle.

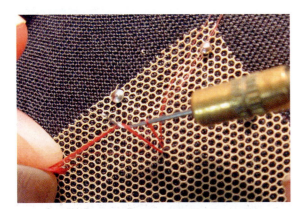

Figure 2-26 Turn the needle a half turn away from you so that it can catch the rest of the hair.

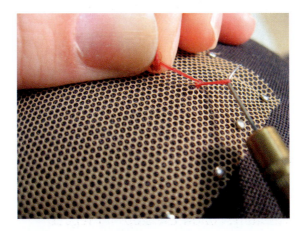

Figure 2-27 Pull the hair you have just caught with the needle through the loop of hair you have made.

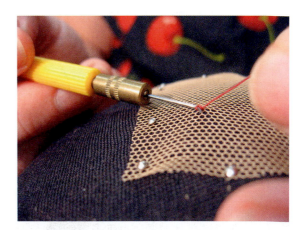

Figure 2-28 Pull the hair partway through the loop and tighten down the knot.

sometimes referred to as a "spider." If you find yourself getting frustrated, put your ventilating down and take a break for a few minutes. It will be easier to return to your project with a clear head.

Some things to remember:

- Always make sure you keep the roots and tips of the hair straight in your mind. Always tie the knot at the root end of the

Figure 2-29 An example of poorly tied knots.

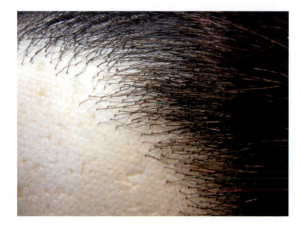

Figure 2-30 An example of well-tied knots.

hair. Use a drawing card to lay out your loose hair—this will hold your hair and keep it organized. Hair that has been cut off the head or thrown into a pile will become "mixed" hair. This means the roots and tips are all jumbled together. *Never attempt to make a wig with mixed hair!* The wig will always want to tangle. The cuticle of a strand of hair has ridges like the shingles on a roof. If the hair is laying in the proper direction, all of the shingles will be pointing the same direction, so the hair can lie smooth. If the hair gets mixed, the ridges or shingles will rub up against each other, causing the hair to tangle. Mixed hair can occasionally be used for facial hair, where texture would be a good thing. Otherwise, avoid mixed hair at all costs.

- As you work, think about where on the lace you are going to start ventilating and where you are going to stop. You always want to be working so that you are not trying to work underneath hair that you have already knotted. For example, when building a full wig, begin working at the nape of the neck and ventilate forward towards the front of the head. This way, you are always working on top of hair you have already put in, not underneath that hair.

DOUBLE KNOTTING

Sometimes you will need to tie a double knot when ventilating. The double knot is a stronger knot, but it is little more bulky, so choose when you use it carefully. Follow the steps for regular knotting listed above until you get to step 11. Instead of pulling the hair all the way through in step 11, do the following:

11. Pull the hair you just wrapped around the needle through the loop you made when you first began the knot. Pull the hair partway through the loop and then tighten the knot.
12. Pull the hook, with the old loop of hair still on the needle, back towards the hair in your hand. Wrap the hair in your hand over the top of the needle again.
13. Turn the hook away from you so that it rests against the hair you just wrapped. Pull that hair through the loop and then tighten the knot. Pull the hair the rest of the way through.

Use double knotting when ventilating hair onto caul net. Because this net has such an open weave, it is easier for the knots to become untied as time goes on. You can also use double knots when knotting hair under the bottom edge of the wig. These knots need to be

Figure 2-31 Turn the needle away from you to grab the hairs you are going to pull through the loop, just as you did when making a single knot.

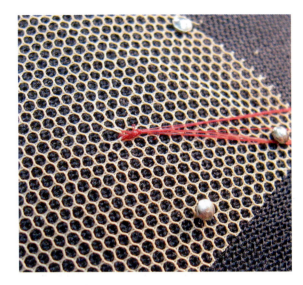

Figure 2-32 A finished double knot. Note how it is a bit bulkier than a single knot.

extra-strong and secure, because they will constantly be rubbing against the nape of the neck. Sometime you can use double knots to join two layers of lace together without sewing them together. Double knotting will also reappear when we discuss sewing with invisible thread. For videos demonstrating both single and double knotting, please visit the companion website to this book at http://booksite.focalpress.com/companion/Ruskai/wig/.

VENTILATING POSITIONS

Every wigmaker eventually finds their ideal position to work in—everyone has their favorite. Try a variety of positions until you find one that you can sit

comfortably in for several hours at a time. It is important to sit so that your lower back is supported and so that you do not have to hold your arms at awkward angles for an extended period of time. Also beware of hunching over

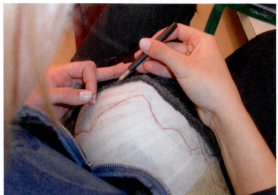

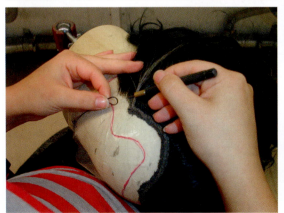

Figures 2-33–36 Examples of different body and hand positions used while ventilating.

your head block so much that your neck and shoulders start to ache.

Most wigmakers prefer to work at or near a table so that they can spread their tools out. Good light is a must. Lamps that clamp to a table and swing into different positions are ideal—you can place the light wherever you need it. Many prefer to work in a chair that has arms so that they can use their arms to prop the head block up between their body and the table (Figure 2-37).

Other people like to put the wig on a pillow in their lap (the pillow keeps the wig from rolling around). Still other wigmakers use specially made boxes with grooves cut in them to rest their wigs in. Some wigmakers find it useful to put their feet up on a box or stool to help balance the wig block on their lap.

Whatever position you choose, it is very important to get up, stretch, and

walk around every so often. This prevents stiffness and muscle cramps.

Another thing to experiment with is the direction in which you pull the hair. Many ventilators tie their knots with an arm motion that goes away from their body towards the front. Other ventilators pull their knots through to the side, and a few rare ventilators even work by pulling the knots towards their bodies. As you become more proficient at ventilating, you will begin to see how manipulating the direction you pull the hair through allows you to control the appearance of the hair. Different sections of hair grow in different directions; adapting your ventilating direction to match will result in a natural looking wig. See the following section for more information about how to control the direction of your knots.

HAIR DENSITY AND VENTILATING PATTERNS

When making a wig, it important to consider where the hair needs to be thick and where it needs to be thinner. Because there is great variety in human heads, you will need to be able to ventilate in different thicknesses and patterns. Whenever you get the chance, observe the heads of hair that are around you. Look at the hairlines, the swirls of hair at the crown, the cowlicks, the little fuzzy hairs around the face—all of these things can be applied to a wig. More information about hair growth

patterns and directions will be covered in Chapters 5, 6, and 7. As a beginning ventilator, you should develop a set of ventilating patterns to use:

1. **Single hair, every hole (Figure 2-38).** Practice tying a section of knots where you tie one hair into every hole. This produces a delicate section of hair that still has good coverage. Use this pattern close to the hairline of a wig. As you reach the very front of the hairline, you should start to thin the knots out to a single hair every other hole, and then a single hair every few holes. Practice tapering out your knots.
2. **Two or three hairs, checkerboard pattern (Figure 2-39).** This is a good pattern to use to fill in areas of wigs that still need to remain delicate, but not as delicate as a hairline. For example, use this pattern from an inch behind the hairline to back over the top of the head to the crown area.

Figure 2-37 Student Beauty Thibodeau balances her wig block between the work table and her body.

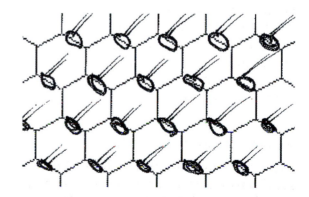

Figure 2-38 A diagram of a single hair, every hole pattern.

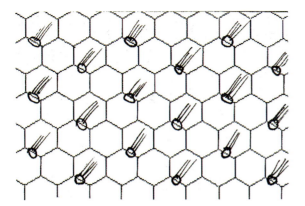

Figure 2-39 A diagram of a two/three hairs, checkerboard pattern.

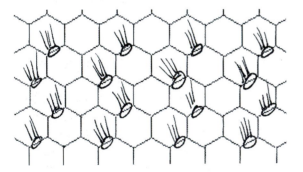

Figure 2-40 A diagram of a four or five hairs, two out of every three holes pattern.

3. **Four or five hairs, two out of every three holes (Figure 2-40).** Use this pattern to fill in the back of wig. The hair in the back is where you need more coverage, less fine detail. Knots in the back can be even bigger—anywhere from seven to ten hairs. Tying these large knots is sometimes referred to as "chunking hair in," because it is a fast way to get hair into an area of the wig that does not need to be delicate.

Keep in mind—these patterns are just meant to guide your work. Ventilating that is too mechanical and evenly spaced starts to look machine-made, which defeats the entire purpose of hand-making a wig! (This is especially true at the front hairline.) As you gain experience, your eye will develop and you will be able to see when your knots need to be more random.

VENTILATING DIRECTION

Look back over the ventilating patterns we have laid out. Notice how the direction that the hair falls in is controlled by tying the hair onto a certain bar that makes up the hexagon of the lace. For example, if you want the hair to fall down and to the right, always tie the hair on the lower right bar of the hexagon.

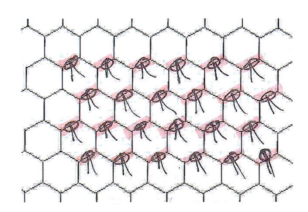

Figure 2-41 The ventilating direction is established by tying all of the hairs on the lower right bar of each hexagon.

UNTYING KNOTS

There will be times when you need to remove knots from your work. The knot may insist on flipping itself in the wrong direction, the knots may be too thick, or you may be altering the existing hairline of a wig so that it fits a different person. There are two main ways of untying/removing your knotted hair—with your ventilating hook and with tweezers.

1. Using a ventilating hook, insert the point of the needle into the center of the knot you wish to untie (Figure 2-42). Make sure you catch all of the hairs in the knot.
2. Pull the knot open with the hook (Figure 2-43).
3. Finish untying the knot by pulling the hairs out in the opposite way they were tied in.

To remove a knot with tweezers, follow the same steps, but use the tips of the

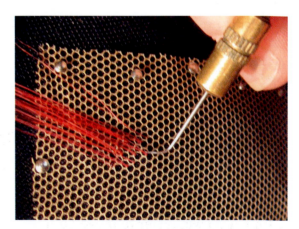

Figure 2-42 Insert the point of your ventilating hook into the center of the knot you wish to untie.

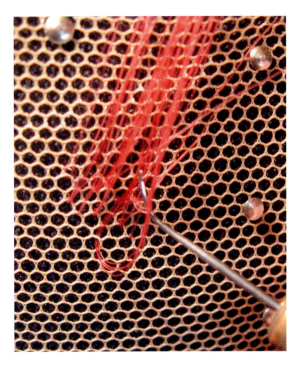

Figure 2-43 Pull the knot open with your ventilating hook.

Figure 2-44 Untying a knot using tweezers.

Figure 2-46 A drawing card containing multiple shades of hair colors, all to be used on one wig.

tweezers to gently pull the knot apart (Figure 2-44).

Use slant=tipped tweezers. Whatever way you do this will require patience and a gentle hand. If the knot is untied improperly, you could also grab a piece of the lace and tear it. It takes more time to untie a knot than it does to tie it.

COLOR BLENDING

After mastering the arts of knot tying, hair density, and ventilating direction, it is time for a wigmaker to move on to color blending. Human heads contain

Figure 2-45 Notice the multiple colors that have been ventilated into this wig.

wide varieties of colors. Although these colors may not be apparent at first glance, they will be more obvious under close examination. Therefore, your wig should contain more than just one shade of hair color—one solid, uniform shade will just scream "big fake wig!" As a general rule, never use fewer than three shades of hair when you are working—the base color, two or three shades lighter for highlights, and two or three shades darker for lowlights. Even better, use at least five or six shades if you have them available; we use as many as ten different shades when we are trying to create a realistic gray. As you practice ventilating, experiment with combining several different colors. This will help to train your eye and give your finished wigs more depth.

Figure 2-47 Invisible thread being used to sew pleats onto a wig front.

Figure 2-48 Hold the invisible thread in the same kind of loop you use when ventilating hair.

Figure 2-49 Insert your ventilating hook in the lace, making sure you catch both the pleat and the lace underneath with your needle.

SEWING WITH INVISIBLE THREAD

Sewing with invisible thread is very similar to the process of knotting hair. The sewing is actually done with invisible thread and your ventilating hook. Invisible thread is a clear, fine thread that is like a very lightweight fishing line. It is used not only to sew pleats in a wig or facial hair foundation, but also to sew layers of a wig foundation together.

To sew with invisible thread:

1. Pin the pleat or lace you are sewing together in place.
2. Hold the invisible thread in the same hand that you hold the hair with when you are ventilating. Fold over the top inch or two to make your loop and turn around (Figure 2-48).
3. Insert your ventilating hook so that you catch both the edge of the pleat

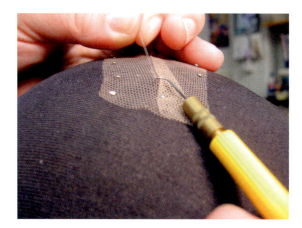

Figure 2-50 Catch the invisible thread with the barb on your ventilating hook.

Figure 2-51 After sliding the invisible thread loop down to the bend of your needle, wrap the invisible thread in your hand over the top of the needle.

and the lace you are sewing it to (Figure 2-49).
4. Bring the thread to the hook and catch the thread with the barb on the end of the needle (Figure 2-50).
5. Pull the thread back through the layers of lace. Slide the loop down to the bend of the hook.

6. Just as you did with the hair when ventilating, bring the ventilating hook back toward the thread. Wrap the thread over the top of the needle—twist the hook away from you so that it catches the thread (Figure 2-51).

Figure 2-52 Pulling the invisible thread back through the initial loop.

Figure 2-53 While holding the invisible thread taut, catch the thread with your needle and pull it through the lace without making a loop.

10. Hold the invisible thread taut. Swing it over to the hook so that it is close enough for the hook to grab. Catch the taut thread with the barb on the ventilating hook (Figure 2-53).
11. Pull the thread through the layers of lace. Follow the steps again and tie a second knot.
12. Continue sewing until you reach the desired end point.

One variation: when sewing, you may not wish to tie a knot every single time. You can simply pull the invisible thread straight through the layers without tying the knot.

The thread going through the layers will help hold the seam together. Tie a knot every third time you pull the thread through. This stitch is very similar to a chain stitch used in sewing. For video demonstrating how to sew with invisible thread, please visit the companion website to this book (http://booksite. focalpress.com/companion/Ruskai/wig/).

7. Pull the thread back through the loop you created when you began the knot (Figure 2-52). Pull the thread partway through this loop, then tighten the knot down. Pull the thread the rest of the way through the loop.

8. You will make your next knot using the same piece of thread. Pick up the thread and hold it close to where you want the next knot to be.
9. Thread the ventilating hook through the lace a few holes down from the first knot.

For any wig to look good, it must—above all—fit the wearer as well as possible. A wig that is too small will always show glimpses of the real hair underneath; a wig that is too large will bubble and gape and reveal all of its secrets. Taking accurate measurements is therefore of key importance to the wig-making process.

PROPER HEAD MEASUREMENTS

There is a basic set of measurements that wigmakers take that is close to universal. Use the measurement chart provided to create a master book of head measurements for your performers/clients.

It is often helpful to have a second person record the measurements as you are working. The beginning of the form is to be used for basic information about the performer—name, contact information, whether they have previously worn a wig, and whether they have any allergies to wig adhesives or removers, foundation materials, or hair

HAIR & MAKEUP INFORMATION

DATE _____   PRODUCTION _____

CHARACTER _____   PERFORMER _____

Makeup Experience: None Basic Intermediate Professional
Have you ever worn a wig? Yes No   Lace Front? Yes No
Any Allergies to makeup &/or spirit gum? Yes No
If yes, Please list _____
Do you sweat a lot on stage? Yes No
Do you wear contacts or glasses? Yes No

<u>HEAD MEASUREMENTS</u>

A. _____ CIRCUMFERENCE OF HEAD

B. _____ NAPE TO FRONT

C. _____ EAR TO EAR

D. _____ TEMPLE TO TEMPLE (BACK)

E. _____ SIDEBURN TO SIDEBURN (OVER CROWN)

F. _____ SIDEBURN TO SIDEBURN (OVER TOP)

G. _____ ACROSS NAPE

H. _____ WIDTH OF SIDEBURN

I. _____ EAR TO EAR (AROUND BACK)

J. _____ TEMPLE TO TEMPLE (FRONT)

K. _____ BRIDGE OF NOSE TO HAIRLINE

L. _____ BRIDGE OF NOSE TO RECEDING POINT

M. _____ EAR TO NAPE

N. _____ TEMPLE TO SIDEBURN

O. _____ BACK OF EAR TO BACK OF EAR

Natural Hair Color _____
Naturally Straight / Curly / Wavy / Permed
Length of hair _____

Figure 3-1 Copy this chart and fill it out for each person you will be working with.

care products. If the person you are measuring has short hair, you can cover their hair with a wig cap and proceed directly to taking their measurements. If the person has long hair, prepare their hair in the same manner that it will be worn under the wig and cover it securely with a wig cap (see Chapter 8 for instructions on different methods used to prepare the hair). This step ensures that the wig will fit properly. (Prepping the hair can add a couple of inches to the final head size if your performer has very thick hair!) After the information is filled out and the hair is prepped, use a tape measure to measure these key points (the letters for each measurement correspond to the measurement chart provided):

A. **Horizontal circumference of head.** This measurement is taken around the fullest part of the head,

Head Size (in Inches)	Hat Size
21	6 5/8
21 1/2	6 3/4
21 5/8	6 7/8
22 1/4	7
22 1/2	7 1/8
23	7 1/4
23 3/8	7 3/8
23 3/4	7 1/2
24	7 5/8
24 3/8	7 3/4
25	7 7/8
25 1/4	8
25 1/2	8 1/8

Figure 3-3 Hat size chart.

parallel to the floor. This is usually around eyebrow level. This is also the measurement used to determine hat size. A hat size chart has been provided for reference (Figure 3-3).

B. **Front to nape.** This is measured from the hairline at the center of the forehead, down the center of the back of the head to where the hairline (where the roots of the growing hair stop, not the ends of the length of the baby hairs) ends at the nape.

C. **Ear to ear.** This is measured over the top of the head (like a headband) from where the ear joins the head on top on one side to where the ear joins the head on the other side.

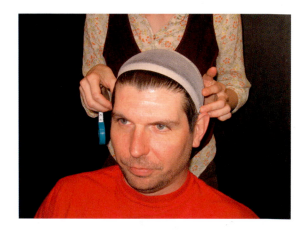

Figure 3-5 Ear to ear.

D. **Temple to temple (back).** This measures one side of where the hair is farthest forward onto the face in the temple area, around the back of the head to where the hair is farthest forward at the temple on the other side. Depending on the shape of the person's hairline, this can be closer to or farther away from the sideburn.

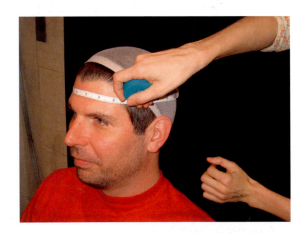

Figure 3-2 University of Texas students Scott Darby and Natalie Maynard demonstrate the horizontal circumference measurement.

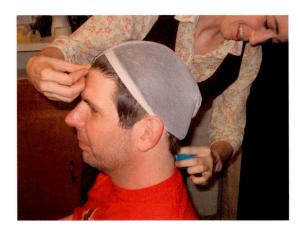

Figure 3-4 Front to nape.

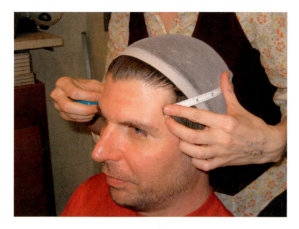

Figure 3-6 Temple to temple, around the back of the head.

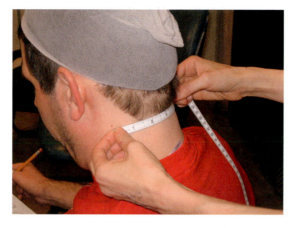

Figure 3-7 Across the nape.

E. **Sideburn to sideburn (over crown).** This measurement is taken from the lowest point of the sideburn diagonally around the head (over the crown) to the lowest point of the sideburn on the other side. We define the crown of the head as the area where the head begins to curve down from the top of the head to the back of the head.

F. **Sideburn to sideburn (over top).** This measures the same lowest point of the sideburn as the previous mea-surement, but this time it is measured directly over the top of the head.

G. **Across nape.** This measures the width of the hair at the nape of the neck at the widest point.

H. **Width of sideburn.** This measures the width of the bottom of the sideburn. There is usually a bare patch of skin between the sideburn and the ear—do not include that patch when taking this measurement.

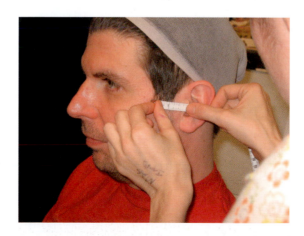

Figure 3-8 Width of the sideburn.

I. **Ear to ear (around back).** This measurement is a little bit tricky—use this measurement to give yourself a general idea of where the ears are located on the head. This measurement is taken from the bump in the front of the ear (called the *tragus*), over the ear, around the back of the head, over the other ear to the bump in the middle of the other ear. Gently flatten the ears to the head when you take this measurement.

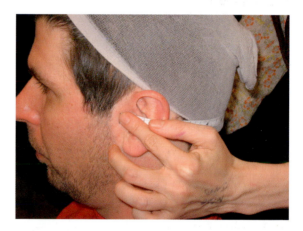

Figure 3-9 Ear to ear around the back of the head.

J. **Temple to temple (front).** This measurement is taken across the forehead between the farthest forward points of the temples. This measurement (temple to temple—back) added to measurement D (temple to temple—front) should be equal to measurement A (circumference).

Figure 3-10 Temple to temple across the front.

L. **Bridge of nose to receding point.** Use the same point at the bridge of the nose to begin this measurement. Angle your tape measure away from the center of the hairline out to a 45-degree angle—this is the receding point. Note that the receding point may not actually recede. The hairline may be a smooth arc in the front or it may be full of irregularities in shape. We are using the term "receding point" because this area commonly recedes back from the center hairline.

K. **Bridge of nose to hairline.** Take this measurement from the center of the hairline in the front straight down to the bridge of the nose.

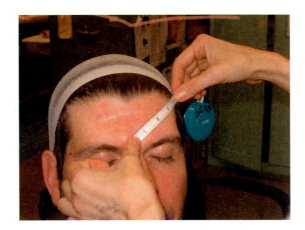

Figure 3-12 Bridge of nose to receding point.

M. **Ear to nape.** This measurement angles downward from where the ear connects to the head down to where the hairline stops at the nape of the neck.

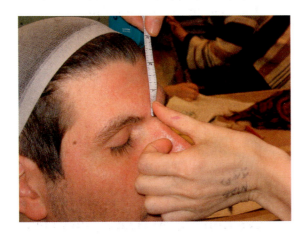

Figure 3-11 Bridge of nose to hairline.

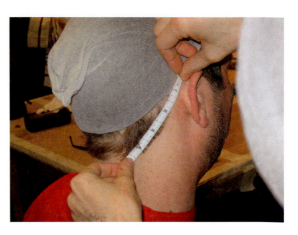

Figure 3-13 Ear to nape.

N. **Temple to sideburn.** This measurement angles across from where the hair is farthest forward at the temple to the lowest point of the sideburn.

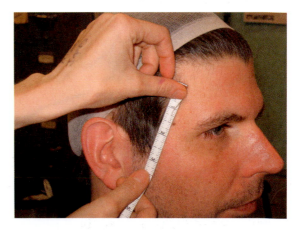

Figure 3-14 Temple to sideburn.

O. **Back of ear to back of ear.** This measurement starts where the back of the ear joins the head, and goes around the back of the head to where the back of the ear joins the head on the other side.

At this time, you should also make a few notes about the performer's own hair. Use a human hair color ring (available from many wig supply companies) to match the performer's natural hair color. You often need to use several hair colors to match one person's hair. This information is useful if you need to use a hairpiece or 3/4 wig instead of a full wig—you will have all the information you need to purchase a good color match for them. Also record if the performer's own hair is naturally straight, wavy, or curly, and how long their hair is from the nape of their neck. Finally, photograph the performer from the front, both sides, and the back so that you can refer to these pictures while you are working. If the person has longer hair, pull it back in a ponytail so that you can see the shape of their head from all angles.

TRANSFERRING HEAD MEASUREMENTS TO A BLOCK

Now that you have all of these numbers written down, what do you do with them? You will want to use a canvas or wooden head form and use the measurements to recreate an accurate model of your wig wearer's head.

1. Select the proper size of head block to work on. The size is determined by the horizontal circumference of the head (measurement A). For example, if the performer has a horizontal circumference of 23 inches, select a size 23 head block. If you have the luxury of owning more than one block in each head size, use your photos to determine which block is shaped more like your performer's head. The best way to determine this is to look at the photo of your wearer's head in profile and compare it to the profile of the head block. Pay special attention to the shape of the back of the block and the back of your performer's head—some heads are flatter, some are more round, some bulge out a bit. Select the block that most closely resembles your person. You may need to pad out the block if the only one you have available is markedly different in shape from your performer's head shape. The quickest way to pad the block is to fold paper towels into rectangular strips and tape them to the block where you need to add fullness. You may also discover as you begin marking your measurements that you need to add more padding or take some away.

2. Cover the block with masking tape so that you can mark directly on the block as you are working. Use a colored pencil to begin plotting points on the head form. (We have included Figure 3-15 as another illustration of where the measurements are located on the head.)

3. Always start with measurement B—front to nape. Again, refer to your photograph to determine where on the forehead of the head form you should place the center of the hairline. Make a mark at this point. Then mark a center line all the way down the head until you reach the measurement where the nape of the hairline should be—make a second mark. The center line is very important—you will refer back to it for many other measurements.

4. Mark measurement C (ear to ear) on the head block. Divide the measurement in half. For example, if the measurement is 12 {½} inches, half of that would be 6 {¼} inches. From the center line that you marked in the previous step, measure 6 {¼} inches (or whatever number you have calculated) down from the top center of the head to where the ears would be on either side of the head and mark each side.

5. Look at your photographs again. Determine approximately how high

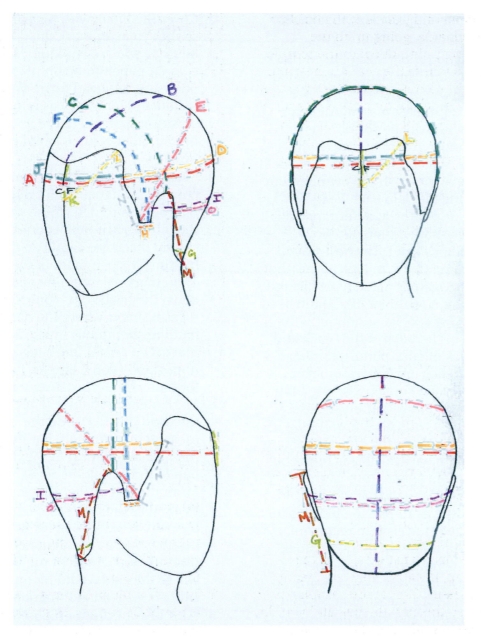

Figure 3-15 Placement of the measurements on the head. Use this diagram to assist you in plotting out the measurements on your wig block.

or low the temples need to be placed on the head. Next, divide measurement D (temple to temple—back) in half. Again, from the center line at the back of the head, measure forward to the temples and mark each side. Check the accuracy of this measurement by measuring the temples across the forehead. This should equal measurement J (temple to temple—front).

6. Mark the sideburns. Divide measurement E (sideburn to sideburn—over crown) in half. From the center line at the crown of the head, measure forward and down to where the sideburn should be. Mark each side with your colored pencil. Double-check this measurement by dividing measurement F (sideburn to sideburn—over top) in half and measuring down from the center line at the top of the head. Look at your sideburn marks from the front of the head and make sure that they are even.

7. Look at the photo of the back of your person's head. Approximate where the widest part of the hairline at the nape of the neck is. Divide measurement G (across nape) in half and mark each side out from the center line.

8. For now, skip measurement H and go to measurement I (ear to ear—around back). Divide measurement I in half and mark the location of the

front of the ear on each side of the head. Once you have the top of the ear and the front of the ear marked, go ahead and sketch in an ear shape that you can use as a reference. This ear sketch should be inside the measurements you have marked. Return to measurement H (width of sideburn) and mark it on either side of the head in front of the ear. Do not forget to account for the bare patch of skin in front of each ear.

9. Go back to the center front of the hairline. From the first point you marked in step 2, measure down the forehead to the number that you have for measurement K (bridge of nose to hairline). Mark the bridge of the nose. From this point, angle the tape measure out at a 45-degree angle to mark the receding point on each side (measurement L).

10. Use the same point where the ear attaches to the head that you marked in step 3. Measure down from this point to where you marked measurement G (across the nape). This number should be equal to measurement M (ear to nape). Do this on both sides of the head.

11. From the temple, measure down to the sideburn. This number should be equal to measurement N (temple to sideburn).

12. Once you have marked all of these many points, it is time to connect the dots! Begin at the center of the

forehead and sketch in the hairline on each side, going up to the receding point, down to the temple, around where the ear attaches, and around the nape of the neck to meet at the center of the nape. Constantly refer to your photographs to copy any shapes or quirks that your performer's hairline has. Don't be afraid to erase and redraw if the measurements are not quite working out. Use your photographs and your good judgment to best match the shape of the hairline you are trying to recreate.

Congratulations—you have transferred your hairline to the block using measurements!

PLASTIC-WRAP HEAD TRACINGS

Another way to copy a performer's hairline is to create a plastic-wrap tracing of their head. This tracing will be an exact copy of your performer's head that you can work from to create wigs. To create this tracing, you will need plastic wrap, invisible tape, and a permanent marker. (Some people substitute clear plastic bags for the plastic wrap, because they are already round in shape. This is fine, as long as you can see through the bag and you do not let the bag slip over the person's face. Also, do not use clear packing tape in place of the invisible tape—many

Figure 3-16 A sample plastic head tracing.

brands allow the permanent marker to be rubbed right off.) Here are the steps to follow:

1. Prepare your wearer's hair the way it will be worn under the wig. Cover it with a wig cap, making sure that the shape of their hairline is visible all the way around.

2. Tear off a piece of plastic wrap that is about 24 inches long. Make sure that it does not stick to itself. (Sometimes this is tricky—this product is designed to stick to

itself!) Smooth the plastic wrap over their forehead and down over their ears. Place a piece of the invisible tape across the forehead to secure the shape. Ask the performer to hold the plastic wrap in place in front of his or her ears (Figure 3-17).

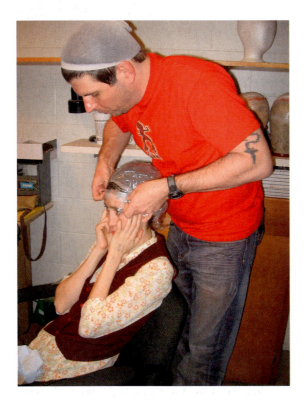

Figure 3-17 University of Texas students Natalie Maynard and Scott Darby demonstrate how to make a plastic-wrap head tracing. Natalie holds the plastic wrap in place while Scott smoothes the shape.

3. Wrap the rest of the plastic wrap around the back of the head. Tuck it and smooth it so it fits the head snugly, with no lumps or wads (Figure 3-18). Use a couple of small pieces of tape to hold the shape in place.

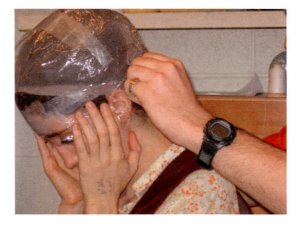

Figure 3-18 Smoothing and tucking the plastic wrap in the back of the head.

4. If there is still a section of hair or wig cap not covered with the plastic wrap, tear off a second, smaller piece of plastic wrap and use it to cover the rest of hair. Smooth it and tuck it to blend in with the first piece of plastic wrap. Make sure your plastic wrap covers all of the hairline around the head—check in front of the ears, at the sideburns, and at the nape of the neck.

5. Use the invisible tape to hold the plastic wrap in the shape of the head. (Make sure the tape is not too shiny. Some clear tapes allow permanent marker to be wiped off of them because they are so slick. This is not what you want.) Place the first pieces of tape across the forehead.

Figure 3-19 The tape being placed across the forehead of student Chelsea Bunn.

6. Continue placing long pieces of tape across the forehead until you get to the ears. Once you are at the ears, switch direction and start placing the tape vertically. Continue covering the plastic wrap with tape until the entire hairline and head is covered. Be careful—do not cover the person's face with plastic wrap and tape! You should also not tape

directly to your performer's hair. Do not layer your pieces of tape too much—you want to be able to see through the tape to the hairline underneath.

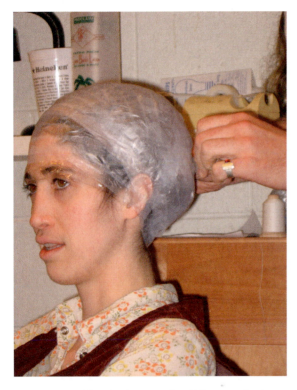

Figure 3-20 The plastic wrap should be completely covered with invisible tape.

7. Once the head is firmly covered (you should not be able to slip in more than one finger into each side of the tracing) with plastic wrap and tape,

it is time to copy the hairline. Use your permanent marker (do not start marking with a black marker—use a lighter color marker such as red or orange) to start marking in the hairline. Mark the hairline with a series of marks that mimic the directions and density of hair growth. Make sure to mark the location of the ears.

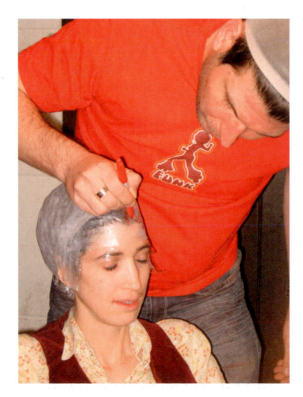

Figure 3-21 Marking the hairline.

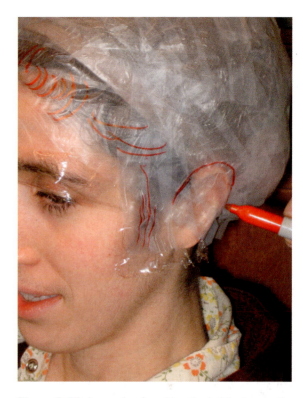

Figure 3-22 A sample of marking the hairline's growth direction and density.

8. When you have finished marking, ease the plastic tracing off of your performer's head. Do this slowly so as not to cause your performer pain. Wiggle the tracing gently upward until it slides off of the head. If your tracing comes off really easily, it may mean that you did not place your tape and plastic wrap tight enough. Double-check this.

Your plastic tracing is finished! The plastic wrap and tape create a perfect copy of your performer's head. You can also use this technique with the plastic wrap and clear tape to make plastic tracings for facial hair. (For more detailed instructions on making a facial hair tracing, please see Chapter 4.) Simply lay the plastic wrap over the chin, upper lip, sideburn area, or whatever area you want to recreate (again, do not cover the nose!). Cover it with tape and use the permanent marker to create the facial hair shape you wish to make. (Work quickly with the marker under the nose—permanent marker smell can fast become overwhelming!) Once you have sent your performer on their way, you will use the tracing to create a custom head block.

PADDING OUT A BLOCK WITH A PLASTIC TRACING

Try your plastic wrap head tracing on a variety of canvas blocks. You are looking for the block that fits the hairline snugly all the way around the head. (This includes the hairline behind the ears and at the nape of the neck.) Once you have found a block where the hairline fits properly, you will need to fill in the gaps between the canvas block and your plastic head tracing.

1. Use five or six straight pins to hold your plastic tracing in the proper place on your block.
2. Use invisible tape to tape down the entire hairline. This shape will be somewhat diagonal. You can tape right over the straight pins. Make sure that you cover all of your marker lines with tape. This will prevent the marker ink from transferring to your wig lace later in the wig making process.

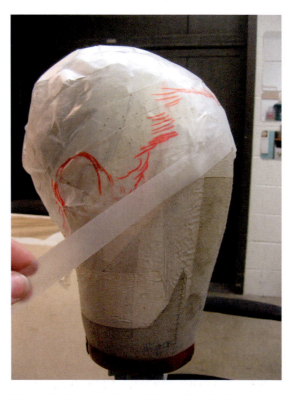

Figure 3-23 Secure the hairline to the wig block with invisible tape.

3. Use a seam ripper or a pair of small sharp scissors to cut a horizontal slit about 4 inches wide in the top of your plastic tracing. This slit should be right on the very top of the head.

Figure 3-24 Cut a slit into the top of the tracing.

4. Begin stuffing your tracing. You can use pieces of torn paper towel, newspaper, or tissue to fill in the shape. Another frequently used stuffing material is Easter grass, the

shiny plastic strips used in Easter baskets. We like to begin with pieces of tissue. Use the end of a rat-tail comb to gently push the pieces of stuffing into place. Use enough stuffing so that the tracing is full. You do *not* need to stuff it so full that it is bursting.

Figure 3-25 Stuffing the head tracing.

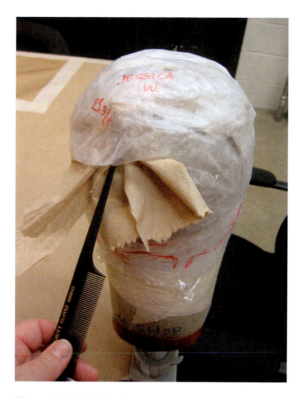

Figure 3-26 Stuffing a second slit, lower down on the back of the head.

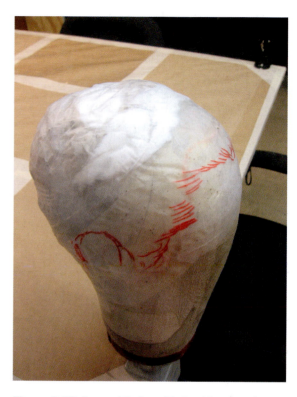

Figure 3-27 A completed, padded-out head tracing.

5. Once you have filled up the bottom of the tracing, reseal the slit with clear tape. Make another slit several inches higher or lower on the head. Continue stuffing. Keep working your way around the head until the shape is completely padded out to match your tracing.

6. After the padding is complete, apply another layer of clear tape. This will smooth out any rough spots and firm up the shape of the head you have created. Your custom head is now ready to be worked upon.

When you decide that you are finished with a head shape, you can peel off the tape, stuffing, and plastic wrap and throw it away. If you may be working with the same performer at some point in the future, you can either take the tracing off gently and save it for future use, or you can take a tracing of the tracing before you remove the original from the block and save that. Once the tracing is removed, your canvas head block will be ready to be returned to your stock.

CHAPTER 4   Facial Hair

Making facial hair is a great first project to start learning the art of wig making. It allows you to practice knot tying, creating hair density, hair growth direction, color blending, and working with wig lace in a smaller, more controlled project. It can also be a great project for using up scraps of lace and small bit of human hair that you might have lying around. It is possible to make a facial hair piece for any area of the face—eyebrows, mustaches, goatees, sideburns, and full beards. There is great variety in facial hair—we will discuss the major trends and characteristics of facial hair that you can use as a guide to making your facial hair look as realistic as possible. The best lace for making facial hair is either super lace or film lace—any other lace is too heavy to move as well as good facial hair needs to move. The best hair for making facial hair is human hair, yak hair, or other animal hair. The solvents that will be used to take off the facial hair piece will eventually ruin synthetic hair, so it is

Figure 4-1 Zachary Ullah wearing facial hair as Charles Guiteau in *Assassins* at the University of Texas.

not a good choice for facial hair. Hair with texture is ideal—permed or creped hair will look more realistic, because most facial hair is a bit coarser in texture than the hair on the head.

CREATING THE PATTERN FOR THE FACIAL HAIR PIECE

After you have determined what facial hair piece you would like to make, begin by making a pattern. Use the same invisible tape/plastic-wrap method that was discussed in Chapter 3 to take a tracing of the person you are making the piece for. Follow these steps:

1. Place the plastic wrap covering the face from below the nose to underneath the chin. Have the person you are working on hold the plastic wrap in place behind their ears. Smooth the plastic wrap under the chin and secure it with invisible tape (Figure 4-2). Make sure it hugs the shape of the chin tightly. Add another piece of tape across the face from ear to ear crossing the face underneath the nostrils.
2. Cover the rest of the plastic wrap with tape (Figure 4-3).

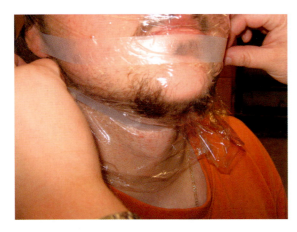

Figure 4-2 Student John Harmon has a facial-hair tracing made, beginning with securing the plastic wrap under his chin and across his face.

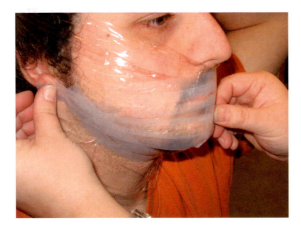

Figure 4-3 The rest of the plastic wrap is secured with tape.

3. Make sure that you mark all of the important landmarks on the face (Figure 4-4):

- For an eyebrow piece, mark the shape of the existing eyebrows.
- For a mustache, mark the shape and location of the upper lip, the location

of the bottom of the nose and each nostril, and mark the nasolabial folds (to locate these, have your performer smile).

- For sideburns or mutton chops, mark the location of the jaw line, and the ears.
- For beards and goatees, mark the location of the lower lip, the sides of the mouth, the jaw line, and the ears.
- If you are incorporating the performer's own facial hair, mark the location of that as well (Figure 4-5).

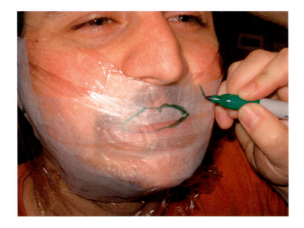

Figure 4-4 Mark in all facial landmarks—lips, ears, nasolabial folds, and any existing facial hair.

You will also want to gather as much information as you can about the person you are making the facial hair for—look for the shape, density, and growth direction of any facial hair or stubble they may already have. (You may be supplementing their own facial hair or you may be trying to recreate their growth pattern in a different color

or style.) You should note where they might have thin patchy areas of hair, or thicker and fuller areas of hair. Also look to see if there is any color differences between the person's facial hair and hair on their head. Use a human hair color ring to match their facial hair if there is enough hair present to get a good sense of the color.

Use your plastic-wrap/tape tracing as a guide to create the pattern for your facial hairpiece. The landmarks should set the boundaries that the facial hair must fit in between. Draw out the pattern of the shape that you want.

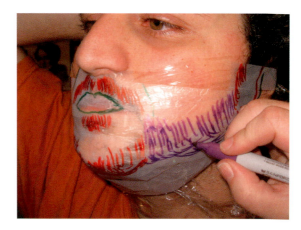

Figure 4-5 The actor's own facial hair was marked in red; the shape of the desired piece was marked in purple.

Do not feel limited by the way the person's facial hair may actually grow. Make use of different styles and facial hair looks to create the character look that suits the design of the production. Once you have drawn your pattern, you

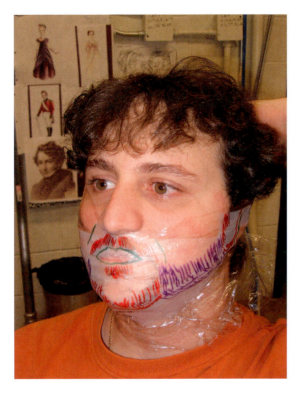

Figure 4-6 The facial-hair tracing, complete with all markings.

Figure 4-7 Truing your facial hair pattern. The markings in magenta indicate where the pattern is different from the opposite side.

Figure 4-8 Tape your pattern piece to a canvas block. Here, an eyebrow pattern has been secured in place.

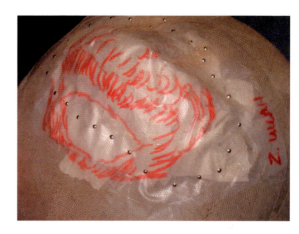

Figure 4-9 A canvas head block with a goatee tracing padded out on it.

will then need to true the pattern up (*truing* the pattern refers to the process of making the pattern symmetrical). Fold the pattern in half and look for where the sides do not match up (Figure 4-7). Choose which side you like the best and mark it on the pattern with a different-colored marker. After your pattern is symmetrical, tape it securely to a canvas head block (Figure 4-8).

Make sure to tape over all of the marker lines—if you do not, you run the risk of having the ink transfer onto the wig lace. If you are working on a chin piece (a beard or goatee), you should pin your pattern to a chin block. If you do not have a chin block, you can tape the edges of your plastic tracing to a canvas head block and pad it out in the same way we described padding out a head block in Chapter 3 (Figure 4-9).

ADDING TEXTURE TO THE HAIR

There are several different methods you can use to texturize the hair you will be using. First, you must decide whether you wish to add texture before or after you ventilate with the hair. Adding the texture before often looks better, because you can be assured that the curl or wave will go all the way to the root of the hair. However, some people intensely dislike knotting with textured hair and prefer to add their texture after the piece is made. If you choose this method, make sure you have enough length to work with.

If you choose to add curl beforehand, you have two choices: perm the hair on rollers or crepe the hair. If you perm the hair on rollers, you should buy a home perm kit from a drugstore or beauty supply store. Roll your hair onto tiny perm rods. Follow the instructions that come with the kit. Once you have permed the hair, rinsed it, and allowed it to dry, you can remove it from the rollers and it is ready for use.

You can also choose to crepe the hair. Crepeing is a method of adding texture to hair by weaving it through two strings in a set pattern and then boiling the hair to set the curl.

1. Set up your crepeing sticks (Figure 4-10). The crepeing stick kit should have come with two metal clamps that screw onto the table. Screw them onto the table about twenty inches apart. Insert the sticks. The stick with the knob goes on your left and the stick with the holes goes on your right. Make sure the small wooden thread bobbins (which come with the kit) are loaded with waxed thread (also comes with the kit).

2. Insert two bobbins into the stick which has the holes in it. There

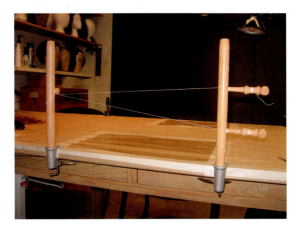

Figure 4-10 Crepeing sticks set up with waxed threads.

should be an empty hole between them. Unwind enough waxed thread to reach to the stick on the right side. Tie both threads to the knob that sticks out of the other stick.

3. Remove one bobbin and make a knot about one inch from the end of the left side (Figure 4-11).

Figure 4-11 Make a knot in the waxed threads.

4. Take a small section of human hair in your hand. The size of the section will affect the size of the creped waves—a larger hunk of hair will create a looser texture, and a tiny amount of hair will make tightly frizzed tiny waves. Wet the hair and thread it through the strings (Figure 4-12).

5. Wrap the root end of the hair over the top string and back through the center (Figure 4-13).

Figure 4-12 Thread the hair through the strings.

Figure 4-13 Wrap the root end of the hair over the top string and back through to the center.

6. Join the short end of the hair to the long end of the hair by smoothing them together in your hand and twisting them (Figure 4-14). You may need to add a little extra water to make them stick together.

Figure 4-14 Join the root end back with the rest of the hair by twisting them together.

7. Wrap both pieces of hair under the bottom string and bring them back through the middle (Figure 4-15).
8. Continue working in a figure-eight pattern by wrapping the hair around

Figure 4-15 Wrap the joined pieces of hair under the bottom string and bring them back up through the middle of the strings.

Figure 4-16 Continue crepeing the hair around the two strings in a figure-eight pattern.

the top string and back through the middle, then under the bottom and back through the middle (Figure 4-16). After you have gone around the strings several times, push the hair to the left in order to tighten the creped braid.
9. When you get near the end of the first piece of hair you will need to add another piece so that you can continue to crepe. Whenever you need to pick up another piece of hair, secure you work with either a clippie or a paper clip (Figure 4-17). Wet another piece of hair and thread it between the strings. Smooth it into the short end that is left from the first piece (Figure 4-18).

Figure 4-17 Whenever you must stop your work use either a clippie (shown here) or a paper clip to temporarily secure your work.

Figure 4-18 When you need to add more hair, do so by bringing a second piece through the middle of the strings and smoothing it into the short end of the first piece.

Figure 4-19 The creped hair is wrapped around the stick.

Figure 4-20 Knot the strings at the end of the braid when you have creped all of the hair you need.

Figure 4-21 On the left is an example of the finished creped texture. On the right is the creped hair being removed from the strings.

10. Continue working in the same figure-eight pattern. When you have creped hair to the middle of the distance between the strings, you will need to stop and wrap the creped hair around the stick. This is because the strings will start getting too far apart for you to wind the hair between them easily. Anchor your work with a clip and then loosen the thread on the bobbins. Loosen them enough so that you can turn the stick on your left away from you until the creped hair begins to wind around it (Figure 4-19). When you have wound most of the length of the hair, tighten your threads back up and continue working.

11. When you are finished with crepeing the amount of hair you want, make another knot in the strings at the end of the hair (Figure 4-20).

12. Cut the strings loose from the crepeing sticks, being careful not to cut the knot at either end. To set the curl, immerse the creped braid in boiling water for 30 minutes. Be sure to keep stirring the hair so that it does not sink to the bottom and cause the hair to scorch. Dry the hair thoroughly—it is ready to use. Cut the end knot and pull the hair free to begin ventilating with the hair.

Once you have dealt with the issue of how to achieve the hair texture, you are ready to begin actually making your facial hairpiece. Gather the colors and texture of facial hair that you wish to use. Ventilate the facial hair with hair that is 5 to 6 inches in length—anything shorter than that is difficult to handle and create good knots with. (If you are making a long, wizard-style beard, you will need to use longer hair, of course.) You will trim off the excess hair length when you are ready to style your facial hair piece.

INDIVIDUAL HAIRPIECE CHARACTERISTICS

EYEBROWS

Eyebrows often need to be made to fit around the performer's real eyebrow. Thus, the lace piece will need to be large enough to glue both above and below the performer's natural eyebrow without gluing the hair of the natural brow. (If you glue an artificial eyebrow directly onto the real eyebrow, the removal process could be quite painful!) Keep this in mind as you are creating the piece. Eyebrows can be neat and trim or wild and woolly. They may be much darker than the hair on the head, or they may go gray before the hair on the head does. Experimenting with eyebrow shapes can help you change a performer's appearance quite drastically.

A typical growth pattern for eyebrows (Figure 4-22):

- The inside corner of the eyebrow (closest to the nose) is a bit sparse and grows straight up and down (or may even angle in towards the nose).
- As you move along the eyebrow away from the nose, the hairs begin to angle away from the nose, moving away at a 45-degree angle.
- Two-thirds of the way along the eyebrow, the growth direction often splits in two.

The top hairs begin to angle downward at a 45-degree angle. The hairs along the lower half of the eyebrow continue to angle up at a 45-degree angle. These hairs often meet in the middle and create a tiny cowlick in the brow.

After taping your pattern to the canvas head block, you will need to lay your lace. For eyebrows, it is best to lay the lace with the grain of the lace going up and down. (Determine the grain of the lace by looking to see which direction the holes of the lace all line up in. That is the grain of the lace. You can either use the lace on the vertical grain, with the holes lining up going up and down, or on the horizontal grain, with the holes lining up going side to side. Which one you choose will be determined by the piece you are making. See the lace direction chart in Figure 4-23 to help inform your decision.)

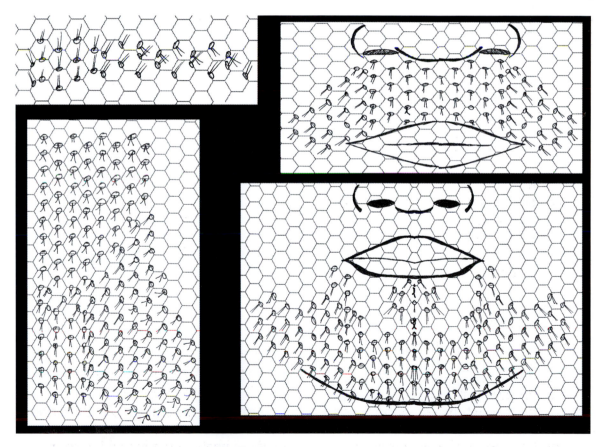

Figure 4-22 Typical growth pattern of the eyebrow.

Figure 4-23 Lace direction chart. Clockwise from top left—eyebrow, mustache, beard, sideburn. This chart illustrates the layout of the lace and the general direction of the knotting. These drawings are not done to scale.

Lay the lace for each eyebrow separately—do not use one piece for both:

1. Use straight pins to pin the lace to the block. Begin by placing one pin half an inch above the center on the piece, and one pin half an inch below the center of the piece.
2. Pin half an inch to either side of the piece.

By using this "north/south, east/west" method of pinning (Figure 4-24), you will keep the tension on the lace even as you work. Make sure that you are pinning far enough away from your eyebrow that you will have enough lace to glue around your performer's eyebrow.

Figure 4-24 Evenly distribute the tension on your lace piece by pinning north/south, then east/west. This technique is demonstrated here on a mustache.

3. Continue pinning around each eyebrow, spacing your pins about a half an inch apart.
4. Once you have pinned around the entire piece, the eyebrow is ready to be ventilated. You can trim off the excess lace that extends outside of your straight pins—this will help you avoid catching your needle in any lace that may be flapping. Begin ventilating the eyebrow at the inside corner nearest the nose. Work your way out towards the end of the eyebrow. Follow the growth direction pattern that has been laid out in Figures 4-22 and 4-23.
5. When you have finished ventilating the eyebrow, style it in the desired style. (More information about this process is in the "Cutting and Styling the Facial Hair" section near the end of this chapter.) Remove the pins when you are done styling and take the piece off of the block. You will need to call your performer in for a fitting before you trim off all of the excess lace. When your performer comes in for the fitting, hold the lace piece up to their eyebrow (Figure 4-25). Carefully look at how much lace you will need to leave in order to glue the piece on properly. (It is difficult to mark facial hair pieces— they are often so small that there is not enough room to mark on them with pen or marker. You will need to trust your eyes.) Trim off a little bit

Figure 4-25 Student Keenan Zarling has an eyebrow trimmed to fit over his own eyebrow.

of lace at a time until you are happy with the final size.

MUSTACHES

Mustaches are fun to make—they have lots of character and can really change the look of someone's face. There have been some outrageous fashions in mustaches over the years—these can be used to make a strong statement about a character's personality. They can also help establish in what period a historical production is taking place. Mustaches are often used to add a little bit of age to a performer's appearance.

Typical growth pattern for a mustache (Figure 4-26):

• Under the center of the nose, in the divot over the upper lip, is usually where the mustache is the sparsest. The hairs usually grow straight down.

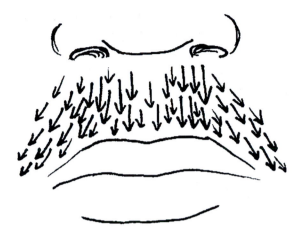

Figure 4-26 Typical mustache growth pattern.

- The hair is much thicker under each nostril. The hairs begin to angle away from the nose at a 45-degree angle.
- As you travel sideways along the mustache towards the corner of the mouth, the hairs may get a tiny bit thinner or they may stay at the same thickness.
- Many mustaches follow the shape of the mouth and curve down slightly at the outer corners. The hair at the corners of the mouth is usually thinner and grows straight down.

Mustache and beard hair is often, in real life, a bit redder than the hair on the rest of the head. It can also be darker, grayer, or the same color as the rest of the hair. When you are making a mustache pattern, you should make it just a little smaller than the area it has to fit in. This will make it easier for your performer to talk or sing. Leave room for the length of the trimmed hair—for example, the knots should end at least a quarter of an inch above the upper lip so that there is room for the hair at the bottom of the mustache to hang down.

1. Tape your mustache pattern to the block.
2. Lay your lace with the grain of the lace going up and down through the mustache. Use the same "north/south, east/west" pinning technique described above for eyebrows to pin the lace securely on top of your pattern. Trim away the excess lace that is outside your pins.
3. Begin ventilating at the center bottom of your mustache and work your way out and up (Figure 4-27).

Figure 4-27 Begin ventilating your mustache at the center bottom of the piece.

Again, follow the direction and density patterns that were discussed previously in Figure 4-23.

4. When you are finished ventilating, style the mustache. When your style is complete, remove the mustache from the block. Call your actor in for a quick fitting and trim the excess lace away using the same method that was described earlier for eyebrows.

SIDEBURNS

Sideburns can make a strong statement about the historical period your production is taking place in. Many periods in history had a very specific sideburn look.

Typical growth pattern of a sideburn (Figure 4-28):

- There is usually a noticeable change in texture where the temple hair stops and the sideburn begins. The hairs grow down and slightly back toward the ear.
- As you move down the jaw line, the hairs angle back more, reaching a 45-degree angle. There is usually a clean strip of skin between the sideburn and the ear. The back of the sideburn (closer to the ear) is usually thicker than the hair closest to the cheek.
- The bottom of the sideburn often angles up and down vertically (parallel to the nose) as it moves onto the cheek. The sideburn hair can be thick here or much thinner—this will depend on how hairy the person is overall.

Figure 4-28 Typical sideburn growth pattern.

Here are the steps for creating sideburns:

1. Tape your sideburn pattern to the block.

2. Lay your lace with the grain of the lace going up and down through the length of the sideburn. Pin your lace securely with straight pins, again making sure that the tension on the lace is even. Trim off the excess lace outside of your pins.

3. Begin tying the hair at the bottom back of the sideburn and work your way up and onto the cheek area.

4. When you finish ventilating, style the sideburn. Remove it from the block and call your performer in for a fitting. Trim away the excess lace.

BEARDS AND GOATEES

Beards and goatees probably have the most variety in shape of any other piece of facial hair. They can be anything from a tiny spot of hair on the chin to a full-coverage grizzled beard. They also require the most attention to pattern and fit because of this. This is the first time you will really have to take a two-dimensional object (the lace) and create a three-dimensional shape (the chin) with it.

Typical growth and density pattern of a beard (Figure 4-29):

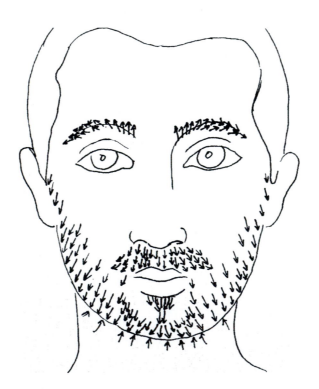

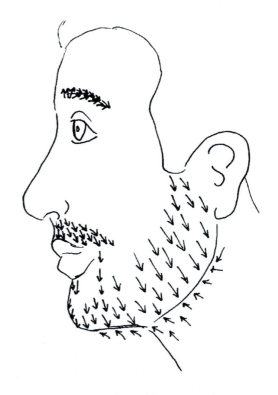

Figure 4-29 Typical beard/goatee growth pattern.

- Under the center of the lower lip, the hair usually grows right up to the lip line. This section of hair is often referred to as a soul patch or chin tuft.
- On either side of the chin tuft, the hair is usually quite sparse—perhaps even nonexistent.
- The hair on the center of the chin is dense and full. Where the hair crosses over the chin line toward the neck, the hair growth direction often changes. It may begin to grow up the neck toward the tip of the chin. This hair growth pattern is often what makes a goatee jut out from the tip of the chin instead of curving down into the neck.
- As the hair moves along the jaw line towards the ears, it angles down and very slightly back. It may be uniformly full until it connects with sideburns or it may be patchy and thin in places. The hair growth may stay fairly close to the jaw line or it may grow up onto the face nearly up to the cheekbones.
- Follow these steps to create a beard or goatee:

1. Tape your beard pattern to a block. You can use either a chin-shaped block or a head-shaped block that is padded out to fit the shape of the chin tracing.
2. Lay your lace with the grain running up and down through the center of the chin. Begin pinning the lace about half an inch above the hair on the chin. (It is often easier to make the chin tuft as a tiny separate piece.)

3. Smooth the lace down under the chin and pin half an inch past where you want the hair to stop. Make a vertical slit in the lace above the first pin; this slit should stop an inch above the pin (Figure 4-30).

Slitting the lace will allow you to open a V-shape in the center as you smooth the lace down over each side of the jaw. The lace over the jaw will be much smoother and more taut after you do this.

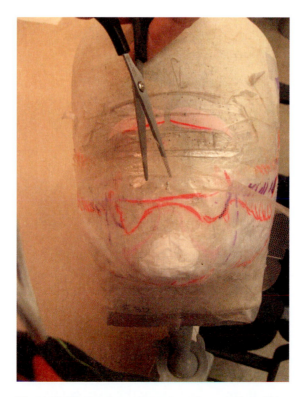

Figure 4-30 Use tiny scissors to make a vertical slit in the lace above the chin.

4. Pin the lace securely around the sideburn and jaw area. Most of the excess lace will end up gathered under the chin. Make pleats on either side of the center (Figure 4-31).

Try to make your pleats as symmetrical as possible—if one is significantly bigger than the other, it may mean that you have pulled the lace off grain. You may need to make two, four, or even six total pleats in order to flatten the extra lace. Sew these pleats securely by using your ventilating hook and invisible thread in the method described in Chapter 2. When you are sewing pleats or darts, you will need to change direction at the top of the dart and come down the other side.

To get rid of a bubble in the lace, you may need to manipulate the dart with the invisible thread. Do this by threading the ventilating hook through lace where

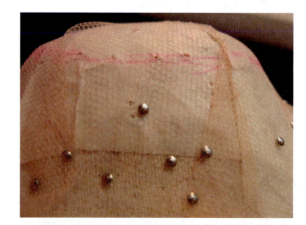

Figure 4-31 Use straight pins to pin down the pleats in the lace under the chin.

you want the fullness to go. Next, thread the hook through the excess lace (Figure 4-32). When you tie the knot with the ventilating thread, it will begin to pull the bubble where you want it go (Figure 4-33). Continue moving and securing the excess lace until the bubble is flat.

Please note: for best results, it is always best if your pleat or dart ends at least half an inch back from the visible hairline. (Under the chin is an exception to this rule, as it is very difficult to see

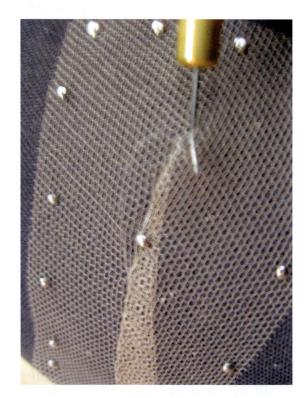

Figure 4-32 Thread your ventilating hook through the lace, skipping over several holes in order to gather up the fullness of the dart.

Figure 4-33 Manipulating the lace with invisible thread to get rid of a bubble.

the edge of the piece if it is in this location.)

5. When you have finished stitching down all of your pleats, you are ready to begin ventilating. Ventilate the hair under the chin of the goatee or beard first and tie the hair up to the jawline. Then you can turn your block around and begin ventilating the hair at the jawline and work your way up towards the cheekbones.
6. When the ventilating is completed, cut and style the beard. If the hair is long enough, you may be able to set it on rollers or perm rods instead of using the Marcel iron method described shortly.
7. Remove your piece from the block and call your performer in for a fitting. Trim away the excess lace. Also make sure the beard/goatee

cups the chin tightly. If it does not, you may have to make a small dart on the inside to tighten up the fit.

CUTTING AND STYLING THE FACIAL HAIR

Once you have finished all of the ventilating on your facial hairpiece, you will need to trim and style the hair so that it looks as realistic as possible:

1. Leave the piece you will be styling securely pinned to the block.
2. Determine how long you would like the hair to be and give the piece an initial haircut that leaves the hair a bit longer than the final look (Figure 4-34). Next, you should pull the hair straight out from the lace and trim a tiny bit off. This will slightly layer

Figure 4-34 Cut off most of the excess hair length before you begin styling.

your facial hair so that it does not look too blunt.

3. Styling the facial hair can be done with tiny rollers or perm rods if the hair is long enough. If using rollers, set them so that when the hair comes off of the rollers it will want to fall in the direction that the hair would grow. More often, facial hair is styled using a Marcel oven and Marcel irons (Figure 4-35).

A Marcel oven is a small electrical oven that becomes very hot when

Figure 4-35 Marcel irons heating up in a Marcel oven.

plugged in. Marcel irons are metal curling irons that are placed in the oven and heated up. They are not like commercial electric curling irons, which heat internally when they are plugged in. They are also available in much smaller sizes than regular curling irons. These smaller sizes allow you to curl even the tiniest, shortest bits of facial hair. Marcel irons can get extremely hot, so it is important to test the heat *every time* you take them out of the oven. Test the temperature of the hair by clamping a small sample of the same hair you used to make the hair piece (Figure 4-36). If the hair crimps and bends, it is hot enough to begin curling the hair.

If nothing happens, the iron is not hot enough. If it scorches the hair, causing it to turn yellow, black, or white, become crispy, and give off a sweet burning smell, your iron is too hot! Wave

Figure 4-36 Hair sample used to test the heat of the iron.

the iron around in the air (please do not hit anyone around you, though) until the iron has cooled off. Keep testing the iron on your hair sample until is cool enough to use. If you do not have any leftover hair from your piece, you can use a single sheet of tissue for heat testing. (you may have to pull the layers of tissue apart until there is only one ply left.) Test the iron by clamping the piece of tissue—if it turns the tissue gold or brown, the iron is too hot. This method is not as reliable as testing on the actual hair that you used and may even start a small fire if you are not very careful!

4. When styling the hair, hold the iron so that your thumb and forefinger are on one side of the handle while your third and fourth fingers control the other side of the handle (Figure 4-37).

5. Your third and fourth fingers will control the opening and closing of the iron. Practice this movement with a cool iron before you start working with a hot iron.

6. Curl the hair in small sections in the direction that you want the finished product to go (Figure 4-38).

Work quickly and avoid leaving the iron on any one piece of hair for too long.

7. When you have curled all of the hair once, comb through it with a fine-toothed comb. This first pass through curling the hair will add the

Figure 4-37 The proper way to hold a Marcel iron when styling.

Figure 4-38 Begin by curling small sections of hair.

texture you need for the facial hair to look good. You may also wish to do a little trimming of the hair at this time. Curl it a second time to finish styling the shape you want.

Experiment with curling the hair in different directions in order to see what kind of styles you can achieve. To make a handlebar mustache or a mustache with waxed and curled ends, you can use mustache wax (available at many beauty supply stores) to help hold the hair in place. Warm a small amount of mustache wax between your fingers. Work it into the section of hair you are styling (Figure 4-39). Comb the wax through and either twist the ends of the mustache with your fingers into the shape you want or use the Marcel iron to curl the ends with wax. (Do not be alarmed if the wax smokes a little.)

Figure 4-39 Work the mustache wax into the hair with your fingers.

If the final shape of the mustache is going to be very stylized, it may be helpful to pin the mustache in the shape you want with straight pins, mist the mustache with hairspray, and allow it to sit overnight (Figure 4-40). This allows the hair to relax into the final position.

Figure 4-40 Pins can be used to direct the style of the facial hair.

If you have made your facial hair with pretextured hair, you may find that you do not need to do as much work to achieve your finished style. You will still need to cut the piece, but the amount of curling you need to do may be much less. Trim the textured facial hair until it is almost the shape you want. Step back and look at it. If you are happy with the style, shape, and texture, finish the trim and you are finished with your styling. If there are areas you are not quite happy with, go back and correct those areas with the Marcel iron.

Figure 4-41 A finished, styled mustache made with textured hair.

APPLYING THE FACIAL HAIR

One of the challenges in attaching facial hair to a performer is dealing with how mobile and flexible the face is. You should put the facial hair on very carefully so that it does not pop off at an inopportune time. Here are the steps to follow:

1. Remove the facial hair from the block. Trim away the excess lace. For stage, leave an eighth of an inch of extra lace around the outside of the piece. For small theatres and for film, you will need to trim the lace as close to hair as possible.

2. Apply the beard, goatee, or sideburns first. Begin by painting a thin coat of spirit gum on the center of the chin (Figure 4-42). Tap the spirit gum with your finger a little until it becomes sticky.

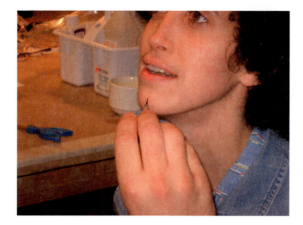

Figure 4-42 Paint a thin coat of spirit gum on the center of the chin.

3. Place the hairpiece on the center of the chin and check its placement to make sure that it is not crooked. Use a piece of chamois cloth or a clean powder puff to press the piece into the glue (Figure 4-43). (This will also remove any excess glue.)

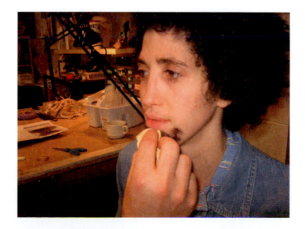

Figure 4-43 Use a piece of chamois cloth to press the facial hair into the spirit gum on the chin.

Work your way towards the edges of the piece by gluing from side to side, away from the center. Always tap the glue before you press the lace in. When you are working on the sections of the hairpiece that are near the mouth, have the performer open their mouth slightly. This will stretch the skin at the corners of the mouth so the piece does not come loose when they speak.

4. Apply the mustache last. Paint a thin coat of spirit gum above the upper lip and tap it until it is sticky. Have the performer smile—this will stretch out his or her upper lip. Position the mustache and press it into the glue with your chamois cloth or powder puff.

5. When you apply eyebrows, make sure you do not put the glue directly into the performer's real eyebrows—this will make for a very uncomfortable removal process. Place a thin line of glue under their real eyebrow, tap it until sticky, and press the false eyebrow into the glue. Finish securing the eyebrow by painting a small amount of glue above their real eyebrow, tap, and press the lace into the glue.

After you finish applying the facial hair, have the performer speak and move their face around in order to make sure there are no places that the lace wants to come loose.

If anything comes loose, add a bit more glue. Please note that the glue

Figure 4-44 Student Natalie Maynard models her finished and applied mustache and goatee.

Figure 4-45 Student Tiffany Knight has her facial hair piece removed.

Once you get underneath the lace, gently roll the cotton swab along the lace and allow the spirit gum remover to dissolve the spirit gum. (Do not use the cotton swab to yank the lace away from the skin.) Once you get all of the lace pieces off, give the performer a cotton ball with spirit gum remover so that he or she can remove any remaining traces of glue.

For information about cleaning lace pieces, please refer to Chapter 14.

should always be added to the performer's skin, not to the lace piece itself. If your performer has very oily or sweaty skin, it may be helpful to clean the skin with witch hazel or rubbing alcohol before applying the glue.

REMOVING THE FACIAL HAIR

To remove the facial hair, use some spirit gum remover on a cotton swab. Soak the cotton swab and use it to work one edge of the facial hair loose (Figure 4-45).

Figure 4-46 Students (clockwise from top left) Beauty Thibodeau, Tiffany Knight, Kara Meche, and Amanda Ramirez model their facial-hair construction projects.

CHAPTER 5 Fronting and Other Adaptations of Commercial Wigs

The fastest method of making a wig with a natural looking-hairline is to add what is called a *lace front* to a preexisting commercial wig. Commercial wigs have a simple generic hairline and rarely do these match the performer's hairline. Commercial wigs also have a very dense abrupt hairline, which does not resemble the very gradual way a real human hairline starts and stops on the face.

TYPES OF FRONTS

There are three basic types of lace fronts:

1. **Quick Front:** A quick front is the fastest and least expensive way to add a realistic hairline to a commercial wig. Nothing is done to the commercial wig before the bare minimum of lace is added. A quick front usually has a very narrow area of hand knotting. Commonly, less

than 1 inch of hairline is added. This type of front should be finished in less than eight hours. A quick front is best suited to hairstyles that involve

volume at the hairline; for example, a Gibson Girl style and eighteenth-century Macaroni style. See Figures 5-1 and 5-2.

Figure 5-1 (a) Gibson Girl (b) Synthetic wig with added quick front styled in Gibson hairstyle. Made and styled by Sarah Baloche Redding and modelled by Marissa Smith.

Figure 5-2 (a) Paintress of Macaroni's. Image courtesy the Lewis Walpole Library Yale University. (b) Profile sketch of classic Macaroni style showing volume at hairline. (c) Peter Strummer as Dr Bartolo; wig and makeup by Georgianna Eberhard.

2. **Standard Front:** This type has approximately 1–3 inches of hand tying and the front of the commercial wig has had the thick ribbon-front edge of the commercial wig removed to make for more gradual transition from ventilated lace to commercial wig. This style is more natural in appearance than a quick front when pulled back into a ponytail or bun. It is not suitable for styles in which a part should appear natural up close, because there will be a noticeable change in opacity where the commercial wig meets the hand-tied area. A standard front will usually take 12 hours to complete from start to finish. This type is useful for the average natural eighteenth-century men's tie-back wig or for a woman's 1980s full curly style that waves off the face.

3. **Deep Front:** Making a deep front involves removing a significant portion of the commercial wig's top and sides. The tops of many styles of commercial wigs are too thick and stiff for the wig to ever be styled to look natural with a part on the top. Removing and replacing between $1/3$ and $1/2$ of the entire wig requires substantial work—sometimes as much as 25 hours. There are methods of making wigs from scratch that require a similar amount of time. However, it is sometimes more cost-effective to purchase a commercial wig made

Figure 5-3 (a) Image courtesy the Lewis Walpole Library, Yale University. (b) Wig on left is a quick front wig on right is a standard front. Wigs designed by Tera Willis and styled by Victoria Tinsman for 1776, presented by the Pennsylvania Shakespeare Festival.

Figure 5-4 An example of a 1980s hairstyle.

from weft than to purchase the amount of weft needed to make a wefted wig from scratch. For a wig with a realistic center part, this is usually a better choice than a quick or standard front.

THE HUMAN HAIRLINE

Because the point of adding any type of lace front is to make the commercial wig look more realistic, it is important to understand what human hairlines look like:

- Normal (nonbalding) healthy hairlines are a variation of a half oval.

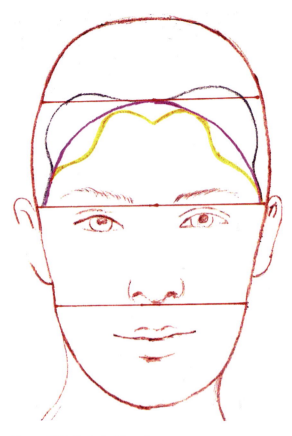

Figure 5-5 Basic hairline shapes.

- No human hairline is ever a perfect solid line. All hairlines have some variation of curvature and density.
- The shape of human hairlines is related to gender, age, ethnic heritage, and occasionally to medical procedures. In general, males with Northern European ancestry tend to have the highest, squarest hairlines. The narrowest and lowest hairlines are found more often in females with Mediterranean ancestry. However, it is possible to find all shapes of hairlines

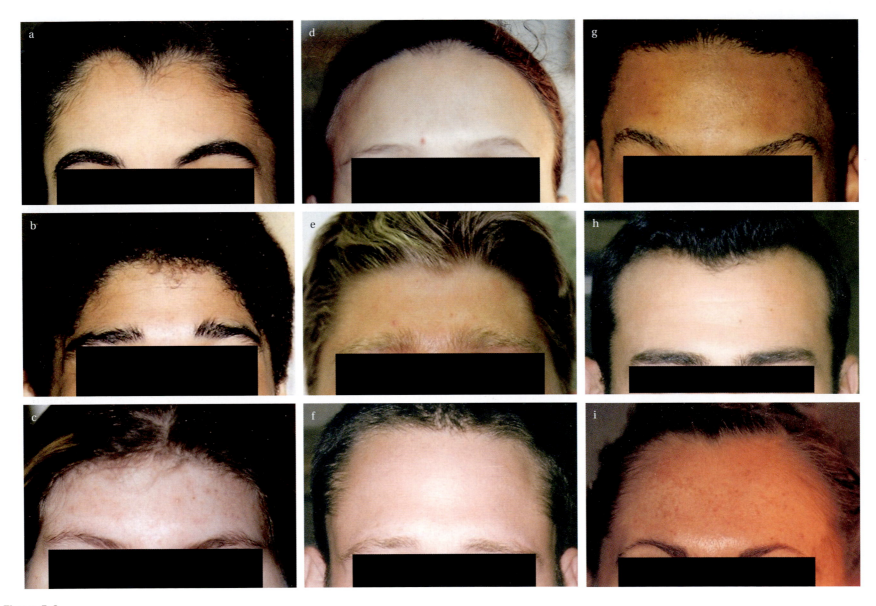

Figure 5-6

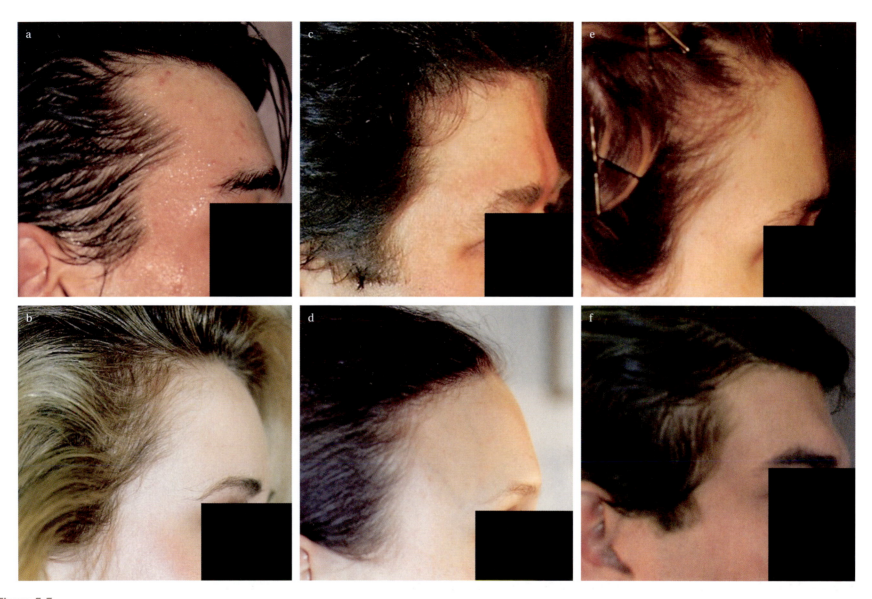

Figure 5-7

and relative locations on the forehead of hairlines on both genders and across ethnic groups. In the melting pot of world travel and cross-cultural marriages, predicting the shape of a hairline long distance is tricky. Good measurements, tracings and photographs are critical to creating the best hairline for a wig.

• Hairlines have different curvature as well as different relative proximity to the eyes. Classical proportions for the ideal adult human head include an ideal for hairline placement.

CHANGING THE HAIRLINE

In many cases, a wigmaker is making a wig that matches the performer's hairline. At other times, the wig hairline needs to be made intentionally different from the performer's own hairline to help create the appropriate look for the character's age, gender, and background.

Because fronting lace is 95 percent transparent, it is important to note that raising the wig hairline to make it significantly higher or wider than the

performer's own hairline will require that the performer's own hair be concealed with makeup, a silk blender, or bald cap. Lowering a hairline generally doesn't require any special hair or makeup preparation for performances. If the wig hair is a drastically different color than the performer's own hair, it may be possible to see through the wig hair to the performer's own hairline. White and very blonde yak, human, and synthetic hair are all somewhat transparent and will let a black or vivid red hairline show through. The density of the knotting also affects the opacity of a wig hairline. The finer and sparser the edge of a lace wig hairline is, the more natural it appears. But if it is too thin and the hair from beneath is visible, it may be distracting to the audience. If a performer is wearing a wig that allows a few of the performer's own hairs show through the lace it will be visible on film, but not in a theater with a large orchestra pit.

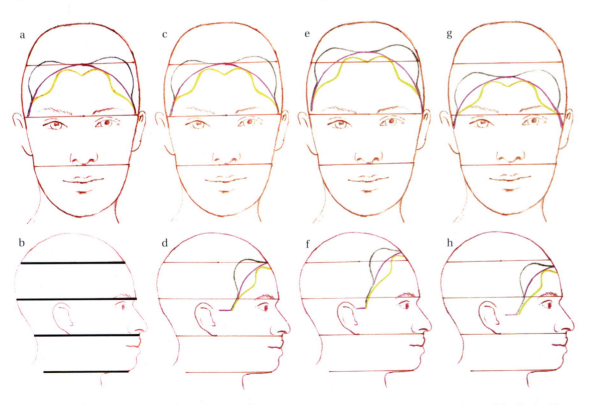

Figure 5-8 (a-b) Face divided in thirds from hairline to between the eyebrows to bottom of nose and finally to chin. (c-d) Normal hairline at the classical ideal location. (e-f) Hairlines higher than the classical ideal. (g-h) Hairlines lower than the classical ideal.

BUILDING THE FRONTS

The first step in adding a lace front to a commercial wig is to create a new hairline on a block of the right size and shape. Follow the directions for taking measurements and plastic tracings as discussed in the previous chapters.

It is a very good idea to place the commercial wig on top of the plastic tracing and mark onto the plastic where the commercial wig edge will be. (Try to

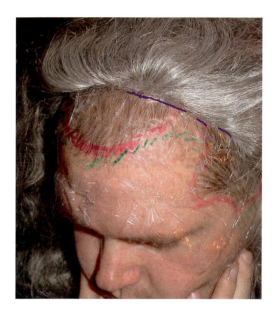

Figure 5-9 Tracing commercial wig line onto plastic.

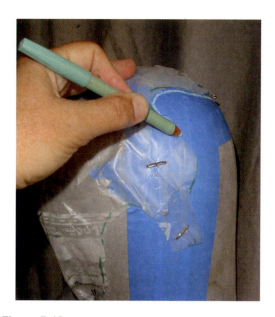

Figure 5-10

avoid getting marker on the wig hair.) It is also helpful to take measurements from where the wig stops to the center front hairline and temple peaks.

There are three ways to use this plastic tracing when adding a lace front.

VARIATION 1

- Cut the plastic wrap off in front of the desired hairline.
- Place on the block and trace the edge with pencil.

VARIATION 2

- Place the plastic wrap on the block and punch through along the hairline with a pin creating a row of dots in the masking tape.

Figure 5-11 Using a pin to punch hairline through plastic into masking tape.

VARIATION 3

- Pin and /or tape the plastic to your block and lay the lace and wig on top of the plastic.

TRUING THE HAIRLINE

Though you will often create a wig that has the performer's own slightly asymmetrical hairline, there are times when it will be better to create a symmetrical hairline on the wig. This is a good choice when the wig will be worn by many people, or when building wigs for short-term rental. In addition, there are hairstyles that look best when the hairline is truly symmetrical. Geisha wigs and eighteenth-century white wigs are both styled symmetrically and look odd if the hairline is noticeably asymmetrical. Creating a symmetrical hairline is called *truing* the pattern. "Truing" is the process of making a pattern symmetrical and more generic.

Truing a hairline can be done by folding the plastic tracing in half while it is off the block. Then hold the plastic tracing up to the light and mark the differences in the hairline with a different color of marker.

Truing can also be done by tracing the hairline twice:

1. The first line will be traced onto the block with the plastic right side out.

2. Turn the plastic cape inside out and place it back on the block. Trace the hairline again.
3. Remove the plastic and connect the dots with a colored pencil or indelible marker. See Figure 5-12.

If the wig hairline and color are close to the performer's own hairline and color, the truing can be done by carefully creating a new line that is in between the two traced lines.

If the wig is significantly lighter than the performer's hair, it is best to true the hairline closer to the lines that are more on the face so that all the performer's own hair will be covered.

- Mark onto the block where the edge of the commercial wig should be placed.

In addition, it is very helpful to mark ventilating directions and where the direction transitions will happen.

LACE DIRECTION AND HAIR GROWTH DIRECTION

When you choose to lay lace for a front, the placement will determine which angles you can ventilate in and the amount of stretch or tension you will get. What directions do you want to be able to ventilate? See Figures 5-13 through 5-22 for examples of variations of growth direction, lace grain and ventilating direction.

Figure 5-14 Hair naturally growing down at the temple.

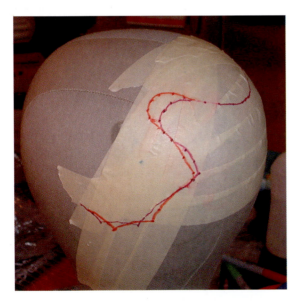

Figure 5-12 The orange line is the hairline traced right-side-out. The pink line is the hairline traced inside-out.

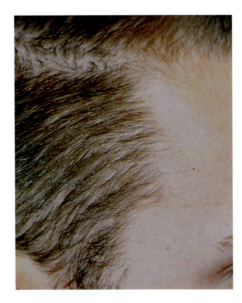

Figure 5-13 Hair naturally growing back and down off face at a 45-degree angle. Notice the cowlick formed on the lower side of the part where forward growth meets the stream of backward growth.

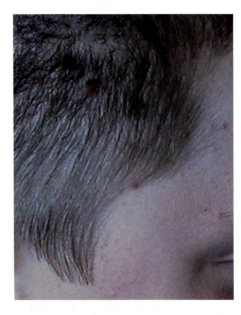

Figure 5-15 Temple hair growing back at peak, then down and forward just above sideburn.

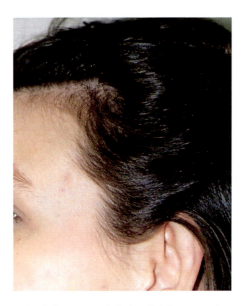

Figure 5-16 Long temple hair will follow growth direction if pulled back loosely.

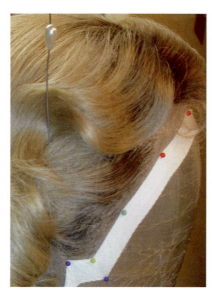

Figure 5-18 *West Side Story's* "Consuela": Knotting on temple follows normal growth pattern of back and down at a 45-degree angle.

Figure 5-20 Forehead hair growth.

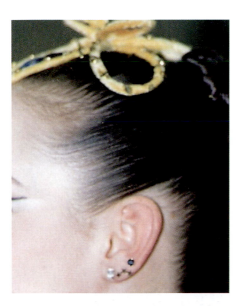

Figure 5-17 Hair pulled back with gel and held securely will appear to be growing straight back.

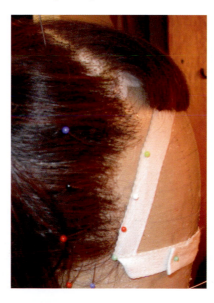

Figure 5-19 *West Side Story's* "Velma": Knotting on temple of wig goes straight back to aid styling. *West Side Story* wigs Designed by Mark Adam Rampmeyer; stylist: Jennifer Bullock.

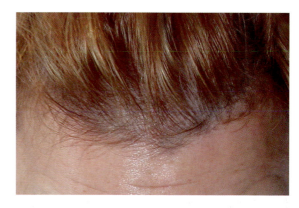

Figure 5-21 Forehead hair growth.

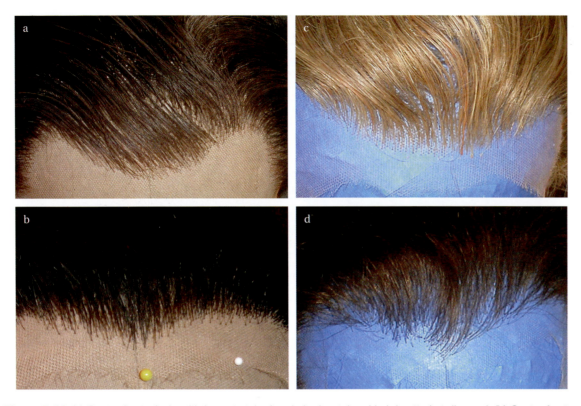

Figure 5-22 (a) Center front of wig with lace stretched grain horizontal and hair knotted at diagonal. (b) Center front of wig with lace stretched grain vertically and hair knotted straight back for a geisha wig. (c) Center front of wig with lace stretched grain vertically and hair knotted straight back. (d) Center front of wig with lace stretched grain vertically and hair knotted both straight back and diagonally back.

For very deep and very curved foreheads, it may be necessary to create a few small pleats to help shape the flat piece of lace over the curve of the forehead.

When stretching the lace for a front, the goal is to have the lace hug the head an average of ¾ inch in front of the hairline, at the hairline, and ¾ inch behind the hairline.

Some types of fronting lace are heat-sensitive and can be stretched, shrunk, and shaped with a heat gun. All heat-sensitive wig laces can burn in a split second. Practice this technique on scraps of lace before attempting it on a large piece laid on a block. You can heat-shrink if a front ends up too big. You can also heat and stretch lace while warm from a heat gun. This is very tricky, and takes practice and patience. If you try to shrink too much, the lace condenses and the threads get closer together and therefore more visible. If you try to pull and stretch too much, the pattern of hexagons distorts significantly, affecting the direction you can ventilate.

- Do you want to duplicate the growth of a particular person's hair?
- Do you want to ventilate in a direction that makes the styling easier to maintain?

When laying any foundation material for any portion of a wig, remember that you are using a flat piece of material and trying to make it fit a curved surface. This includes laying the fronting lace. Lace does stretch and for small areas will conform to the curvature of the block.

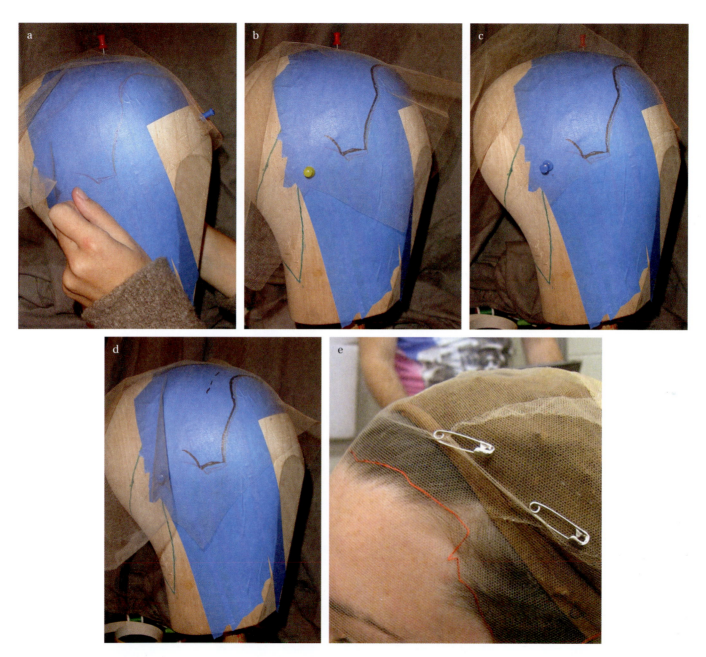

Figure 5-23 (a) Stretching lace for front. (b) Tension of the lace is too high and vertical and is causing the lace to "shelf" over the forehead. (c) Tension of the lace is too low and horizontal and will cause bubbles behind the hairline and possibly make the wig too tight. (d) Tension of the lace is just right. It hugs the head in front of and behind the hairline. (e) Even in the best-stretched foundations, it is sometimes necessary to make small adjustment darts before adding hair.

QUICK FRONT: A STEP-BY-STEP EXAMPLE

This quick front is going to have a copy of a wig hairline that is known to fit the performer:

1. The hairline is traced by punching holes into a layer of masking tape.

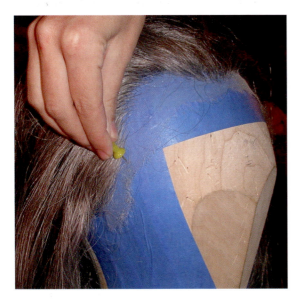

Figure 5-24 Copying existing hairline by using pin to trace hairline into masking tape.

This quick front has a narrow area between the desired hairline and the hard front edge of the wig.

2. The commercial wig is placed directly over the lace and secured to the block.

3. Sew the commercial wig to the fronting lace using a short diagonal stitch. Keep stitches short and make

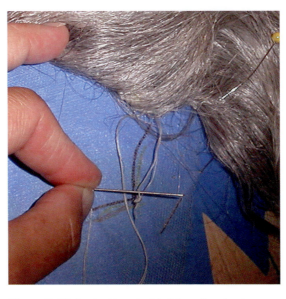

Figure 5-25 Start with a doubled thread and put needle through loop. This will help ensure that the thread does not pop through the open-weave ribbon of the wig.

Figure 5-26 Sew front edge of commercial wig to lace with short diagonal stitches.

sure that each stitch catches both the foundation fabric of the commercial wig as well as the fronting lace. Some people prefer to use a strong straight needle, thimble, and finger guard; others prefer to use a curved needle and pliers.

4. Ventilate very densely close to the commercial wig hairline. Make the knots with at least three hairs. This will help create an area that has hair density similar to the commercial wig. Then gradually decrease to single hairs and wider spacing at the front edge of hairline.

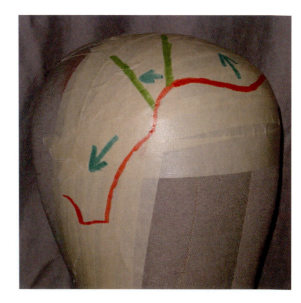

Figure 5-27 Ventilating directions and transition lines drawn on block.

Figure 5-28 Closeup of completed quick front.

Figure 5-29 Lace folded under and stitched.

5. Once the ventilating is finished, remove the wig from the block. Turn a short hem under and sew in place. It is always best to have two rows of stitching holding a front in place. Remember to keep stitches tiny so that they won't catch on the pin-curl prep of the performer as the wig is put on and taken off.

The wig is now ready to set and style!

STANDARD FRONT

This is the most common method used to add a lace front to a commercial wig. When adding a standard front you will be adding 1–3 inches of hairline by hand. One of the details that distinguishes a standard front from a quick front is that the lace is put on top of the foundation in a standard front. It works best if you remove all hair from the edge of the commercial wig to create $1/8$–$1/4$ inch of hair free foundation. The fronting lace is then placed over the bare strip of wig foundation.

The lace is then sewn to the very edge of the wig foundation, turned under, and stitched again where the folded edge meets the wig hair. This method provides a smoother transition from lace edge to bulk of commercial wig.

1. In some cases, the easiest method is to use a seam ripper to remove the ribbon binding the front edge of the wig. This will usually reveal about $1/8$ inch of foundation fabric that is then ready to have the lace applied.

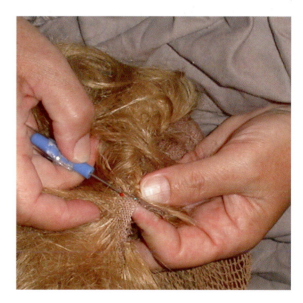

Figure 5-30 Removing front edge ribbon from commercial wig foundation, revealing $1/8$ inch of foundation that is free of hair.

However, often the wig has no real foundation and is merely vertical ribbon with rows of weft sewn horizontally and a row of elastic providing the back edge.

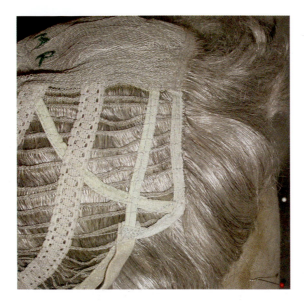

Figure 5-31 Inside view of commercial wig showing weft sewn only to ribbon. Do not remove ribbon from this wig; only remove hair from ribbon. Then lay lace on top of "bald" ribbon.

Figure 5-32 Lace overlapping the front edge of wig foundation.

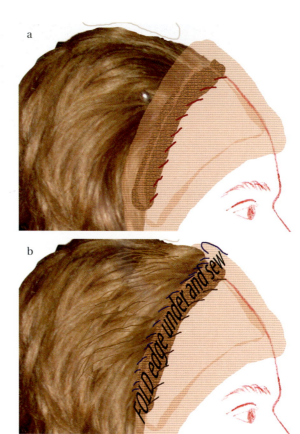

Figure 5-33 (a) Lace sewn to foundation along front edge, (b) Fold back edge of lace under and stitch.

If one removes the ribbon from the front edge of this style of commercial wig, then there isn't a foundation left to attach the lace. In this situation, it is best to leave the ribbon and remove the weft as far back as necessary to provide $^1/_8$–$^1/_4$ inch of foundation over which the lace can be laid.

2. Once the front edge of the wig foundation is free of hair, pin the foundation onto the appropriate block. Make sure to line up the edge of the wig with measurements or tracing.

3. Stretch the lace as described earlier in this chapter.

The lace should extend about $^1/_2$ inch behind the edge of the wig foundation.

4. Sew the lace to the front edge of the wig foundation using either regular needle and thread or invisible thread.

5. Trim and turn under the lace so that the folded edge lines up with the first hairs. Sew the folded edge down.

6. Ventilate hair into lace, including the portion that overlaps the heavy foundation.

In general, start ventilating at the point that will be "underneath" when you are finished. For a wig that will be styled pulled back off the face, it is best to do the ventilating where the lace overlaps the commercial foundation first. Then move to the sideburns and work up to the center front.

Figure 5-34 (a) Kristopher Irmiter as Don Giovanni, wearing a standard front wig. Opera Carolina/photo by Greg Cable. (b) Side view of wig on block. (c) Center front detail of wig.

DEEP FRONTS

Many commercial wigs in recent years have solid plastic tops that are supposed to look like a scalp if the wig hair is parted. These plastic tops are stiff and often not the color of the person's skin. It can be cheaper to take the top off and add lace and hair to the top and front compared to making a full wig from scratch with weft.

DEEP FRONT VARIATION 1

1. Remove edge ribbon from ear to ear.
2. Remove weft that is on top of the plastic with a seam ripper. Be careful not to tear the fabric, often a stretchy lace, below the plastic.
3. Place the wig on the block. Check against your tracing, measurements and hairline to make sure that you are creating the right size and shape. Once the plastic top and edge ribbon come off, it can be very easy to stretch out the shape and size of the wig. (It is sometime helpful to stay stitch the stretch lace or make a rolled hem, especially if the ear to ear measurement of the person is less than 12 inches.)
4. Lay fronting lace over the hairline and extend back to cover and overlap the stretch lace top. It generally takes at least two darts to make this work. Sew the darts on both sides and then sew the fronting lace to the foundation of the wig.

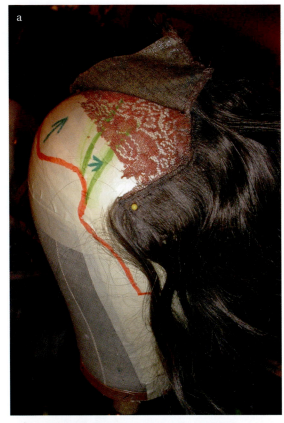

Figure 5-35 (a) Remove plastic skin top from commercial wig. (b) Fronting lace over foundation fabric.

5. Trim and fold a rolled hem that just overlaps the first row of weft that is visible.

This type of deep front is great for men's natural-colored eighteenth-century ponytail wigs that will have a small side curl or two. It is also a good way to get a flat top of head for very natural Cavalier wigs for women.

VARIATION 2

In this version, all of the wig foundation on the top and front edge of the wig is removed. A heavier lace is placed under the remaining section of commercial wig. Finally, the fronting lace is added over the front edge.

VARIATION 3

When a natural part is desired with little volume on the top of the head, the best way to achieve this is to remove all of the top and front edge and replace with only fronting lace. See Figure 5-36.

Figure 5-36 Plastic skin top is replaced with pieces of fronting lace. Three pieces were used to use up scraps. This can also be achieved with one piece of fronting lace. Courtesy UNCSA.

hair to pull back tightly and hold the wig onto the performer's hairless head, but the side-curl styling can cover the temples. See Figure 5-37.

Figure 5-37

Figure 5-38

MINI FRONTS

Sometimes there just aren't enough skilled hands or time for each person on stage to get a completely new front. Some styles only show part of the hairline. For these styles it is possible to get away with *mini fronts*. Mini fronts have only the visible part of the hairline ventilated. The lace is usually complete across the face.

A style that this works for is eighteenth-century wigs when you need enough lace and ventilated forehead

Another kind of style that can have a mini front are those with bangs across the forehead, but the sides will be pulled off the face, as in this iconic style of the 1940s. See Figure 5-38.

For such a style, a full lace can be laid but in a pinch, only the sides really need to be ventilated.

SILK BLENDERS

There are times when the person's hairline is too close to the eyes or their hair is too dark and would be seen through even the densest of ventilating.

There are three solutions to this problem:

- Apply a bald cap.
- Put lighter makeup in the performer's hair (either to make the performer's roots match the lighter wig hair color or to look like the skin tone).
- Use wig silk to make a "blender." A blender is an opaque fabric sewn into the front of a wig under the lace. Usually a special weave of silk, it covers the performer's hair and mimics skin.

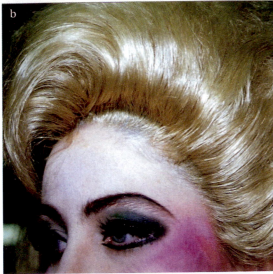

Figure 5-39 (a) Dark hair showing under white wig hair. (b) Dark roots of performer have been covered in makeup under pale blonde wig hair.

Full or partial silk blenders can be used in proscenium stage situations, but never for film. Wig silk will reflect light differently from skin or makeup. It is important to check the color carefully in performance lighting and not rely exclusively on workroom lights.

A blender is added to a wig in the same way that a quick front is added. It can be added at the same time as the fronting lace is added or after the wig is completed.

Wig silk is a special weave and weight. Wig silk is purchased white and dyed if desired. The silk will dye easily to an appropriate beige for Caucasian performers using either a dilute solution of orange pekoe tea or an extremely dilute mix of Tintex fabric dye in beige and pink rose. For performers with dark olive or dark brown skin tones, a mix of beige, gold, orange, red, and/or brown dye will be needed. The exact color needed must be determined by how the makeup foundation color or skin tone of the performer looks compared under stage lighting. Sometimes wig silk needs to be pinker and darker than the foundation of the performer. This occurs often under bluish lighting. Other times, under low-level bastard amber light, any differences between the silk and the skin will not be noticeable to the audience.

It is also possible to color the silk with foundation. Makeup also adds more opacity to the wig silk. Cream makeup is messy and will transfer to the underside of the lace, but it does add a bit of sheen

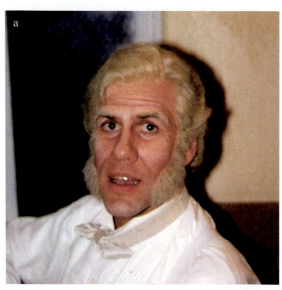

Figure 5-40 (a) Wig with silk blender worn by baritone Jeffrey Morrissey in *La Traviata*, the Atlanta Opera. (b) Wig with silk blender worn by John Muriello as KoKo in the *Mikado*, Opera Carolina.

that can be helpful in reflecting light. Pancake also works and is less likely to transfer to the underside of the wig. However, some brands of pancake will change color if the wig silk is wet with sweat. But only after first dress rehearsal will you know for sure how the silk is reading compared to the skin color.

NAPE LACE

Commercial wigs are made to be worn hanging down with the nape of the foundation covered by hair. Many period and contemporary looks have the nape hair pulled up. The normal everyday commercial wig was not made for these styles.

Sometimes all that is needed for this type of hairstyle requires creative solutions to conceal the performer's

Figure 5-41 Standard inexpensive commercial wig with hair pulled up tight exposing the elastic and rounded shape of wig, compared to the square or W shape of a human nape.

Figure 5-42 Commercially made wig with elastic and weft styled to cover elastic edge of wig and the dark hair of the performer.

nape hair and the edge of the foundation. Simply draping the hair into the hairstyle and cutting and curling "nape wispies" is sometimes sufficient.

Adding a row or two of weft to the inside of the wig can be quite helpful in concealing the elastic and providing more hair for draping and wisps. Make sure that the elastic on the inside of the wig is stretched out before you stitch on the hair; otherwise, you may make the wig too small, because the elastic will not be able to stretch after you have stitched the weft inside the wig.

Sometimes the only solution is to add an extra piece to the nape of the wig. One version of this is a *nape lace*. If you have time, it is better to build a

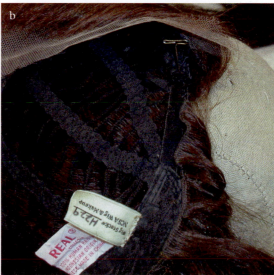

Figure 5-43 (a) Inside of commercial wig with extra weft sewn in and the elastic back stretched out. (b) Same wig with elastic relaxed to normal.

great-fitting wig with a shaped nape. If you have to add a nape lace to a commercial wig, follow these steps:

1. Start by taking measurements, a tracing, or cutting a paper pattern of the performer's neck and back of head, as described earlier.
2. Place the wig on top of the tracing and mark where the edge of the wig will sit.
3. Lay the lace as you would lay a front lace, leaving the edge toward the neck raw.
4. Place the wig over the lace.
5. Sew the lace to the edge of the wig. See Figures 5-44 through 5-46.

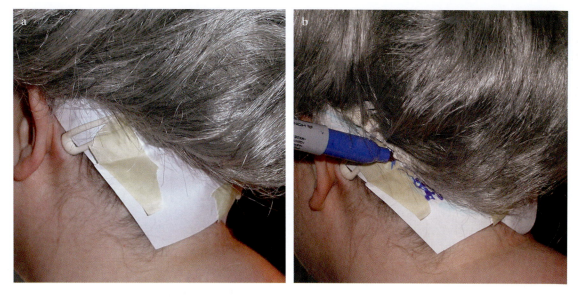

Figure 5-44 (a) Paper pattern showing the shape of the lace to be added. (b) Tracing the location and shape of the commercial wig edge onto paper pattern.

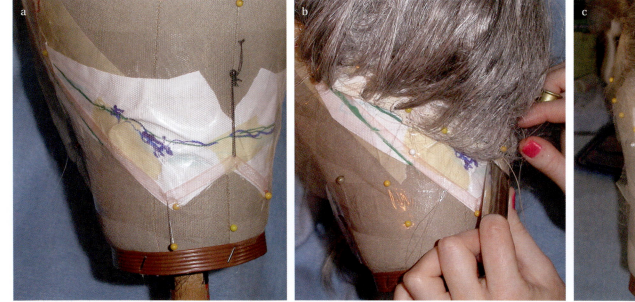
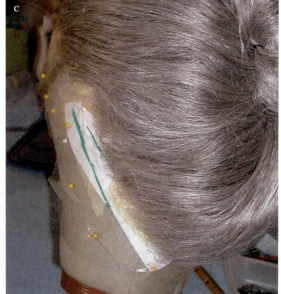

Figure 5-45 (a) Pattern transferred to block, lace stretched in place. (b) Sewing nape of commercial wig to lace. (c) Hair added to nape lace.

Remember that if you are sewing to elastic, the wig will no longer stretch as much where sewn to the wig. This is why the tracing including the edge of the wig on the performer is so useful.

6. Ventilate hair in the direction desired.

It is very rare that nape lace is actually glued to the performer. The neck is far too mobile for a glued lace to stay well. Usually the pin-curl prep or toupee clips provide an anchor spot for the lace to be pinned into.

Whether pinning or using skin-grade adhesive, have the performer look to the left while you secure the right side of the nape. Then they should look to the right while you secure the left nape. This will

Figure 5-47 Variation with hard-edge addition to commercial wig nape. A trapezoidal piece of heavy wig lace is added and has hair added on the outside and weft added on the inside edge as well.

hopefully provide enough give that as the performer moves, the wig will stay anchored.

PIECING TOGETHER WIGS

You can piece commercial wigs together to quickly create period hair hairstyles. One example that we will illustrate is creating a full-bottom wig. (Making a foundation and a full-bottom wig from scratch will be covered later in the book.) A decent style of later seventeenth- and early eighteenth-century full-bottom wig can be made using several commercial synthetic wigs. Because resetting a full-bottom wig is time-consuming, we prefer to use a

Figure 5-48 *Five Orders of Perriwigs* by Hogarth. Image courtesy the Lewis Walpole Library Yale University.

Figure 5-49 One of many styles of commercial synthetic wigs suitable for making full-bottom wigs. Style shown is "Posie" from Wig America.

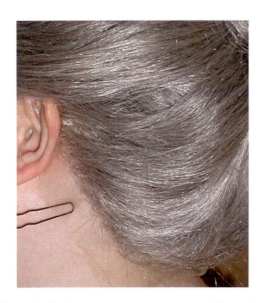

Figure 5-46 Nape lace complete and pinned in place.

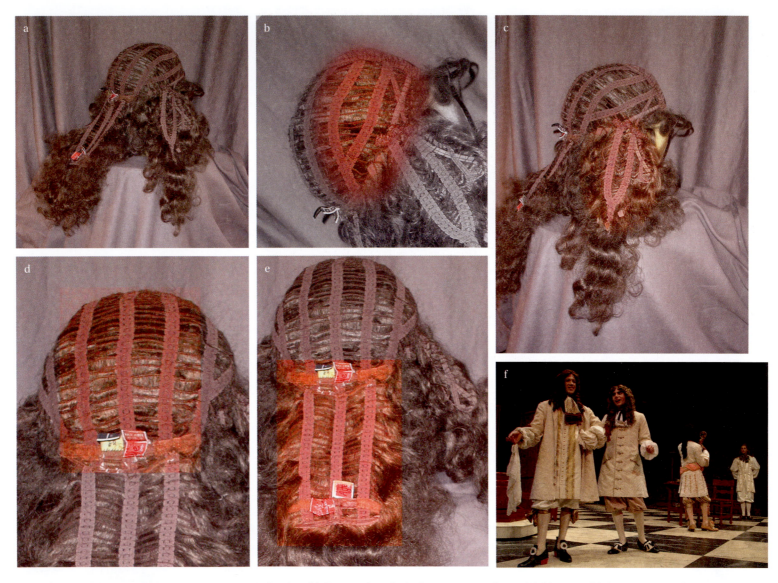

Figure 5-50 (a) Inside of full-bottom wig made from two synthetic wigs. (b) Cut temples of wig 2 to create ear flaps of full bottom. (c) Cut out temple fragments sewn to bottom of temple of wig 1. (d) The center back portion of wig 2 becomes … (e) … the center back hanging tab of the full-bottom wig. (f) Full-bottom wigs in *Man of Mode*; wig designer Sarah Landbeck; photo.

synthetic wig that comes with a factory curl texture as close to the finished style as possible.

Because long, curly commercial wigs are usually being sold to women as hair replacement, these wigs are sized for an average woman's head with little or no hair. These commercial wigs will generally fit someone with a 19.5–22.5 inch head circumference with a small tuck or small elastic piece added to the nape back. The average opera baritone head is somewhere between 23.5 and 24.5 inches. When the wigs need to fit a head of those proportions, more significant alterations might be needed. Adding a lace front or a lace nape will allow you to add quite a lot of size. But sometimes the wig needs to remain a "hard front" and match others onstage. This happens with opera chorus and supers quite often. These two pictures are just two of the many ways in which two inexpensive commercial synthetic wigs can be cut and pieced together to fit a 25-inch head.

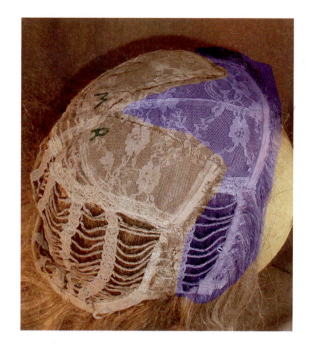

Figure 5-51 To make a larger hard front, wig 1 was split center-front (shown in yellow). Wig 2 (blue) was cut to overlap and stitched in place. The wig now fits someone with a 25-inch head.

CHAPTER 6 Building a Wig from Scratch

The word "foundation" refers to the cap or base to which hair is attached to make a wig. Custom theatrical wig foundations for wigs that are supposed to look like "real" hair growing out of the head are usually made of special lightweight, open-weave fabrics called *lace* or *net*. Laces and nets come in many weights, stiffness, densities, and levels of stretch. Sometimes special opaque silk fabrics or a type of leather called *chamois* are used.

The choice of whether to build a full wig or to adjust a commercial wig depends primarily on the available labor. Decent-quality hair in both human and synthetic is available in bulk, in a commercially available hand tied wig, and in weft. It will take an experienced wig maker anywhere from 24 to 60 hours to build a full wig. The work goes faster if the foundation is colored, the hair is medium to dark in color, short, and the density moderate. The longer the hair, the lighter the hair, the finer the foundation material, and

the more exquisite the workmanship needs to be, the longer it will take to build the wig. One of the most important times to have a fully hand-tied wig on a custom foundation is when only one man in a cast will be wearing a wig. If this one wig is not beautifully done, the actor will stand out like a sore thumb and his wig will be obvious. This is the most difficult of situations. This is when everything from the hair prep to the foundation material to the last hair knotted into the front counts to make the wig appear completely natural. Another critical time for a wig to look completely natural is when a principal actor has to be reshot in a movie after they have gone onto another project and cut and dyed their hair. In these situations, a fronted commercial wig just doesn't look natural enough.

The foundation you choose to build depends on several factors. Wig makers have developed and adapted foundation patterns and assembly methods to suit production, performer, staff, and

company needs. There is no one "perfect" foundation. In this chapter, you will find examples of some of the more

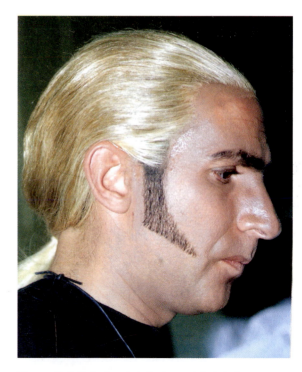

Figure 6-1 Fully hand tied wig over dark hair.

common foundation patterns, materials, and methods along with instructions on how to make them and a discussion of the advantages and disadvantages of each. There are many variations of foundations available. Many are shown at the end of the chapter.

TYPES OF FOUNDATIONS

All foundations begin with the concept of wrapping flat fabric around a round head. If you have ever tried to wrap a soccer ball with gift-wrap paper, you will understand the predicament. When making a lace-front wig, the fine lace is added to a foundation "back." In this chapter, the term "foundation" refers to the back of the wig. We will discuss the four basic types of foundations:

1. **The circumference band foundation.** A traditional foundation. Two pieces of fabric are used, one of which is a continuous band that goes around the diagonal circumference of the head. See Figure 6-1b.

2. **A nape-piece foundation.** A foundation that is made with a shaped piece at the nape of the neck. This style has become more common in recent years. This type of foundation will have a nape, crown, and front. In some cases the crown area may be in two or more pieces. See Figure 6-1c.

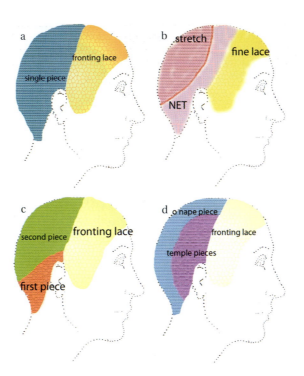

Figure 6-1 (a) One piece. (b) Circumference band. (c) Nape band. (d) Coif.

3. **One-piece foundations.** These foundations are made of one piece of lace that is darted and stretched around the head. These require that the fabric either be stretched from flat to round or be gathered or darted wherever there is too much fabric. See Figure 6-1a.

4. **The hatmaker's coif foundation.** This foundation idea is taken from the idea of a close-fitting skull cap that has been used in fashion and costume for centuries. See Figure 6-1d.

Before beginning constructing any foundation, ask yourself these questions:

- What does it need to look like?
- What does it need to do?
- What materials do I have or can get?
- Who is going to do the work?
- How long does it need to last?

All of these things are very important, because the "best" wig for the only actor in a realistic play that takes place in a small 250-seat theater is going to need to be very fine hand-tied work on a very thin, well-fitting all-lace foundation made with good-quality human hair. Such a wig, while very nice-looking, is probably not practical for the chorus woman standing in the back of a crowd scene of 200, wearing a large-brimmed hat over the wig and involving a quick change in and out of the wig by herself with a volunteer dresser for the community holiday pageant that performs three times. For her, a much sturdier, less-expensive wig is more practical.

Foundations can be grouped by materials used in the construction, by the way the piecing and patterning is done, and by the method of construction.

Pattern Style	Lace Type	Seam Style	Ribbon	Sewing Method
circumference	all fine lace	overlap, no fold	galloon	machine straight stitch
nape	vegetable and caul net	single fold overlap	invisible mesh ribbon	machine stitch zig zag
one piece back	medium weight laces	double fold overlap	twill tape	hand sewn straight
coif	Fosshape	french seam	bias tape	hand sewn diagonal whip stitch
other	buchram		none	invisible thread "crochet" stitch
	opaque silk			invisible thread straight stitch
	chamois			
	felt			

Chart 6-1 For each foundation, pick one from each column.

BUILDING A CIRCUMFERENCE-BAND FOUNDATION

Here are the steps used to build a circumference-band foundation using traditional wig-making methods and materials.

VEGETABLE NET & CAUL NET/ CIRCUMFERENCE BAND/ RIGHT-SIDE-OUT/HAND SEWN

In this example, the foundation will be constructed right-side-out, or as it will sit on the performer's head. This method is well suited to custom wigs that need to fit very well. In addition, this type of foundation will hold up for many performances. This foundation style is sturdy and will support many rows

of weft. It is a foundation that can withstand hundreds of performances with heavy hats pinned on and off during quick changes, because the vegetable net on the top is so durable.

1. Establish the hairline pattern on the block by using a plastic tracing or measurements as described earlier in the book. Then add lines for the location of the seams where materials will change. The vegetable net ring will go all the way to the back edge of the nape. The transition from fronting lace to vegetable net can be anywhere from 1 inch to 4 inches behind the front hairline. The vegetable net can be anywhere from 1 inch wide to 4 inches wide.

2. Lay the silk ribbon down over the block. The silk ribbon will follow the edge of the foundation, where pieces of netting will be joined and wherever additional stability is wanted. Make sure to place the silk

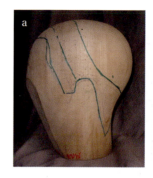 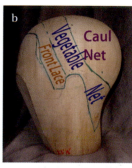

Figure 6-2 The pattern of the foundation has been drawn on the head block (a). The types of lace used have been added in (b).

Figure 6-3 Silk ribbon held in place with points.

Figure 6-4 When you get to a corner, place a point on the outside of the ribbon at the very corner and then create the dart by folding the ribbon in without flipping over.

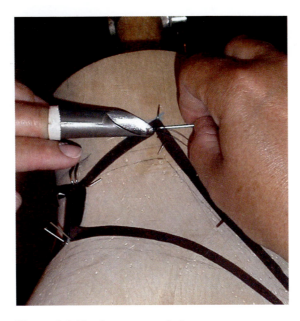

Figure 6-6 Hand-sew corner darts.

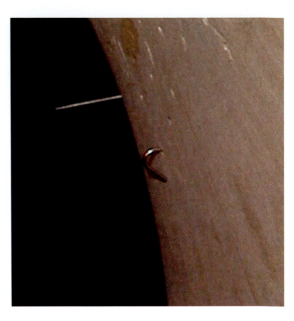

Figure 6-7 Point loop for bracing threads.

Figure 6-5 Around the ear curves, use points to hold the longest line in place. Later on, you will gather or dart the short edge and stitch.

ribbon so that it is flat but not pulled so tightly that it might shrink when removed from block.

When you are working with the silk ribbon, you may wish to wet it so that it will stick slightly to the wooden block as you work. Pay careful attention to the corners and curves.

3. Brace the ribbon to the block. After sewing the corner darts, short curve gathers, and any places where ribbon needs to be joined, it is helpful to switch from points to "bracing threads." Bracing threads are used wherever you need to hold ribbon or fabric to the block but where a point or a pin would get "locked in." Start

by putting a point into the block in an area where no lace will be placed. Then fold the point over and tap the other end into the block to create a small loop or "eye" that your sewing needle will be able to go through easily. See Figure 6-7

To make the bracings, choose a bright color of thread that will be easy to see later when it is time to remove the threads. Double the thread and knot the ends together securely. Next, go through the point loop and secure the thread by taking the needle back through the loop of thread. Take the needle and catch the ribbon and go back to one of the eyes. It will take some practice to figure out the right angles of tension to hold the ribbon in place with bracings. The goal is to keep the ribbon from sliding up, down, or off the block. Anchor outside corners and tips away from the foundation. Anchor the ear curve so that the curve is held up and away from the ear.

4. Place the caul net on the block and secure the center of the crown with a point. Gently continue to smooth the caul net and point it in place. Ease, gather, or pleat any fullness. It is very important to smooth rather than stretch the caul net over the crown of the head. If the caul net is stretched too tightly on the block, when the foundation is removed from the block the caul net will shrink back and will create

Figure 6-9 Darts in caul net.

Figure 6-8 Bracing threads to hold silk ribbon in place once points are removed.

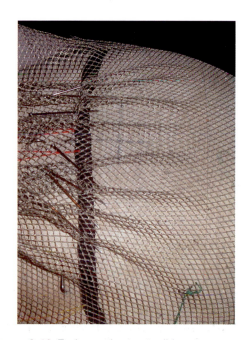

Figure 6-10 Easing caul net onto ribbon.

a foundation that is too small. Easing and gathering will create a crown that has more forgiveness for pin curls and bulky hair. Darting creates a more form-fitting crown that will hug the head under flat styles.

Figure 6-11 Sewing caul net darts.

Figure 6-12 Sew the caul net to the edge of ribbon away from the center of the crown.

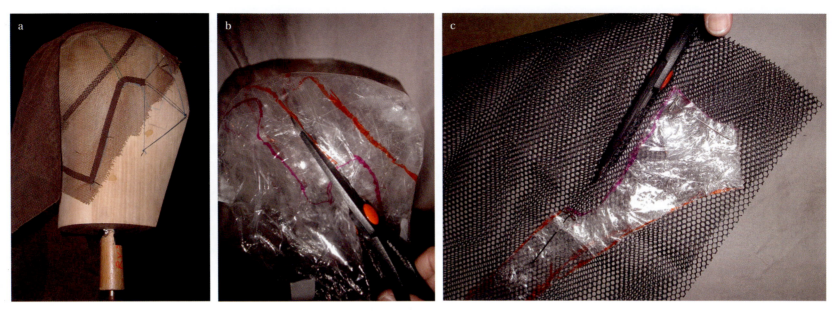

Figure 6-13 (a) Drape vegetable net over block. (b) A pattern for vegetable net circumference band made by cutting the plastic tracing. (c) Cutting net using pattern created out of plastic tracing.

5. Sew the caul net to the ribbon. If there are darts in the caul net, sew along both sides of the dart.

Trim away any excess caul net.

6. Place vegetable net over the block. Normally the "grain" is placed running along the line from center of forehead to center of nape.

It is possible to place the "grain" running from ear to ear. This decision is most often made based on the best way to get the piece out of the fabric. It is best to keep the vegetable net symmetrical. If the grain is diagonal in any way, the foundation will torque on the head. The vegetable net can be draped as shown in Figure 6-13a or a pattern can be created by wrapping plastic or paper over the block, or cutting up the plastic head tracing of the performer, as shown in Figures 6-13b & 6-13c.

Wetting the vegetable net with plain water will make it more malleable and easier to place on the block smoothly.

7. Hand-sew the vegetable net to the sides of the silk ribbons that face each other first: in other words, the inside edge of the outer ribbon and the outside edge of the inner ribbon.

8. Trim the vegetable net and fold under. Fold so that one row of vegetable net extends over the ribbon edge. Sew folded edge of vegetable net along ribbon edge.

9. Add fronting lace. Stretch and lay your lace front, as discussed in previous chapters. In this instance, the front edge of the vegetable net has been left raw to provide a minimal bulk where the fronting lace and vegetable net will overlap.

Figure 6-14 Blue thread has been used to make it easier to see in the photo. When making a wig foundation, use thread that matches the foundation fabric.

Figure 6-15 Stitches have intentionally been made larger and in contrasting thread to help make more visible. When making a foundation, keep the stitches as small as possible and use thread that matches foundation fabric color.

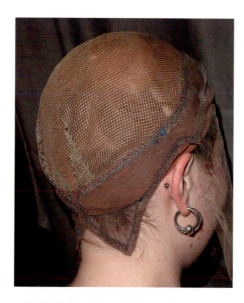

Figure 6-16 Finished foundation on head.

VARIATIONS ON CIRCUMFERENCE BAND FOUNDATIONS

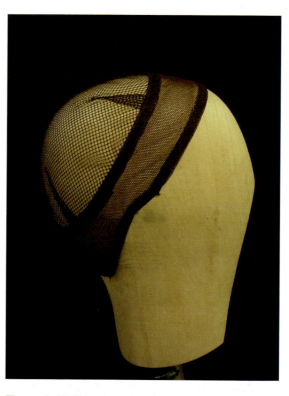

Figure 6-17 This circumference-band foundation has ribbon and hemmed vegetable net all around its outside edge. It is now ready to have a lace front added.

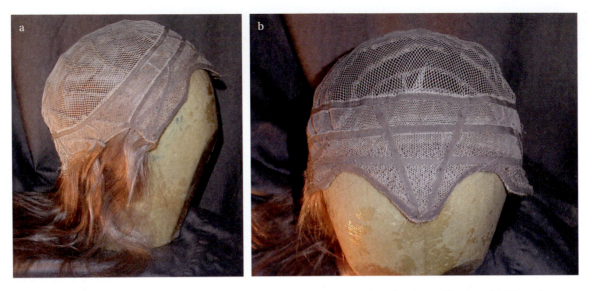

Figure 6-18 (a) Circumference-band foundation for shaped edge hard front for eighteenth-century tie-back-style wig, profile view. (b) Circumference-band foundation for eighteenth-century-style wig showing male pattern–shaped hard front edge.

Figure 6-19 (a) Lace-fronted circumference-band foundation made from vegetable net and lightweight dance power net. (b) The center back of this wig has power net to the nape edge to create a foundation that would stretch over the bulky prep of shoulder-length dreadlocks. (c) The front edge of the vegetable net has been folded toward fronting lace to create a smooth-finished inside edge.

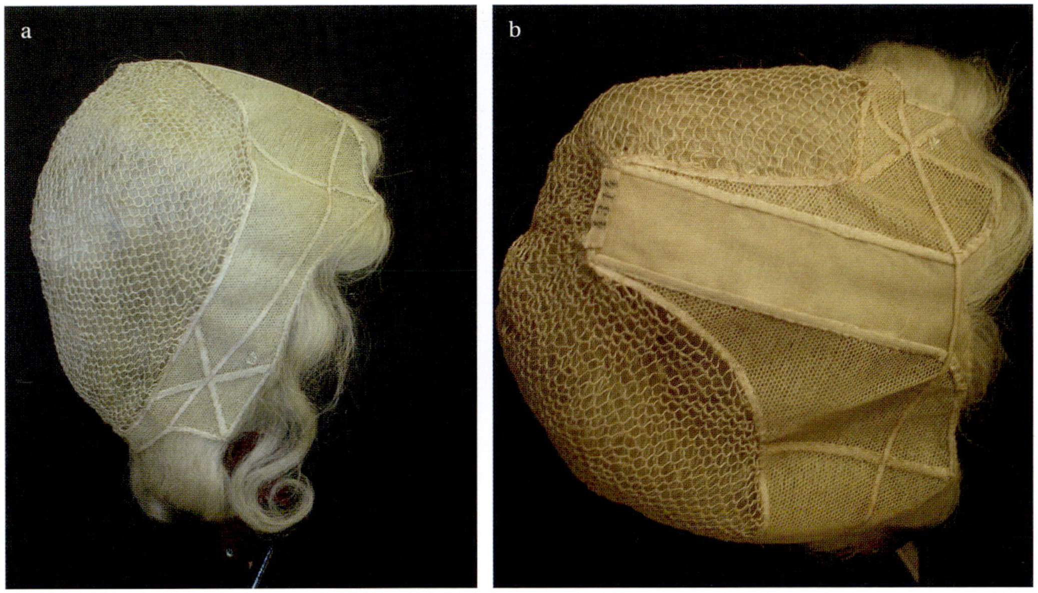

Figure 6-20 (a) Profile view of antique (1920) circumference-band foundation with hand-knotted caul net. (b) Top view of antique circumference-band foundation with silk parting and shaped front edge.

Figure 6-22 Circumference-band foundation made from vegetable net with dyed silk back and flesh silk blender and lace front. Made for chorus and dancers in *Turandot*, Atlanta Opera. Dark silk was used for foundation back to completely cover blonde hair with minimal rows of weft.

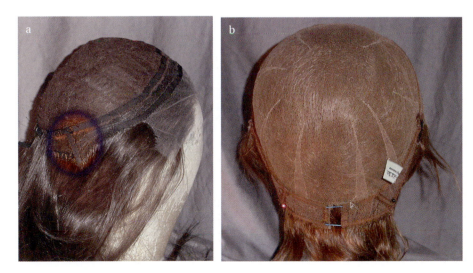

Figure 6-21 (a) Circumference band foundation made from dyed net lace. Nape corners have galloon covered stays. (b) Vegetable net nape showing center back split with elastic running through tubular galloon (silk ribbon) casing and covered stays to hold nape corners out.

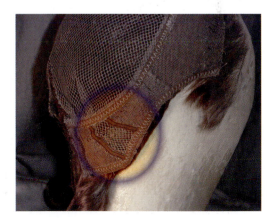

Figure 6-23 Vegetable and caul net foundation with caul net gussets at nape corners to make pinning the nape easier.

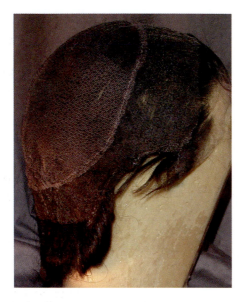

Figure 6-24 Circumference band made from wonder lace with lightweight power net on crown. Ribbon around outside of nape only.

Nape-Piece Foundation

There are several shape variations commonly used in nape band foundations.

A nape band foundation can be created out of a wide range of materials. It can be created using the technique and process order of the previous example with ribbon going on the block first. This example, however, will not use any ribbon, in order to show how to make a foundation without ribbon.

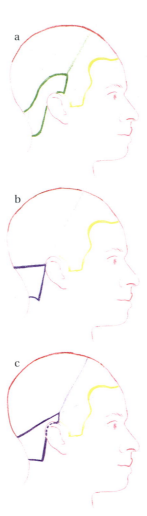

Figure 6-25 (a) Ear curve nape band. (b) Trapezoid nape band. (c) Hairline tension nape.

1. Nape-piece foundations start with a piece of lace at the nape. This piece may be draped over a pattern drawn on the block or patterned. Grain may run up the center back or across the nape. Avoid diagonal grain, as it always torques on the head.

2. Cover the crown of the head with lace. Place a wig point in the center of the crown first. Then place a point at the center front and center back, followed by a point near each ear. Next, gently stretch the lace creating ease or darts where needed. Darting or easing should be symmetrical to help the foundation stay in place on the head.

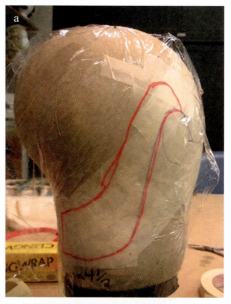

Figure 6-26 (a) Creating pattern with plastic on top of padded block. (b) Free-draping net onto nape of block.

3. Sew the two pieces together by hand with either a standard needle and thread or a ventilating hook and invisible thread. Create two parallel lines and trim back the lace to the sewing.
4. Finish the outside nape edge by turning net up and sewing.
5. Trim front edge of crown and stretch/lay the fronting lace. Refer to previous chapters for detailed information on how to stretch lace for a front.

The nape-piece foundation is now ready to have the hair added.

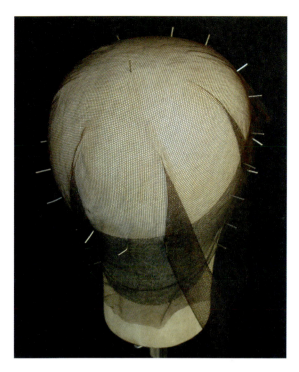

Figure 6-27 Crown covered in net.

Figure 6-29 Trim and fold around bottom edge to create a finished outside edge.

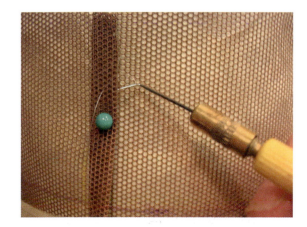

Figure 6-28 Two layers of net sewn together with invisible thread.

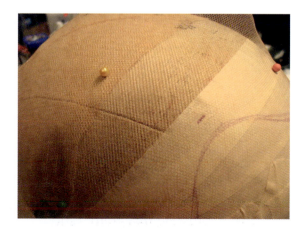

Figure 6-30 Fronting lace stretched over crown lace that is pinned.

Figure 6-31 Using the bracing technique to hold the front edge of the crown net in place if the pin heads get in the way.

VARIATIONS ON NAPE-PIECE FOUNDATIONS

Figure 6-32 Nape band made from net lace with film lace front. Ribbon used on outer nape edge only. Crown is in two pieces.

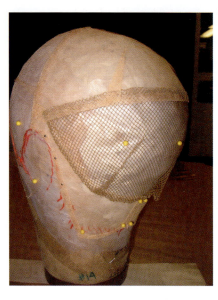

Figure 6-34 Wonder lace nape and two part crown.

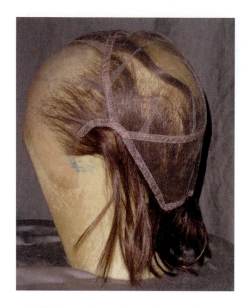

Figure 6-36 Foundation of super lace with monofilament ribbon.

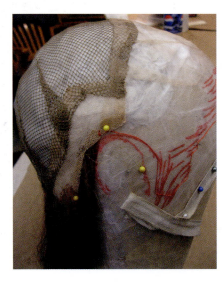

Figure 6-33 Caul net crown and net lace nape. Notice hair coming from both inside and outside of nape.

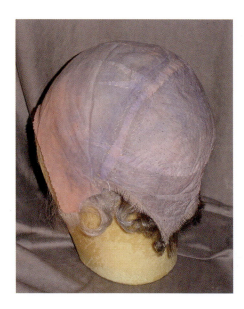

Figure 6-35 Foundation made with three pieces of wig silk for nape, crown, and blender.

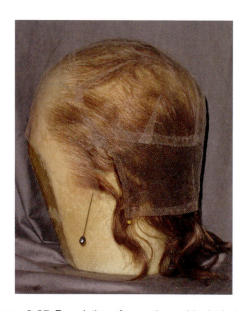

Figure 6-37 Foundation of super lace with single-layer seams and single turned edge.

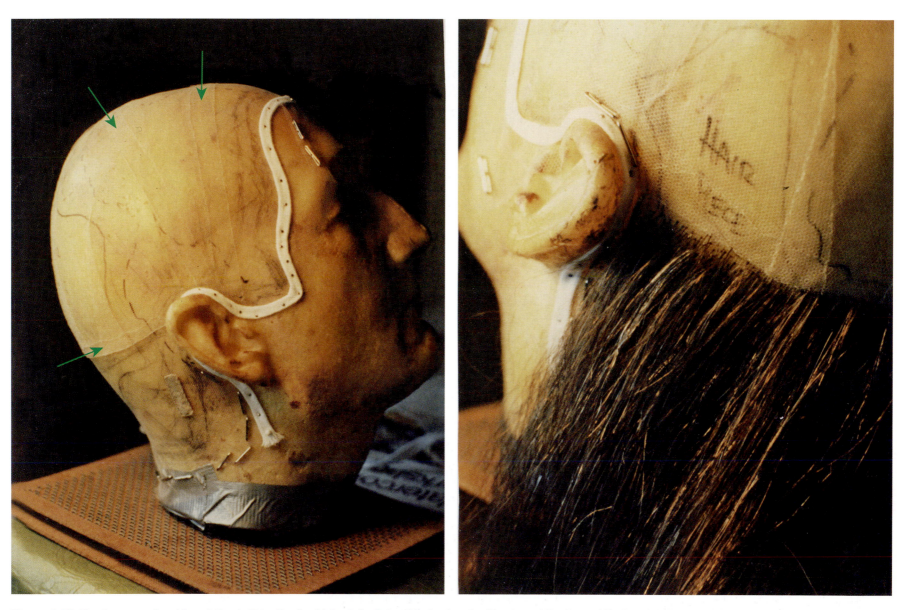

Figure 6-38 Fine-lace nape-band foundation built by Bradley M. Look for Robert Englund as the Phantom of the Opera. Wig foundation was built in 4 pieces on rigid polyfoam copy of actor's head. Arrows indicate location of lace to lace seams stitched with invisible thread.

One-Piece Back Foundation

One-piece back is the fastest type of foundation. This type of back has more darts than the multipieced foundations described previously. This example will be made inside-out and partially machine-stitched, but can also be made right-side-out and hand-stitched. All seams and edges will be covered or folded. This type of foundation is best suited to hairstyles that have hair hanging down over the ears and the neck. In this example, the type of lace available at local wig stores sold as "weaving cap material" is being used. This type of foundation can also be made in lighter-weight laces.

1. Begin by establishing a hairline on the block using any of the methods described previously. (Figure 6-39)
2. Lay a large piece of net approximately 15 × 15 inches over the crown of the head and secure the center. See Figure 6-40

Figure 6-39 Establish your hairline on the wig block.

3. Place push pins down center line and on either side, paying great attention to grain and symmetry. See Figure 6-41
4. Create darts where needed. Your darts should end up being symmetrical. If they are not, check

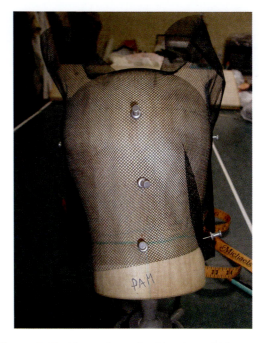

Figure 6-40 A large piece of net has been laid over the back of the head and secured with points.

your straight of grain and the symmetry of the block. Extra fabric at nape corners will help the foundation hold shape.

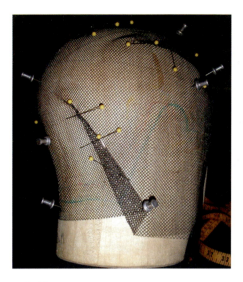

Figure 6-41

Figure 6-42 The outside edge the of ribbon is lined up with the line on the block.

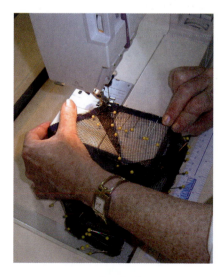

Figure 6-44 The hem of the lace is folded up and over the ribbon.

5. Place ribbon around the foundation back, lining up the outside edge of ribbon to line on block. Pin securely with sewing pins. See Figure 6-42

6. Trim the edge back to ½ inch beyond the ribbon. Clip curves as needed. See Figure 6-43

7. Fold "hem" up and over ribbon. Pin. See Figure 6-44

8. Remove the foundation from the block and machine-stitch along both edges of ribbon using the narrowest zigzag stitch possible. Stitch the darts by machine as well. See Figure 6-45

Using a straight stitch will cause the foundation to shrink slightly. Zigzag stitching stretches, and is therefore better to use on wig foundations.

Figure 6-43 Trim to ½ inch and clip curves.

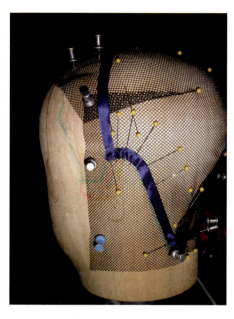

Figure 6-45 After removing the foundation from the block, machine stitch the edges of the ribbon with a narrow zigzag stitch.

VARIATIONS ON ONE-PIECE FOUNDATIONS

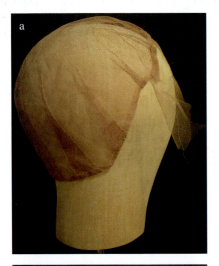

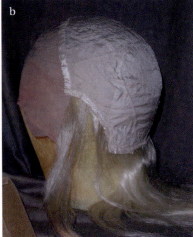

Figure 6-46 (a) One-piece back made from beige net lace with monofilament ribbon around nape edge. (b) One piece back of white shantung silk with wig silk blender at front. The use of opaque fabric for the foundation makes it possible to have a white yak wig without seeing the shadow of dark hair under translucent white yak hair. Putting in enough white yak to provide the coverage with hair alone creates tremendous bulk in the wig.

NOTES ABOUT ADDING HAIR

The fastest method of adding hair is to sew rows of weaving or weft that you buy from a hair supplier. The most realistic-looking method is to tie each hair individually.

It is fine to mix both weft and hand-knotting hair into a wig. If time is a great concern, start by hand-knotting the section that absolutely has to be hand-tied. This is usually around the face and the top of the head. These areas may also include a center back strip for a wig that will be braided. If time runs short, the less important areas can be filled in with weft. Perfect? Not really, but it is certainly a practical solution when you have limited time. See Figure 6-47

In general:

- The shorter the hair, the more important it is to hand-tie.
- The more natural the wig needs to look, the more important it is to hand-tie.
- The more movement wanted in long hair, the more important it is to hand-tie.

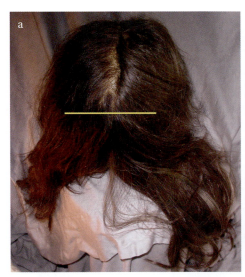

Figure 6-47 (a) Wig with hand-tied front, top, and crown. Nape filled in with weft. Yellow line indicates where transition occurs. (b) Wig worn by Greg Wood as Cyrano de Bergerac with Allison McLemore as Roxanne, presented by the Pennsylvania Shakespeare Festival. Wig built by Ming-yen Ho and Ashley Hardy. Photo by Lee A. Butz.

NOTE ABOUT SEAMS AND EDGES

Wherever two pieces of wig net overlap, the foundation becomes thicker and more opaque. Raw wig net edges will fray over time. Which type of foundation you choose to make depends on your needs for the wig:

1. The sturdiest foundation will last the longest. A foundation made with galloon, folded seams, and tightly stitched with double thread is sturdier and may look elegant from the inside, but adds a bit of bulk to the head.

or:

2. The thinnest, least visible foundation made by using the finest net, single-layer seams, no ribbon, and sewn with single invisible thread will look more realistic on the head, but have a much shorter lifespan.

PARTS, CROWN SWIRLS, AND COWLICKS

Parts, crown swirls, and cowlicks can be put into any style of foundation. Decide the directions and locations of these hair quirks and draw their placement on the block before you lay the wig net. This way you can make sure that the seams are not going to show through a part and that the darts will not make the crown swirl act even crazier.

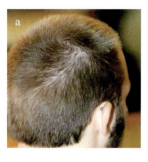
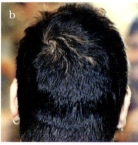

Figure 6-48 (a–c) Double-crown swirl visible in thinning hair.

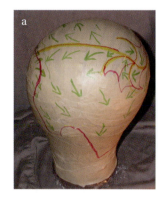

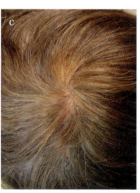

Figure 6-49 (a) and (b) Example of ventilating direction drawn on block. (c) Closeup of crown swirl on lace over silk.

MISCELLANEOUS FOUNDATIONS

Each situation requires a different solution. Here are a few more full-wig foundations with unique details.

Figure 6-50 Foundation of vegetable net with caul net pocket for wireless microphone pack.

Figure 6-51 Foundation built for Grandmother in *The Nutcracker*. The foundation was built with a hole in the crown to allow space for a bun, because the dancer had a quick change into a role that required a high bun in her own hair. The character wears a frilly cap that conceals the hole and the performer's own bun.

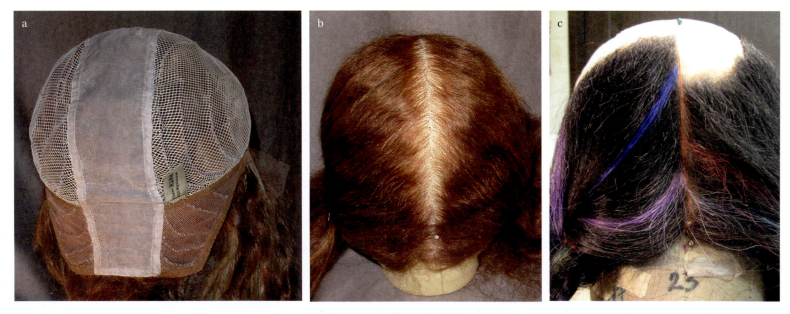

Figure 6-52 (a) Foundation with silk insert running center back to create a clean part. Notice rows of weft aiming for the ear area for the braided pigtails. (b) Outside view of wig designed by Kelsey Contois and built by Bree Schaller, UNCSA. (c) Another parting built on silk.

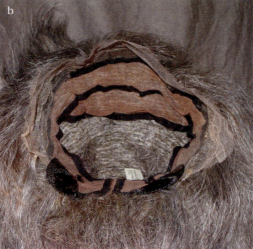
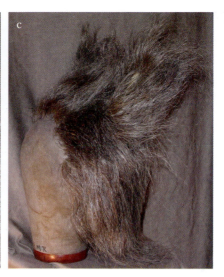

Figure 6-53 (a) Wolf from *Sleeping Beauty*. Wig, prosthetic, and makeup by Christina Grant, UNCSA. (b) Inside view of circumference band with extra-wide vegetable net at the top and extra silk ribbon sewn in to provide a stable place to sew ears. Over the vegetable net circumference band, stretch fur from National Fiber Technology was sewn. The same stretch fur from National Fiber Technology was also used on parts of the costume. (c) Side view of the Wolf wig, showing the hand tied human hair front blending into synthetic fur back.

BALDING WIGS

Although wigs are often used to add hair, there are times when the point is to make someone appear as if they have less hair growing. A balding wig can be worn over a latex, Glatzan, or balloon rubber bald cap, or it can have silk or chamois built into the foundation to imitate the skin under the balding areas.

A great deal of information is readily available on the subject of male pattern baldness. The Hamilton-Norwood scale was first developed in the 1950s and then revised in 1975. (The complete article can be found in *Southern Medical Journal*, November 1975, Vol. 68, No. 11.)

Bald areas begin in two areas of the head: the crown and the front hairline. In some men, the hair recedes from the front hairline with minimal loss of hair on the crown. In other men, the crown thins faster than the hairline moves back. Each pattern requires a different solution from the wig maker.

Foundations for balding wigs can be made using any combination of the materials described previously. In addition, chamois is occasionally used for the crown of a tonsure wig or for the balding pate. Most balding wigs utilize a nape band foundation. Just as foundations meant to have full heads of hair can be made with or without

ribbon, so can balding wigs. It is also possible to drape the lace directly on the block as well as create a pattern to use to cut the lace.

When making thinning or balding wigs with lighter salt-and-pepper mixes or entirely of white hair, use the lightest-weight lace or a medium-weight lace dyed to match the skin tone of the performer. Under scattered white or light gray hair, most single layer seams are not noticeable. One of the most common mistakes people make is putting too much hair in a balding wig. How the pieces get sewn together is very important as well. Regular thread that matches the foundation or skin tone will

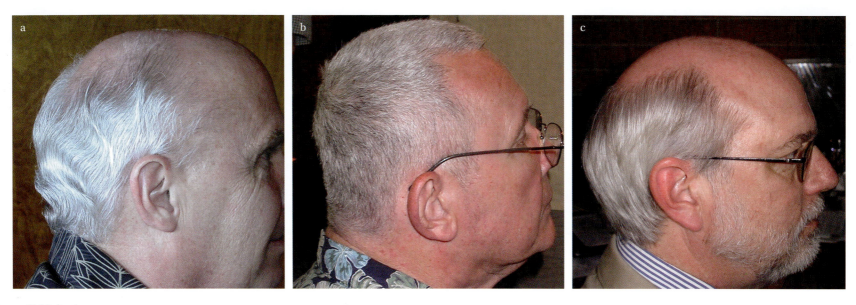

Figure 6-54 (a-c)

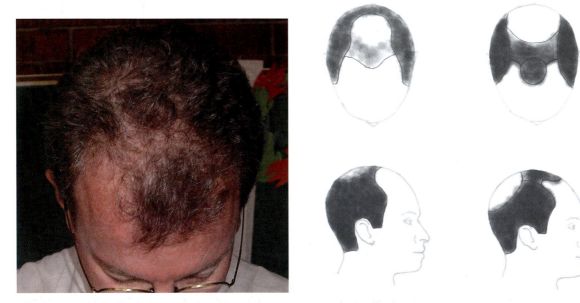

Figure 6-55

Figure 6-56 Basic male balding patterns.

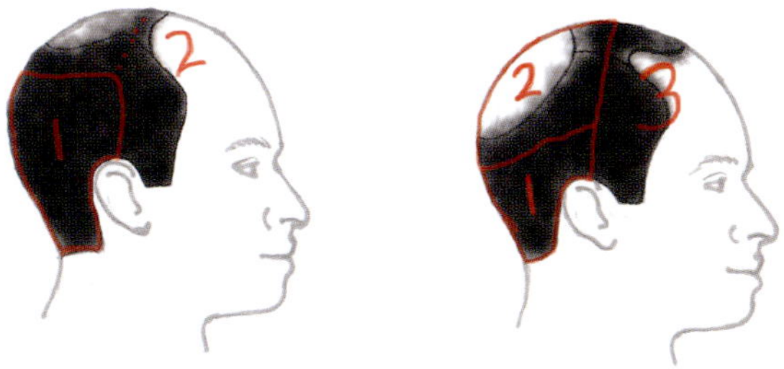

Figure 6-57 Possible patterns for the wig net piecing.

work. Invisible thread works better if done correctly. Keep either type of thread free of tension. Pulling invisible thread too tightly will create a ridge that will catch the light and actually make a line of shadow.

FRINGES

A fringe is a hairpiece, usually worn over a bald cap or shaved head, that has hair only on the lower back and sides. This type of wig leaves the top of the head completely bare.

When choosing materials and methods consider all factors: the time and skill of the building crew, the time and skill of the styling crew, who is running the show and handling the wig each night, what materials are available at what cost (including shipping or

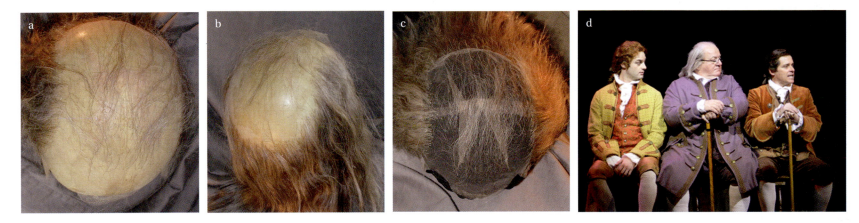

Figure 6-58 (a) and (b) Gray wig on fronting lace foundation. Built by Tera Willis. (c) The same wig, laid over black to show darts and seams more clearly. (d) The wig as worn by Richard Pruitt (center) as Ben Franklin in *1776*, presented by the Pennsylvania Shakespeare Festival. Also shown are Spencer Plachy as Thomas Jefferson and Richard B. Watson as John Adams. Photograph by Lee A Butz.

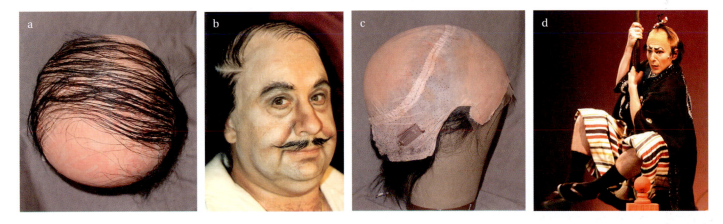

Figure 6-59 (a) Silk foundation with lace front. (b) Thomas Hammons as Benoit in *La Boheme*, Atlanta Opera. (c) The inside of the wig. (d) Wig worn by Jonathan Patterson as Koko in *The Mikado*, Brevard Opera, styled by Tera Willis.

Figure 6-60 Inside view of fringe using net lace and fronting lace. Edges were left raw and glued to bald cap.

Figure 6-62 Styled samurai by Tera Willis, model Isaac Grnya, UNCSA.

Figure 6-61 Inside view of samurai-style wig.

travel time to shop), the design concept and style of the show, and the length of the run are all factors that will influence what the "best" wig might be each time.

SUMMARY

What the "best" choice is for a wig for a leading lady in a Broadway show may not be practical for a regional theater's waitress in the beehive at the back of the ensemble.

CHAPTER 7 — Partial Wigs, Toupees, and Hairpieces

Anything smaller than a full wig is a hairpiece. What distinguishes one hairpiece from another is where on the head it will be worn, how it is made, length of hair, or the hairstyle it is used to create. There are many varieties of hairpieces for sale at the local mall, beauty supply stores, and online wig stores. The biggest reason for making a hairpiece or partial wig is be able to make it the exact color and texture to match someone's own hair. In some theatrical lighting situations, differences in the color of the performer's own hair and the piece may not be noticeable. In film and TV, any difference in color between performer's hair and that of a hairpiece is very evident.

One of the most common custom made hairpieces is the toupee. Toupees are partial wigs made to add hair to the crown and/or top of the head. The reason for adding hair may be to cover a balding or thinning area or to add length, as in Figure 7-1.

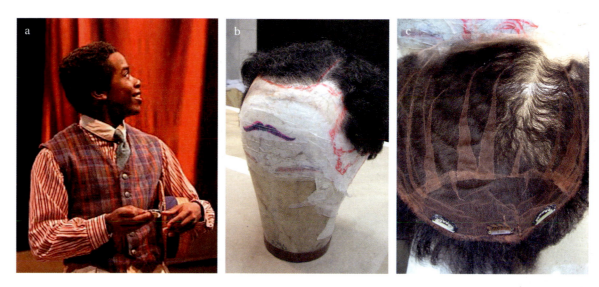

Figure 7-1 (a) (b) and (c) Lace Toupee worn by Shawn Patrick Tubbs. Photo by Mark Rutkowski for UT-A.

TOUPEE

Start by determining what part of the head needs to have additional hair. For transformations, toupees, and men's falls it is good to take a plastic tracing as well as a few measurements.

If you are making a toupee, be sure to mark the performer's own hairline as well as the desired the new hairline. You will want the back edge far enough over into the hair of the wearer that it will be possible to attach with toupee clips.

Figure 7-1 (d) Inside view of lace toupee.

GRAYING TEMPLE PIECES

White hair reflects light differently than hair-whitening sprays and liquids. For situations in which a performer may have to age during a quick change, gray temple pieces may be the solution. Similar to sideburns, these include a small piece of lace that has white or a

Figure 7-2 Philip Cokorinos wearing hand tied temple pieces over his own dark hair as Capellio in *I Capuletti e I Montecchi* backstage at The Atlanta Opera.

mix of white and natural hair color tied into the lace. These are then glued and brushed into the performer's own hair.

PULL-THROUGHS

A "pull through" is an open work hairpieces worn on the top of the head to add thickness or a color change. Pull throughs have a foundation of thread or monofilament ribbon onto which hair is tied or to which weft is sewn. Figure 7-3a shows a pull through made for a

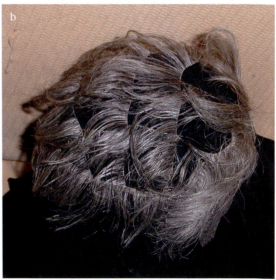

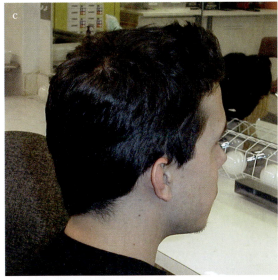

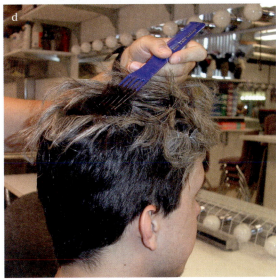

Figure 7-3 (a) Pull-through made on wig lace ribbon by Bradley M. Look. (b) Pull-through made by knotting human hair onto thread by UNCSA student Ming-yen Ho. (c) UNCSA wig student Michael Ferguson's own dark hair. (d) UNCSA wig student Leeanne Catena pulling dark hair in between rows of gray hair. (e) lace front pull through secured in place.

FALLS

TYPE 1

Falls are another type of hairpiece that can be purchased but are also often custom-made. Falls and extensions have much in common. Both are used to add length to hair.

Some falls are manufactured with a stiff, domed base to help create lift at the crown of the head. These were very popular in the 1960s and 1970's. This style of fall is unsuitable for adding hair for men's eighteenth-century styles.

Figure 7-4 (a) This style of commercial fall is built on a stiff, dome-shaped base that adds height at the crown of the head. (b) Dome-based fall and 2 switches used to create an 1865 style.

woman to add thickness and highlights. Figures 7-3b-e show a pull through with lace front used to add grey to a young full head of hair.

TYPE 2

A "ladder-back" fall is one that has horizontal rows of weft sewn to vertical rows of ribbon. See Figure 7-5c.

1. Start by pinning a vertical ribbon to a block or cork board.
2. Starting at the bottom-left corner, sew the beginning of a weft to the left-hand ribbon.
3. Take across and sew to middle ribbon and right-side ribbon at #2.
4. Then angle weft up to left approximately 1 inch above the starting point and sew weft to ribbon, pull across, and sew wherever ribbon and weft meet.
5. Continue as diagrammed. This will create a 5×10-inch "base."

When 20-inch-long hair weft is used and the hairpiece is sewn to the bottom of a wig with 20-inch hair, an additional 10 inches of hair is added to total length.

TYPE 3

Quite often, falls are made to add length to men's hair for eighteenth-century productions. Men's falls for adding length to 1770-style ponytails are made to sit from the nape up to the occiput or crown without adding any volume. These can be made on wig net foundations or diamond-pattern "ladder backs." See Figures 7-6 & 7-7.

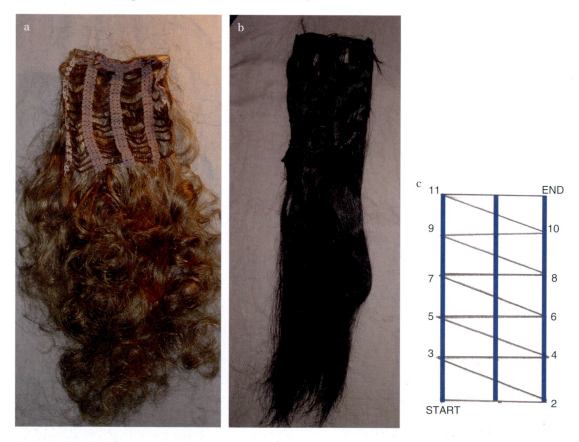

Figure 7-5 (a) This ladder-back fall with horizontal rows of weft is actually the center back section of a commercial weft wig. (b) This custom-made ladder-back fall uses 21-inch hair sewn to three vertical ribbons in a zigzag pattern. (c) Guidelines for making a ladder-back fall.

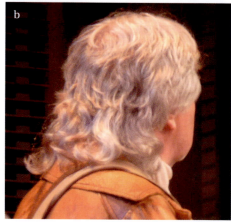

Figure 7-6 (a) Commercial weft sewn to toupee clips. (b) As worn onstage.

Figure 7-7 Fall pulled into queue.

Figure 7-8 3/4 wig.

point of attachment, weft, needles, and strong thread. Here's how:

1. Secure the ribbon or cording to the table or counter. If you plan on making a number of stem switches, you might consider buying a winding machine from a wig-making supply house.
2. Twist the ribbon left over right until it twists up on itself.

Figure 7-9a

3. Fold the end of the ribbon up and stitch. Then stitch the end of the weft to the ribbon.

Figure 7-9b

TYPE 4

A 3/4 wig is a type of hairpiece that is similar to a fall and to a wig. A foundation of wig net is made and hair is either tied into the wig net or weft is sewn to the wig net. The use of a foundation fabric give this piece more stability and more locations to pin to the head. See Figure 7-8.

SWITCHES

Switch, pigtail, and ponytail are terms used interchangeably for any number of hairpieces that have small bases and long hair.

A *stem switch* is a hairpiece made of weft wrapped around a central ribbon or cord. By wrapping weft up a central cord in a spiral pattern, it is possible to give the illusion of a braid or ponytail that is longer than the length of the actual hair. It is common to find "three-stem switches" that are made specifically to make a traditional three-strand braid.

To make a single stem switch, you will need a ribbon or cord, a secure

4. Slowly untwist the ribbon left over right; simultaneously the weft will wrap itself around the ribbon. Stop and sew the weft to the ribbon at each full rotation.
5. When the switch has reach the desired length, cut both weft and ribbon with 1.5 inches left.
6. Fold the ribbon over to create a small loop.

Figure 7-9c

7. Sew the ribbon loop and fold and wrap remaining weft over the ribbon.
8. To finish the stem loop, cover with button-hole stitches.

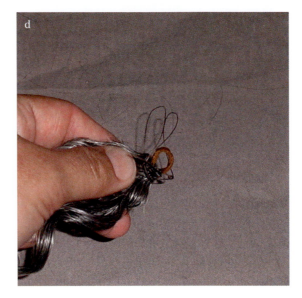

Figure 7-9d

KABUKI-INSPIRED LION WIG

One of the most practical uses for making a switch is making a Kabuki-inspired "lion wig."

The foundation for the lion wig was made entirely with vegetable net using a nape band, shaped front edge, and pieced crown. Additional layers of vegetable net and ribbon were added for stability. Stays are used at the sideburns and nape corners. A lace front was sewn on to provide extra tension, as this wig is so back-heavy.

- Rows of weft with 12-inch-long hair are sewn in a circular pattern every {3/4} inch.

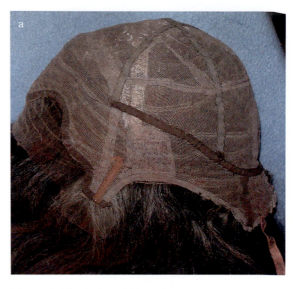

Figure 7-10a Inside of Lion wig.

Figure 7-10b Switch made on 1/2 inch thick cording for tails of Lion wig.

- Three-stem switches are built using the same gray human hair weft, bought at a local wig store.
- The side stems are approximately 25 inches long.
- The back tail has a stem of 50 inches.

- The stems are 1-inch-diameter nylon rope from the hardware store. This was chosen for strength, open weave, and price.

Figure 7-10c

FULL-BOTTOM WIGS

In addition to cutting up commercial wigs to make men's full-bottom wigs, this style can be created by adding fall-like additions or switches to a full foundation wig. In this case, the ladder-back fall extensions are made by sewing commercial weft to vegetable net rectangles. See Figure 7-11.

Figure 7-11 Inside view of far left wig in Figure 5-50f.

MAKING CUSTOM WEFT

When making a partial piece or planning extension work of any kind, the most important thing to consider is the color of the hair.

The color of hair as it grows on a human head is tricky to duplicate with total accuracy. The average human head has far more color variation than most people realize. Most of us have far more than three colors of hair naturally. Take a really close look at several natural, undyed redheads and medium blondes. You will see strands the color you think of as "their color" plus strands much lighter, darker, and sometimes even noticeably different in color. Natural redheads will often have strands of the base red, plus orange, yellow, and even an ash (almost green) dark blonde!

In addition, each strand comes out of the head a specific color and may change color toward the tip from dye, bleach, nicotine stain, swimming pool chlorine damage, sun exposure. And they can even vary because of health or diet reasons.

Hair also varies in color from one part of the head to another. Long hair is likely to be darker on the nape than around the face or on the top of the head. If someone always has a part in the same place, the hair near the part is almost always noticeably lighter than the hair from the nape.

In addition, most hair dyes do not come in truly natural colors. An extremely skilled professional colorist can create a wide range of colors, but generally the color will be more even and flatter than "nature-made." Medium-blond to medium-brown are particularly hard to match. The natural colors are usually a mix of warm brown and almost khaki green or muddy gray. Most brown hair dyes appear red or purple in comparison to natural brown hair, because who wants to pay to have hair the color of old algae? A skilled professional colorist has access to professional products, including pure hue additives to adjust color. Sometimes a dip in fabric dye can shift the brown hair being used in the hairpiece to the right spot on the color wheel.

Finally, lighting can play tricks on you: the hairpiece that matches perfectly in the fitting room, dressing room, or with daylight streaming through the studio window, can look bright purple on stage next to the performer's own natural brown hair. Whenever possible, test color in the type of lighting that the piece will be worn. If it is for wearing to work under fluorescent lighting, then match the color under the same type of fluorescent lights. If it will be worn on a film in daylight, then match it in daylight.

The easiest way to make sure that a hair piece and the person's hair match is to color both. This is not always possible. So be very careful about what part of the head you are trying to match and incorporate the right color in the right place.

For any hairpiece or wig made out of weft, it is possible to use commercial single-weft, double-weft, or hand-made weft. Here are the steps for creation of these pieces:

1. Start winding the bobbins with strong thread. Hymark or other button or carpet threads work well.

Figure 7-12 (a) Tying thread around a bobbin. (b) Tape the thread to the bobbin with masking tape to keep the thread from sliding. (c) Wrap the thread around the bobbin, using even tension. Be sure to wrap all three bobbins the same direction.

2. Set up the wefting sticks with the knob on the left and the bobbins on the right. Insert the bobbins in three holes shoulder height. Tie all three threads to the knob on the left pole.

Figure 7-13 (a) shows wefting stick set up. (b) creating a stop knot.

3. It is helpful to make a single button-hole-style knot to create a "stop" in the thread.

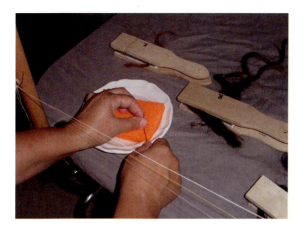

Figure 7-14 Wetting hair on sponge.

Figure 7-15a

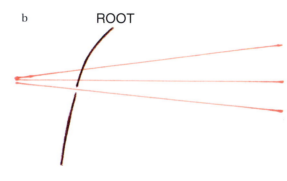

b   ROOT

Figure 7-15b

Figure 7-15c

The tension of the three threads should be equally taut. If plucked, each thread should sound the same note. If the threads are too taut, they will snap. If too loose, they will twist.

4. Pull a few strands of hair from the drawing cards and wet the hair by drawing over a sponge sitting in a saucer of water. (Be sure to wash the sponge and saucer with antibacterial soap and rinse completely before each use. This sponge should only be used for this purpose and never for cleaning.)

5. Hold the hair between the left thumb and index finger slightly behind the bottom thread. Use the thumb and index finger of the right hand to pull the root end of the hair in front of the middle thread.

6. Slide the hair as far to the left as possible.

7. Bring the root end over the top thread. Using the index finger of the left hand, push the root end forward between the top threads. Catch this with the right hand.

8. Pull hair down in front of bottom two threads.

9. Slide the hair to the left.

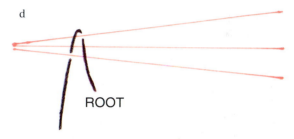

Figure 7-15d

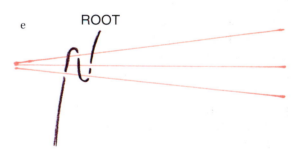

Figure 7-15e

10. Wrap the root end of the hair around and behind the bottom threads. Bring it forward between the top two threads and wrap over the top thread. Slide the hair to the left.

f

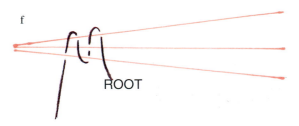

ROOT

Figure 7-15f

g

ROOT

Figure 7-15g

h

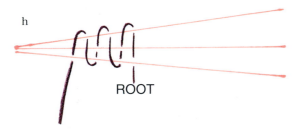

ROOT

Figure 7-15h

11. Repeat steps 7-15f & g if desired and finish by pulling the root ends behind the top and bottom threads but in front of the middle thread. Slide the hair to the left and lock tightly by pushing with the right thumbnail.

i

Figure 7-15i

12. Well-made hand weft will not show any of the top thread between hair loops. If you see the top thread, you are not pushing the hair to the left tightly or frequently enough. It is also possible that the threads are too loose and are gathering between hair loops.

j

Figure 7-15j

Figure 7-16 Fall made with both machine weft and hand weft. The bottom six rows of weft are commercial weft in the root color of performer's hair. The top two rows are hand-made weft with the same base color, plus streaks of lighter brown and dark red to match the highlights in the performer's hair.

HAIR PREP

Hair prep is important to how a wig looks and feels. Hair prep helps hold and hide the performer's own hair out of sight, and provides the anchor points that the bobby pins and wig pins go into to hold a wig in place. The traditional method is to make a series of pincurls around the head.

The most important locations to have pincurls or anchor points are:

1. **Center front forehead.** This is important to help keep wig from sliding backwards.
2. **Over each ear.** These two keep the wig from flapping at the sideburns.
3. **Corners of the nape of the neck.** These provide secure points, especially for very short wigs or wigs styled up off the neck.
4. **Crown of the head (Martian antennae points).** These two provide the basic security points. In quick changes, these are often the only location wig pins are placed.

Figure 8-1 Short hair in pin curls for wig.

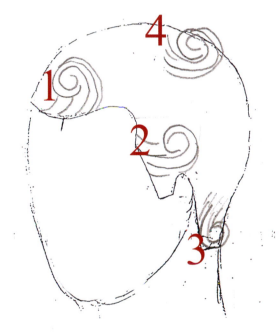

Figure 8-2

LONG HAIR

Long hair will sometimes make pincurls that are bulky and make the head unnaturally large under a wig.

Figure 8-3 Large sections twisted and clumped create lumps under a wig and can add as much as 2 inches to the circumference of the performer's head. When this happens, the wig will not fit correctly.

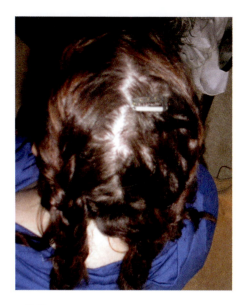

Figure 8-4

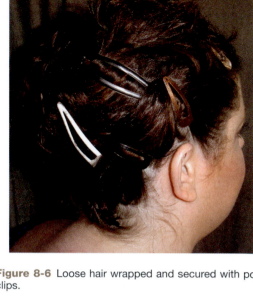

Figure 8-6 Loose hair wrapped and secured with pop clips.

A better way to prep long hair is to wrap most of it or braid the hair:

1. Section the hair into two or four parts. Loose braids can make this easier; however, braids that are too tight will create ridges.
2. Criss-cross the sections, securing with pop clips.
3. Cover the hair with a wig cap. The color of the wig cap should match either the hair color of the performer or the color of the wig.

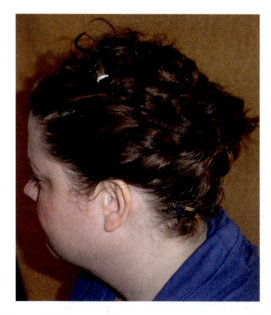

Figure 8-5 Loose braids crossed and securely pinned.

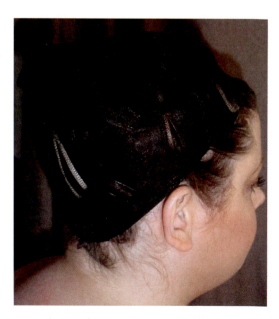

Figure 8-7

4. Pin the edges of the cap.

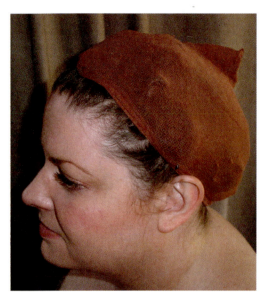

Figure 8-8 The front edge of a wig cap should be pinned securely behind the hairline. If this step is skipped, the cap can slide forward and become visible through the wig lace.

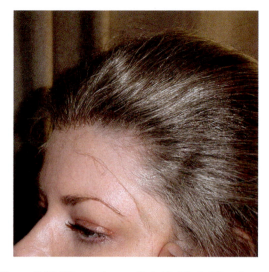

Figure 8-10 When a wig cap sits behind the hairline, the lace and wig hair transition into a performer's skin seamlessly.

Figure 8-11 Small rubber bands can create small secure spots in short hair.

SHORT HAIR

Sometimes hair is too short, fine, and/or straight to make pincurls easily. There are several ways to create secure anchor points. Hair that has extra-hold hairspray or cement spiking gel is easier to twist and fold into pincurls than clean slippery hair. Be very cautious about the use of conditioning pomades, because they can make the bobby pins slide right out of the hair. Cheap freeze-hair products and hair-cement glues work much better when creating hair preps for wigs.

Hair that is very short can be held securely with small rubber bands, pop clips, or toupee comb clips. See Figures 8-11 and 8-12.

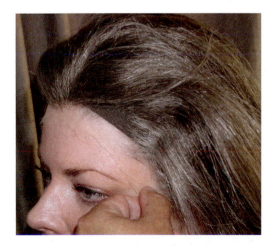

Figure 8-9 A wig cap placed too low in front of hairline, and thus visible through lace.

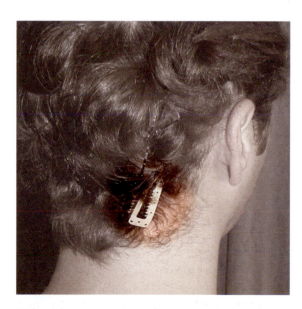

Figure 8-12 Toupee comb clips hold very short hair tightly.

Figure 8-13 Hair only half an inch long can still have toupee clips for anchor points.

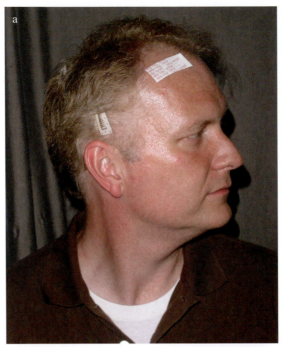

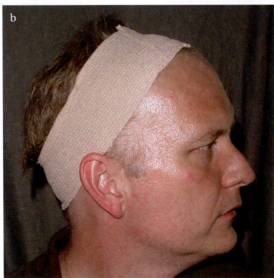

Figure 8-14 (a) Comb clips and toupee tape in place. (b) Sports wrap in place.

When there just isn't hair to pincurl or toupee clip, it is still possible to create something to anchor the wig. Sports wrap, such as a self-adhesive lightweight ACE®, Coban or Vet Wrap bandage, works very well when there is little or no hair. The addition of toupee tape helps the self adhesive wrap hug the head more securely. Sports wrap comes in white, tan, black, and assorted bright colors. It is found in first-aid sections of most drugstores; the bright colors can also be found in tack and veterinary supply stores.

Even cheaper alternatives to sports wrap are bridal tulle and nylon net. Simply secure one end to hair or skin and wrap around twice. Secure second end. Nylon net is a bit scratchy, and some sensitive performers may object. But it does create a sort of hook-and-loop connection to short hair and the inside of a wig.

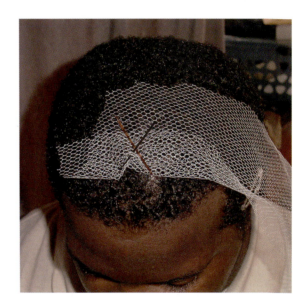

Figure 8-15 Nylon net bobby-pinned CF and then wrapped around the head to provide areas that will hold wig pins.

Wig caps made of nylon-stocking-like material serve several purposes. In addition to holding all the hair in place, the caps protect the inside of the wigs from sweat and from the performer's own hair. Human hair has an outside layer of cuticle that functions like little Velcro®. When a wig is made of virgin human hair that still has a cuticle, if the wig hair and the performer's hair are allowed to rub up against each other, the cuticles will grab on, the way two pieces of Velcro® stick together. Over time, this results in the wig hair being pulled inside the foundation. This is called *reversing*. A wig stocking cap creates a layer between the two and prevents reversing. So if possible, use a wig cap over the sports wrap or tulle.

HOW TO HOLD AND PUT ON A LACE-FRONT WIG

Here are directions for putting on a lace-front wig:

1. Remove all the blocking pins that are holding the wig to the canvas styling block.
2. Carefully grasp the wig by holding the back edge or other portion of sturdy foundation material. Do not carry around a styled wig by the hair or the lace front. Slip it off the block and hold it open with two hands. See Figures 8-16a & b.
3. Position yourself behind the performer, after sitting the performer in front of a mirror.

Figure 8-16

Figure 8-17

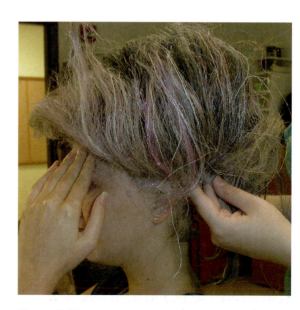

Figure 8-18

4. Place the CF lace slightly in front of the hairline. See Figure 8-17.
5. Once you have adjusted the position of the wig, have the performer place two fingers on the lace CF forehead. See Figure 8-18.

6. Gently lower the back of the wig into position. Carefully keep a tiny bit of space between the wig and the head, so that the wig does not catch on any pincurls. Whenever possible, hold the wig foundation rather than the styled hair or lace front.

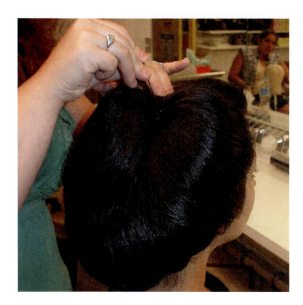

Figure 8-20

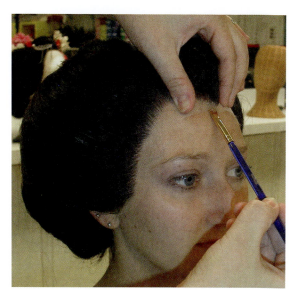

Figure 8-21

Figure 8-19

7. The first pins that go in the wig should be those on the crown of the head. These pins hold the wig in position while the edges get glued and finishing pins are attached. See Figure 8-20.

8. The front of the wig should get pinned or glued in place. Spirit gum goes on the skin under the lace. Gently pinch the CF lace and lift the sides to apply the glue. For most stage situations, only a small portion of the front lace needs glue. For film, the front edge is trimmed back and the entire edge is glued.

9. Press the lace into the spirit gum or Telesis adhesive while the adhesive is still wet and tacky. With spirit gum, a clean velour puff will press the lace down as well as remove any excess spirit gum from between the lace threads. A small piece of real chamois or clean nylon stocking cap also works. For film, a porcupine quill is a great tool for pressing lace down in between the hairs. This or any other pointy slender object will not mash the hairs into the glue, which will be visible on screen.

Figure 8-22

10. The final step is to pin the back of the wig. Always check the nape of a wig from underneath. Remember that the front row of the theatre is usually lower than the stage the audience members sitting in those seats will be looking up at the wig. Have the performer stand up while you squat down to get the right perspective on the nape of the neck as you pin it in place. The correct way to pin a nape is to insert a hairpin through the foundation aiming the ends toward the earlobe. Then reverse the ends of the pin and point them toward the CB of the nape. Do not place pins with the open end up toward the ceiling, because gravity will pull these out before the end of the first scene.

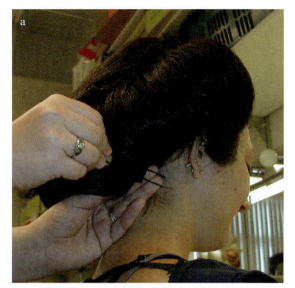

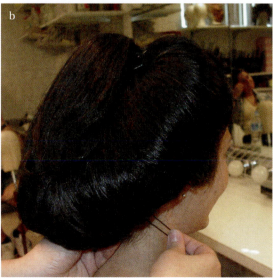

Figure 8-23

APPLYING HARD-FRONT WIGS AND FALLS

Any wig or fall that will have the performer's own hair styled over the front is applied in the same way:

1. Start by prepping the hair with pincurls, pop clips, tiny rubber bands, or toupee clips. Cover with a wig cap if the section is large enough to warrant. Leave out the front hair that will be used to cover the edge of the wig or fall. See Figure 8-24.

Figure 8-24

2. Place the wig behind the hairline but with the front edge covering the pincurls. Pin the crown and front edge of the wig. Then pin the nape.

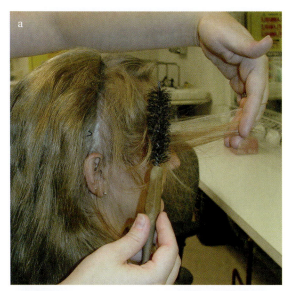

Figure 8-26

Figure 8-25

3. Sometimes it is helpful to lightly tease and spray the underside of the hair to be styled.
4. Brush over the edge of the wig. Pin and spray as needed.

Figure 8-27

REMOVING WIGS AFTER A PERFORMANCE

At the end of a performance, there is a desire to yank off the wig and get out of the theatre as fast as humanly possible. This is a bad idea for both the performer and the wig. A wig should be removed with the same care used to apply it at the top of the show. If the same locations are used each night for the pins that secure the wig to the head, it will be easy to remove.

1. Reverse the order and remove the nape pins.
2. Unpin or unglue the front and/or nape lace. Use the safest but most effective solvent to do this. For standard spirit gum, 99 percent alcohol will work. For Telesis, use the remover sold by the manufacturer. Apply the solvent to the lace with a brush, cotton swab, or cotton ball. Allow the solvent to soften the glue and then carefully run the rounded end of a large wig pin under the lace to check that it is completely loose. Do not rush this step. The performer needs to have all the glue removed from the skin and the wig lace will need to be completely cleaned before the next performance. An extra second or two is all it takes to complete both tasks at once.
3. Remove the pins in the crown that are holding the wig in place.
4. Slip your hands up from the nape and carefully lift the wig up and slide it off the head. Most of the time, the wig will slide back off the head easily. Work slowly, just in case the inside of the wig has caught onto one of the bobby pins holding a pincurl.
5. Place the wig back on the correct block and pin.

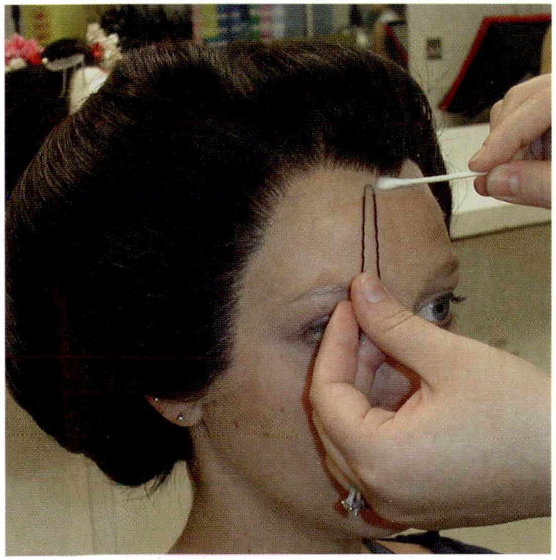

Figure 8-28

A WORD ABOUT QUICK CHANGES AND TAP DANCING

There are characters and stagings that require that the wig be pulled on during a fight. In this situation, you should use more pins and more glue. There are situations in which a performer is playing eight different characters in the course of a play and all of them simply walk around talking. For this performer, it would be best to use only a few pins to hold the wig in place and perhaps a bit of transparent double-stick tape. Combine and adjust the techniques described in this chapter as needed to suit the needs of the performance.

CHAPTER **9** Wig Styling Techniques

Figure 9-1 Jena Maenius models a wig with a 1930s style.

ELEMENTS OF A HAIRSTYLE

Before you attempt to style your wig, you need to be able to perform a variety of different techniques and skills in order to create the hairstyle you want. Most hairstyles are some combination of four different elements:

- Straight hair
- Wavy or crimped hair
- Curly hair
- Braided, coiled, or dreadlocked hair

By knowing how to create these four elements, you will be able to create an infinite number of hairstyle possibilities. These elements are tools that will work for both male and female hairstyles, and for both period and contemporary looks.

A WORD OF CAUTION ON STYLING WIGS

Before you begin styling your wig, you must know what kind of hair is in your wig. If you apply the wrong technique to your hair fiber, it could be melted or ruined beyond all recognition. If you are unsure about the material of your wig, there are a couple of different ways to check what it is. The most obvious is to check the tag. Nearly all commercially made wigs have a tag, usually located at the nape of the neck. If it says anything other than "100% Human Hair," it must be treated as a synthetic wig. Other terms you might see if your wig is synthetic include "Kanekalon," "Elura Fiber," and "Yaki," or your wig may simply be labeled as "Synthetic." If the label has been removed from the wig for some reason, you can test the hair by pulling out a strand and burning it. When doing this, be sure to put out the fire before the entire strand has burned. If the hair burns away into ash and has a distinctly animal smell, it is most likely human hair. If the hair burns into a hard bead and has a chemical smell, it is most likely synthetic hair.

In general, human hair is styled by either applying some kind of heat (hair dryer, curling iron, and so on) or by thoroughly wetting it and drying it with heat. These same elements of heat will often melt a synthetic wig. Synthetic wigs are styled either by wetting the hair thoroughly and allowing it to air dry (often a time-consuming process that does not set the curl as securely) or, more often, by using steam. When in doubt, *always test a section of the hair before styling*! Take a tiny section of hair from the underside of the back and test out your styling method. This will save you a lot of heartache and wig repairs.

STRAIGHT HAIR

Straight hair is defined as hair that hangs in one direction with little or no bend or shape. There are several different ways of achieving straight hair on your wig.

WETTING AND DRYING

If the hair you are working with is human hair that is naturally straight, all you have to do to straighten it is wet it and allow it to dry:

1. Make sure that the wig is securely blocked.
2. Wet the hair thoroughly and comb through it first with a wide-toothed comb, then with a fine-toothed comb. Any tangles that are left in the wig will dry as kinks in the hair, so be sure that your wig is tangle-free. Be sure to handle the wig gently while it is wet—the foundation materials may stretch because of the

extra water weight. You should also be extra careful when untangling the hair—do not rip through the tangles with your comb. Rather, use the comb to gently unknot the tangles strands of hair.

3. Place your wig in a place to dry so that the hair is free to hang straight while it is drying. For example, do not place the hair on a shelf to dry with the hair sitting on the shelf. If you do, the hair will dry with a large L-shaped kink from the shelf. Instead, place your wig with the hair hanging straight down off of the shelf. You can also place your wig in a wig dryer with the hair hanging down and dry it that way.

FLAT-IRONING AND ROLLER SETTING

If the hair you are working with is human hair that is naturally curly, permed, or simply has waves or kinks that you wish to remove, you can straighten it with either a flat iron or with large rollers—rollers that are larger than one inch in diameter. The larger the roller, the straighter the hair will be. To flat-iron:

1. Make sure that the wig is securely blocked.
2. Wash and dry the hair so that it is totally dry. Apply a frizz-control hairstyling product.
3. Separate the hair into sections. Make two sections in the front by dividing the top across the head from ear to

ear, near where a headband would sit. Divide this section in half at the center front of your hairline. Make two more sections behind these two sections. Secure each section by twisting it loosely and holding it with a large duckbill clip. Leave about two inches of the wig hanging down loose in the back.

4. Beginning with hair hanging down, take sections of hair slightly narrower than your flat iron and begin flat-ironing. Start at the root and drag the flat iron downward along the hair. Keep the iron moving—do not let it sit on a section of hair or you risk scorching the section of hair. There are various products available to aid in flat ironing. They are usually specifically marked for this purpose and many of them help to protect the hair from the heat of the flat iron.
5. Continue ironing and smoothing sections of hair, working from the back of the head toward the front of the head.
6. Finish with a light coat of hairspray to hold the hair straight and control frizz.

You can also use a flat-iron on human hair that is naturally straight if you want the hair to be super-sleek.

To roller-set the hair straight:

1. Make sure that the wig is securely blocked.
2. Wash the hair or wet it thoroughly, if the hair is already clean.

3. Take a section of hair at the center front and roll it on an extra-large roller. Secure the roller with a T-pin or corsage pin.

4. Continue rolling the hair on extra-large rollers, working from the front of the wig back toward the nape of the neck. Do this until all of the hair is rolled. The rollers should all remain parallel to each other.

5. Put the wig into the wig dryer to dry.

6. Take the rollers out and brush through the hair. This method does need yield super-straight hair, but instead hair that is mostly straight with a slight amount of bend. This is a more natural straight-hair look than one you will get from flat-ironing hair.

STEAMING THE HAIR

If the hair you are using is synthetic, the best way to straighten the hair is to use steam. Steam heat softens the plastic hair just enough so that it can be reshaped. The nice thing about using steam on synthetics is that it sets the wig the way you have styled it until you steam it into another shape. Small travel steamers are the easiest to use, because they have a handle and you can control where you are steaming. You can also steam a wig with a table-top steamer (such as those used in hat making) or a

commercial clothing steamer, but you are more likely to burn yourself with these kinds. Remember—steam is very hot and causes a particularly painful burn! When you are working while seated at a table, put a towel across your lap as an added bit of protection from drips. Even the best steamers drip hot water occasionally. Here are the steps:

1. Make sure that the wig is securely blocked.

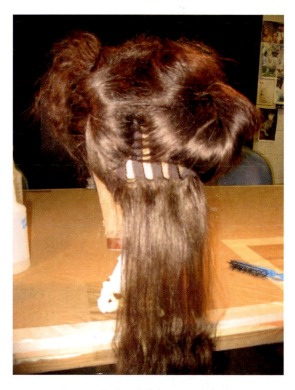

Figure 9-2 The wig is divided into sections before it is steamed.

2. Wet the hair and divide it into sections in the same way as described earlier for flat-ironing (Figure 9-2).

3. Beginning at the nape of the neck, hold the steamer in front of the hair. Make sure that the steamer is couple of inches away from the hair. With your other hand, use a smoothing brush or rat-tail comb to pull the hair straight (Figure 9-3). This works best if you hold a section taut and then steam it. The tension on the hair helps it to straighten out entirely.

Figure 9-3 Pull the hair taut with a comb as you steam the length.

4. Continue straightening sections of hair, working from the nape of the neck forward to the front of the hair (Figure 9-4).

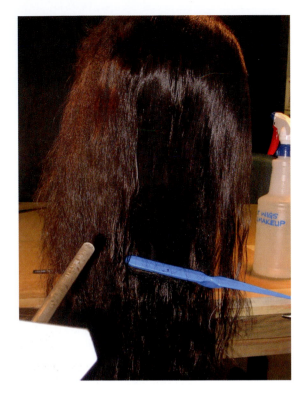

Figure 9-4 Work your way up to the front of the wig, straightening as you go.

Figure 9-5 Wigs that have been steamed straight, drying in a wig dryer.

5. Once all of the hair is straight, you can either put the wig in the wig dryer (Figure 9-5) or allow it to air-dry.

WAVY HAIR

Wavy hair undulates in a series of curves from the roots to the ends. Wavy or crimped hair is one of the most versatile and varied elements of a hairstyle. Waves have been used in styles ranging from Ancient Greek looks to 1930s finger waves and a great many styles in between. Waves can be large and loose, just enough to give movement to hair, or they can be small and very tight, in order to create volume in the hair. Because of the variety in kinds of waves, waving hair can be achieved using several different styling techniques.

FINGER WAVES/WATER WAVES

This type of waving can be done on either human hair or synthetic hair. This type of wave can be styled using your hands and a comb, or you can use duckbill clips or clippies to help you hold the hair in place. The hairstyle will be very close to the head, with little volume. Follow these steps:

1. Make sure that your wig is securely blocked.
2. Thoroughly soak the wig with water—it must be saturated in order to get good results with this technique. You can also add a styling product into the hair at this time—setting lotion and gel are good products to use for this. A styling product will help get the crisp look that is often seen in 1930s hairstyles.
3. Figure out where you want the waves to begin at the hairline—determine whether you want to have a part or if you want the waves to begin softly. Comb all of the hair on the wig in the direction that you want the wave to go (Figure 9-6). It is important that you comb *all* of the hair—not just the surface layer of hair.

Figure 9-6 Comb all of the hair the direction you want to begin.

Figure 9-7 After the hair is combed back in the other direction, use a finger to hold the wave in place. If you use your fingers to pinch the wave, it will accentuate the ridge.

(Figure 9-8); this is the starting point of your wave. Once you have created the first wave, secure it with the ribbon by pinning it down every inch or so (Figure 9-9).

Figure 9-9 The first "c" of the wave has been pinned in place. Notice how the comb is being pushed to create a ridge.

4. Place your finger or hand at the crest (or "c") of the wave you have just combed (Figure 9-7). Hold the hair tightly in place as you comb all of the rest of the hair back in the other direction. You will probably need to move your hand or finger along the wave as you comb the wave into place—just be sure to hold the hair going in the first direction tightly. If you do not, you will pull out the wave you are trying to create. Do not be discouraged—this technique takes practice!

5. If you want to emphasize the ridge between the waves (such as in a 1930s hairstyle), you can either use your comb to push back the ridge or you can pinch the ridge between your fingers.

6. When you are doing this technique, there is a trick you can use to cheat a

little bit. As you form the waves, use either a piece of narrow ribbon or a piece of bias tape to hold the waves in place. Anchor the ribbon by pinning it down at the hairline

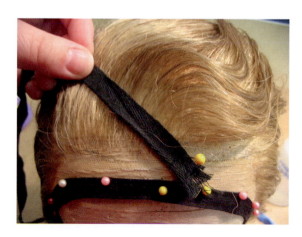

Figure 9-8 Anchor the ribbon at the beginning of the first wave.

Figure 9-10 The second, reverse "c" of the wave has been pinned in place.

7. Continue waving back and forth around the head (Figures 9-10 and 9-11). When you reach the bottom, you can either continue waving until you run out of hair or you can finish with small pincurls. (see later in this chapter for instructions on how to pincurl).

Figure 9-11 A top view of a wig with continuous water waves going back and forth around the entire head.

8. If you are working on a human-hair wig, all you need to do is dry the wig thoroughly. This can be done in a wig dryer set on high. If it is a synthetic wig, you should steam the hair so that it will hold its shape. Using a hand steamer, direct the nozzle towards each section of hair for about 30 seconds. Use the end of a rat-tail comb to hold the waves down while you are steaming them. The wig may then be dried in a wig dryer set on low.

9. Once the wig is dry, remove any ribbon or tape holding the waves in place. Make sure you begin removing the ribbon in the place that you started with it, *not* where you ended with it (Figure 9-12).

Figure 9-12 Remove the ribbon starting where you first pinned it in, *not* where the ribbon ended.

If you pull the ribbon up where you ended it, you will be pulling against the direction of the wave, which can mess up your hairstyle. If you choose to brush out the hair, the wave will be very soft. If you leave the waves as they are, the waves will be very flat and crisp.

MARCEL WAVES

The Marcel method of waving hair was introduced in 1872 by Marcel Grateau, a French hairdresser. His irons and technique significantly changed hairstyling. Prior to this technique, hair was curled by wrapping it around hot curling irons. Grateau pioneered the idea of turning the curling iron upside down and clamping the hair in it instead of wrapping the hair around. He created a special kind of iron where the center was a barrel with a curved plate that fit over it (Figure 9-13).

Figure 9-13 Two modern Marcel irons, on which you can see the barrel and the curved plate.

In order to do this method of styling, you will need a Marcel oven, a metal comb (or a plastic comb, but metal is less likely to melt), and Marcel curling irons. These irons are different from newer curling irons in that they do not have to be plugged in. The oven is plugged in instead, and the irons are placed inside to heat up. Newer curling irons have a temperature shut-off point—they will only ever get to a set temperature. Marcel irons will get much hotter. *Always test the temperature of your Marcel iron before using it!* You can test it in two ways—either directly on a sample of the hair you are using or on tissue. Use a single-ply piece of tissue (most tissue is two-ply, so you will likely need to peel the tissue apart). If the tissue turns brown when you clamp the iron on it, the iron is too hot. Marcel irons lose their heat very quickly, so you will need to put the iron back into the oven fairly often. These high-temperature curling irons caused many heads to be singed in the 1800s, so test your temperature often. (See Chapter 4 for more information about Marcel irons.) This technique should only be done on human hair—the irons will quickly melt any type of synthetic hair. Here's how to curl hair with a Marcel iron:

1. Make sure that your wig is securely blocked.
2. Heat up an iron that is the size you want the wave to be. Test its temperature.
3. Take section of hair and clamp the Marcel iron into it very close to the roots of the hair. Make sure the barrel of the iron is on the top and the curved part of the iron is on the bottom.
4. Gently push the iron in the direction that the wave is pointing.

At the same time, use a metal comb (the heat will melt a plastic comb, so if you use plastic, be careful) to push the hair just below the curling iron in the opposite direction from the way you are pushing the iron (Figure 9-14). This helps the wave shape to be strongly defined.

Figure 9-14 Push the hair (using a comb) and the iron in opposite directions to define the wave.

5. Remove the Marcel iron from the hair. Flip the iron over so that the barrel of the iron is on the bottom and the curved part of the iron is on top (Figure 9-15).
6. Clamp the iron into the hair in the opposite direction of the first section or "C" shape of the wave.

Figure 9-15 Flip the iron over and approach the section you are waving from the opposite side from where you started waving.

Push the iron in that direction. Use the metal comb to push the hair just below the iron in the opposite direction (Figure 9-16).

Figure 9-16 Turn the iron upside down and insert it from the opposite side of the wave you are creating, pushing in the opposite direction with the comb.

7. After doing this, you should have completed the first "S" shape that makes up the Marcel wave. Continuing alternating the iron and the waving direction in this manner until you reach the ends of the hair.

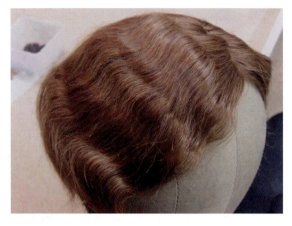

Figure 9-17 The finished section of hair after Marcel waving.

8. To do continuous waves around the head, make sure you follow the exact same pattern that you established on the first section of hair all the way around. Be careful to line up each wave.

PIN CURLS

Like in a Marcel wave, the idea of a pin curl is to create C- or S-shaped waves. This styling technique is particularly successful on layered hair. Pin curls can be done on human or synthetic hair:

1. Make sure that your wig is securely blocked.
2. Decide where you want the first wave to begin. The hair should be thoroughly wet. Styling product, such as setting lotion or gel, is very helpful. Section out a piece of hair that is approximately 1 inch by 1 inch square. Comb the section of hair smoothly in the direction of the wave:

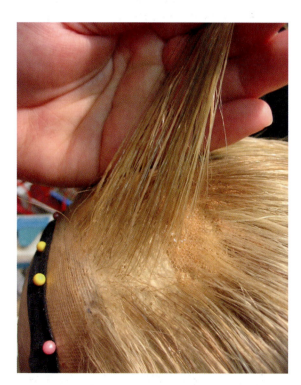

Figure 9-18 Comb the hair in the direction you want the wave to go.

3. Hold your fingers about 2 inches from the roots of the hair:

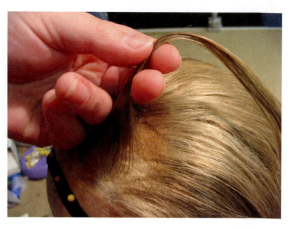

Figure 9-19 Grab the section of hair about 2 inches from the roots.

Wrap the hair around your fingers, using your thumb to hold the hair together each time you wind it around your fingers:

Figure 9-20 Wrap the hair around your fingers. Use your thumb to hold the hair in place.

An alternative method for doing this is to wrap the hair around a smooth rod instead of your fingers (Figure 9-21).

Figure 9-21 An alternative method is to wrap the hair around a smooth rod.

A piece of broomstick or dowel rod that has one end sanded down so that it tapers is ideal for this process. This results in a very sturdy, perfectly round pin curl. By using different sizes of wooden rods, you can achieve smaller or larger waves.

4. When you reach the end of the hair, tuck the ends into the rest of the pincurl. Gently slide your fingers out of the pincurl while holding the curl with your other hand (Figure 9-22). Rotate the hair until you get the root and place the curl flat against the head.

5. Once you have formed the curl, secure it with a clippie. (You can also use bobby pins or hairpins to hold the pin curl in place.) Pin carefully— you need to make sure that all of the hair is clipped or the pin curl will unravel (Figure 9-23). Also, try to avoid pinning in such a way that you will leave marks from the clippies in the hair once the set is dry.

6. Divide out the section of hair immediately beside the first pin curl. Form the pin curl and pin it in the same way that you did the first curl (Figure 9-24). Continue working in a horizontal line.

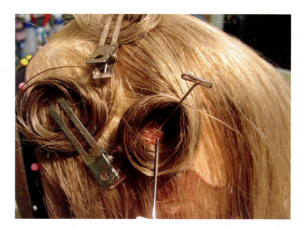

Figure 9-24 Make the next pincurl directly beside the first one.

7. When you are ready to move down on the head, divide out a section of hair. Comb it straight in the opposite direction from the first section of curls. Roll the hair up in the opposite direction (Figure 9-25). For example, if you rolled the first row of hair from the left, you will do the next row of hair from the right.

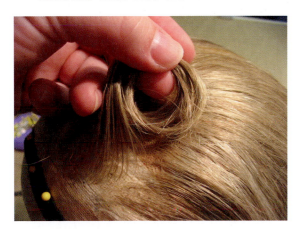

Figure 9-22 Slide your fingers or the rod out of the pincurl and place it flat against the head.

Figure 9-23 The pincurl is secured with a clippie.

Figure 9-25 The second row of pincurls should be rolled in the opposite direction from the first row.

8. Continue working around the head in horizontal lines, alternating each line's direction.
9. Once you are finished pincurling the hair, dry the wig in a wig dryer set on high if it is human hair. If it is synthetic hair, steam each pincurl for 30 seconds, then put it into a wig dryer set on low.
10. When you comb out the hair, it will look like a series of S-shapes. You can reinforce the shape of these waves with either duckbill clips or by pinning the hair in place with bias tape (Figure 9-26), as demonstrated in the section "Finger Waves/Water Waves."

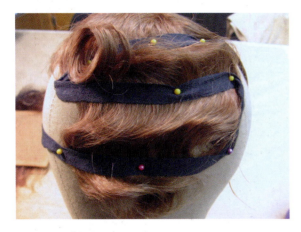

Figure 9-26 A pincurled wig, using bias tape to reinforce the waves.

WAVING AND CRIMPING IRONS

Waving and crimping irons are a fairly new tool to use in waving hair. It is easiest to use a triple-barreled curling iron, which is like a curling iron, but with three barrels instead of just one. Crimping irons usually have plates with multiple wave shapes—these shapes can be rounded, triangular, or square and are smaller and closer together than a waving iron. This results in a tighter, frizzier wave. Because these tools curl using heat, they can only be used on human hair. *Do not* use these on synthetic-fiber wigs! Here are the steps to wave/crimp hair:

1. Make sure the wig is securely blocked.
2. Divide the hair into sections. Do a center front section, a section over each ear going up to the center of the top of the head, and four sections in back. Securely fasten each section so that it is out of your way.
3. Begin waving the hair at one of the sections that is at the nape of the neck. Place the waving iron as close to the root of the hair as you can. Clamp it tightly and hold for 15 seconds to make the first section of wave. The iron can be used either horizontally or vertically, depending on the look you desire. Using the iron vertically makes the undulation of the waves more visible.
4. Carefully line up the iron below the first wave you have made. Be careful

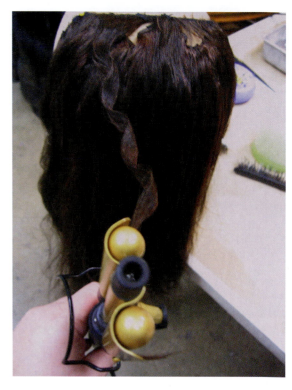

Figure 9-27 Using a triple-barrelled curling iron so the waves go side to side.

that the waves continue in a regular pattern and that you do not break up the wave with poor placement of the iron.
5. Continue making the waves until you reach the ends of the hair (Figure 9-27).
6. Wave each section of hair, working your way up the back of the head until you reach the front.

This method of waving requires very little comb-out. Just run your fingers through the hair to break up the waves. Any brushing or combing with a fine comb will result in frizz.

CURLY HAIR

Curly hair is defined as hair that has an evenly round shape from root to end. With naturally curly hair, the shape of the hair shaft itself is different from the hair shaft of naturally straight hair. Curls, like waves, come in different shapes and sizes, so you will need to employ a variety of techniques in order to achieve the results you want.

ROLLER SETTING

Roller setting is any technique used to set hair involving rollers or curlers. Use end papers when you set hair with rollers in order to make the curl look natural all the way to the ends of the hair. One huge benefit of setting wigs is that you can use T-pins or corsage pins to secure the rollers. This gives you a much tighter, neater curl. Just don't use this method on real live human beings—they tend to scream when you jam pins into their scalps! Another common mistake people make when they set hair with rollers is trying to force too much hair into each roller. The section of hair you separate should be no wider than the roller and no deeper than the roller (Figure 9-28).

Figure 9-28 The section of hair you roll should be no wider and no deeper than your roller.

Before you begin roller setting, it important to understand a couple of terms:

- **On base**—the process of setting a wig so that the curler is even with the roots of the hair. This ensures that the curl goes evenly all the way to the roots of the hair.
- **Forward of base**—hair that is set by pulling the hair forward before putting the roller in. The roller then sits on top of the roots of the hair, flattening them forward a little bit. This technique is useful for any hairstyle that has a pompadour.

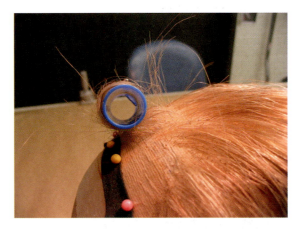

Figure 9-30 Forward of base.

- **Off base or set with "drag"**—hair that is set by pulling the hair backwards before putting the roller in. With this technique,

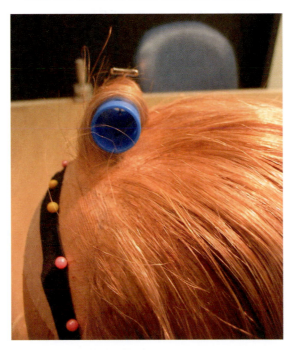

Figure 9-29 On base.

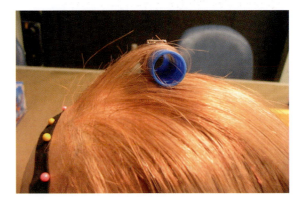

Figure 9-31 "Dragged" back from base.

there are usually about 2 inches of straight hair before the curl begins. This is very useful when you are trying to control the volume in the hairstyle.

Proper rolling technique is as follows:

1. Make sure that the wig is securely blocked.
2. Divide out the first section of hair (Figure 9-32), depending on your desired style. When roller-setting, begin at the front hairline and work your way down to the back of the wig, ending at the nape of the neck.

Figure 9-32 Divide out the first section of hair.

3. Wet the hair. Comb through the section until it is completely tangle-free. Hold it on base, forward of base, or off base. Make sure you keep tension on the section of hair so that it is taut the entire time you are working with it (Figure 9-33).

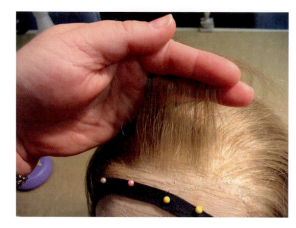

Figure 9-33 Hold the hair out from the wig, maintaining tension.

4. Place the end paper a couple of inches from the end of the hair:

Figure 9-34 The end paper is placed a couple of inches from the ends of the section of hair.

5. Fold one side of the end paper over towards the center:

Figure 9-35 Fold one side of the end paper over towards the center.

6. Fold the other side of the end paper over towards the center and spritz it with water. This will help all sides of the end paper stick together:

Figure 9-36

7. Slide the end paper towards the ends of the hair until all of the ends are contained inside:

Figure 9-37

8. Put the roller at the end paper and begin rolling it towards the scalp:

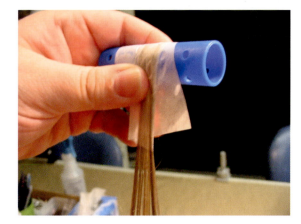

Figure 9-38

It is especially important to keep the tension on the hair during this step:

Figure 9-39

Losing the tension will result in a floppy or mashed curl. When styling, you will nearly always roll the hair under (put the roller behind/under the end paper and roll down). You will rarely roll the hair up unless you are trying to create some sort of flip.

9. When you reach the head, secure the curler with a T-pin:

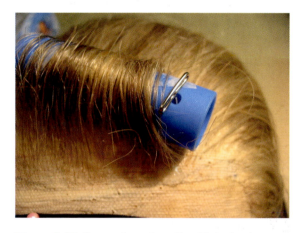

Figure 9-40 Secure the roller with a T-pin that is turned in the direction of the hair.

Make sure that the pin is turned in the direction of the hairs. This will avoid snagging the hair and leaving any indentations on the hair when it dries.

10. Continue rolling sections of hair until you have set the entire wig. The pattern you set the rollers in will be determined by the style you want. For more information about setting

patterns and how to figure them out, please see Chapter 10.

11. If the wig is human hair or yak hair, dry it in a wig dryer set on high for 60 to 90 minutes. If the wig is synthetic fiber, steam each curl for 30 seconds. Then put the wig in a wig dryer set on low for 60 to 90 minutes.

Pay careful attention to the hair when taking out the rollers. Start taking out the rollers at the nape of the neck and work your way forward to the front hairline of the wig. Carefully unroll each curl. Once again, the amount of combing or brushing that you do depends on the desired look. If you want the hair to remain very curly, simply pull each curl apart with your fingers into two or three sections. For a softer look, brush the curls out with a wide-toothed comb. These methods work best if you are trying to achieve the look of naturally curly hair. One thing to watch out for is roller breaks, which are the areas or gaps between each roller. If the wig has been set properly and neatly, these gaps will sometimes still be visible when all of the rollers have been taken out. Sometimes you will even be able to see the foundation of the wig through these gaps. Obviously, we do not want to see the foundation. You may need to go in with a smoothing brush or a comb and just comb the inch or two of the hair closest to the root to break it

up and make it work together. If the roller breaks are severe, you may even need to lightly tease or back comb the sections together at the root.

Another method often used when styling a roller set wig is to brush the entire thing out and then reshape the curls around your fingers. This method is most useful for creating period hairstyles and hairstyles that are meant to look like set hair, not naturally curly hair. Use a large wooden hair brush and brush through all of the curls. This will seem scary and like you are destroying all of the curl in the wig—do not be afraid. The curl will come back if you have set the wig properly. As you arrange each piece of hair, use a smoothing brush to brush the curl around one or two of your fingers, depending on the desire size of the curl. You can then either let the curl hang down or pin it into whatever cluster or arrangement you wish.

ROLLER SETTING: RINGLETS/ SAUSAGE CURLS

Hairstyles from many different periods in history feature the sausage curl or ringlet. This term refers to a curl that hangs in a solid coil, as opposed to being a loose curl that has been brushed out. Setting hair in order to achieve a sausage curl is slightly different from setting a regular curl:

1. Make sure that your wig is securely blocked.
2. Divide out a section of hair. When setting a sausage curl, use a vertical section of hair instead of a horizontal section. Wet the hair and comb through this section so that it is free of any tangles. If you want a really crisp curl that lasts, add setting lotion or another styling product at this point. Comb through the hair after applying the product so that the product is evenly distributed through the hair.
3. Apply an endpaper using the same technique described previously.
4. Hold the roller vertically, parallel to the section of hair. Begin rolling

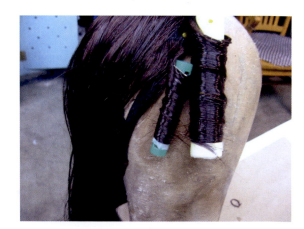

Figure 9-41 Roll a sausage curl from the bottom of the roller up.

with the ends of the hair and the endpaper at the bottom of the roller. Rolling the curler in the direction you want the curl to fall, work the hair up the curler by layering the hair over the hair below it by half of its width. This way, there will be no gaps in the curler.

5. Continue wrapping the hair upwards on the roller until you reach the roots (Figure 9-41). Pin the roller in place with a T-pin. Continue adding rollers until you have set all the hair you want.

6. If the hair is human hair, dry it on high for 90 minutes. If the hair is synthetic, steam each curl for 30 seconds, then dry it on low for 90 minutes.

Once the curl is dry, you are ready to remove the roller. Carefully unroll the hair in the opposite way from which you rolled it. (You will essentially be removing the roller by unwinding it downward.) If you are satisfied with the appearance of the curl, you can leave it as it is. If you would like for the ringlets to not look so crispy, use a slightly different method. After you unwind the curl, brush out the section of hair. Then recurl the ringlet by brushing it around your finger or an appropriately sized dowel rod (Figure 9-42).

Gently remove your finger from the ringlet and then set the curl with

Figure 9-42 Recurling a ringlet around a dowel rod.

hairspray. Make sure to spray underneath as well so that hairspray gets inside of the ringlet. Another helpful tip: do not store the ringlets so that they can hang down if you want them to remain tight (example: storing a wig on shelf with the ringlets hanging over the edge). They will stretch out and become loose curls if you do this. Either make sure the ringlets are resting on a flat surface or use a hairnet to hold the ringlets in place when the wig is not being worn.

ROLLER SETTING: SPIRAL ROLLING TECHNIQUES

Spiral rolling techniques are used when the desired curl is even in size from root to tip. We use two different types of spiral rolls—one we call the "sprocket set" and one that we call the "Medusa" set.

Sprocket Set

We call this set the "sprocket set" because when it is finished, the rollers are sticking out all over the head like the spokes on a wheel. This technique is best for creating a naturally curly-haired look. Because the hair is rolled starting at the root, it looks like the hair is growing out of the scalp curly instead of hair that has been set into curls. Proper technique includes following these steps:

1. Make sure that the wig is securely blocked.

2. Divide out a section of hair that is square—no bigger than 1 inch by 1 inch. Wet this section and comb through it so there are no tangles.

3. Place the roller so that the open end is actually resting on the scalp.

4. Begin rolling the hair at the root upwards around the roller (Figure 9-43). You are rolling this in the same way as the sausage curl, but you are rolling the hair up and away from the roots instead of towards the roots.

Figure 9-43 Wrap the roots of the hair around the base of the roller and work your way up.

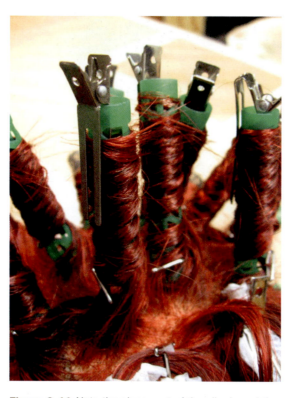

Figure 9-44 Note the placement of the clippie and the T-pin for anchoring this roller.

Figure 9-45 The finished sprocket set.

5. If the hair is wet enough, the end will usually stick to the rest of the wet hair. If it does not stick, secure it either by wetting it or by using a clippie to hold the end in place. Secure the roller with a T-pin. (This can be a little tricky. It sometimes takes several stabs to get the T-pin to hold the roller at the correct angle.) (Figure 9-44)

Continue adding rollers until you have set all the hair you want.

6. If the hair is human hair, dry it on high for 90 minutes. If the hair is synthetic, steam each curl for 30 seconds, then dry on low for 90 minutes.

Once the curls are dry, the rollers can be removed. Unroll them from the root, unwinding them and pulling them away from the scalp. Because you are trying to achieve a naturally curly look with this set, just pull each curl apart with your fingers to style.

3. Twist the hair so that it is twisted from close to the root down to the ends (Figure 9-47). Do not twist the section so tightly that it begins to loop back up on itself. Put an end paper on the end.

Figure 9-46 Paul Hebron (wearing a comb over a hairpiece) and Suzanne Curtis (wearing a wig that was set with a sprocket set) in *Season's Greetings*, presented by the Alabama Shakespeare Festival.

Figure 9-47 Twist the hair before rolling it on the roller.

MEDUSA SET

We call this set the "Medusa set" because the curls look sort of like snakes when the rollers are taken out. This set is best for achieving a wavy curl that has more of an S-shape rather than a perfectly round curl. This set is very similar to the set for a sausage curl:

1. Make sure that your wig is securely blocked.
2. Divide out a section of hair that is no larger than the size of the roller. Wet the hair and comb through it to remove any tangles. Like the sausage curl set, use vertical sections of hair for this technique.

4. Hold the roller parallel to the twisted section of hair. Begin wrapping the hair around the bottom of the roller. Continue rolling upwards, keeping the coils of hair touching one another (Figure 9-48). When you reach the root, secure the roller with a T-pin.

Figure 9-48 The twisted hair wrapped around the roller, starting from the bottom.

Continue adding rollers until you have set all the hair you want.

5. If the hair is human, dry it on high for 90 minutes. If the hair is synthetic, steam each curl for 30 seconds, then dry the wig on low for 90 minutes.

When the hair is dry, unroll each curl from the root down to the ends. If the snaky look is what you want, leave the hair as it is. For beautiful, even waves, pull the curls apart with your fingers or carefully comb out each section with a wide-toothed comb.

BRAIDS

Braids are a very secure way of holding hair in place. Because of this, they have been used throughout history in hairstyles. Having a good set of braiding techniques in your arsenal will serve you well.

Figure 9-49 Betsy Cummings as Annabel Lee in *Still Life with Iris*, presented by the University of Texas. Her wig was styled using the Medusa set.

STANDARD BRAID

FRENCH BRAID

REVERSE FRENCH BRAID

REVERSE FRENCH BRAID
DONE IN A CIRCULAR PATTERN

ROPE BRAID

HERRINGBONE/FISHTAIL BRAID

Figure 9-50 Examples of different types of braids.

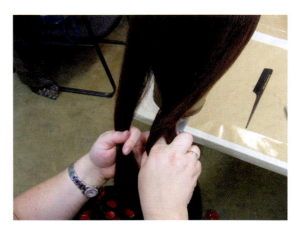

Figure 9-51 Cross the outside section over the middle section.

3. Cross the opposite outside section (section 3) over the middle section (now section 1):

Figure 9-52 Cross the outside section from the other side over the new middle section.

4. Continue alternating sections until you reach the ends of the hair. Secure with a rubber band.

THE STANDARD BASIC BRAID

A braid or plait consists of three sections of hair that are woven together:

1. Divide the hair into three sections.

2. Cross one of the outside sections (section 1) over the middle section (section 2). This will move the outside section, causing it to become the new outside section:

FRENCH BRAIDS

French braids are braids the sit very closely to the scalp. This is because the hair is added to the braid gradually, so that the braid can start right at the edge of the hair.

1. Decide where you want the braid to start. Divide the hair into three small sections as close to the edge of that section as you can get.
2. Begin braiding as you did with the basic braid. Cross each outside section over the middle section once.
3. The second time you go to cross the outside section, pick up a little more hair and add it to section 1 (Figure 9-53). Cross it over the middle section. On the opposite side, pick up a little more hair and add it to section 3. Cross it over the middle section.
4. Continue working your way to the end of the braid, adding a little more hair to each section as you go along. When you reach the end, secure the braid with a rubber band.

Because the braid is essentially contained on the inside of the hair, this is a good braid to use on layered hair. The braid will hold the ends of the layers tight to the scalp and keep the hair from falling out of the braid.

Figure 9-53 Small pieces of hair are picked up and added to each section as you work.

REVERSE FRENCH BRAID

In a reverse French braid, the braid is actually visible from the outside; it looks as though it is sitting on top of the hair. To achieve this braid, follow the same steps as the regular French braid, with one exception: Instead of crossing the outside section over the middle section, cross it *under* the middle section. Do this each time and the braid will end up on the outside instead of on the inside.

ROPE BRAIDS

Rope braids are braids that are made with two sections of hair instead of three. These braids are sometimes referred to as "Renaissance" braids:

1. Divide the hair into two sections.
2. Twist one section as tightly as you can without the hair looping back onto itself.
3. Twist the second section of hair in the same direction as the first section of hair (Figure 9-54). For example, if you twist the first section of hair to the left, you must also twist the second section of hair to the left.

Figure 9-54 The two sections of hair are twisted in the same direction.

4. Twist the two sections of hair around each other in the opposite direction from the direction you twisted each

Figure 9-55 Twist the two sections of hair together in the opposite direction.

section (Figure 9-55). For example, if you twisted the sections of hair to the left, twist them together to the right.

5. Continue twisting the hair together, making sure the hair stays twisted. You may have to twist the hair a little bit as you go along in order to keep the coils tight. When you reach the end, secure the braid with a rubber band.

HERRINGBONE BRAIDS

The herringbone braid is another braid created using two sections of hair. It is sometimes referred to as a fishtail braid. Follow these steps:

1. Divide the hair into two sections.
2. Take a small section of hair from the outside of one section; cross it over to the inside of the opposite section (Figure 9-56).

3. Take a small section of hair from the outside of the other section and cross it over to the inside of the first section. Continue doing this until you reach the ends of the hair. Secure with a rubber band.

This braid is simple, but time-consuming. The braid looks very intricate when done with small sections of hair. It just requires patience to keep going until you reach the end.

DREADLOCKS

Sometimes it is useful to know how to create dreadlocks in a wig. We have a

technique that can be done *only* on a synthetic wig. A word of caution—once you have put dreadlocks in a wig, it is extremely difficult to remove them. Most of the time, removing the dreadlocks ruins the wig. This technique has been most successful on a fully ventilated synthetic wig that has a lot of hair. Because you will lose some length, start with a wig that is a few inches longer than the final result you want:

1. Divide out a small square section of hair. Start at the nape of the neck and work your way up the back of the head.

Figure 9-56 Take a small section of hair from the outside of one side and cross it over to the inside of the other side.

Figure 9-57 Anna Fugate as the Goddess of Mercy in *410[GONE]* at the University of Texas, wearing a dreadlocked wig. Photo by Mark Rutkowski.

2. Start at the root and tightly tease the hair along the entire length of the hair (Figure 9-58).

Figure 9-58 Tease the section of hair.

3. Twist the teased section of hair (Figure 9-59).
4. Hold the teased, twisted section of hair in one and a handheld steamer

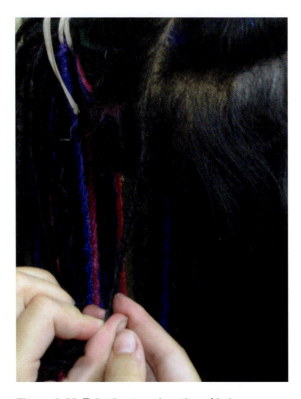

Figure 9-59 Twist the teased section of hair.

in the other hand. Begin steaming at the end of the hair, being careful not to burn your fingers.

The hair magically begins to twist itself up towards the root of the hair (Figure 9-60). We don't know why this works, but it gets the job done.

Figure 9-60 As you begin applying steam to the end of the twisted hair. The hair will begin to twirl and lock itself in place.

5. Continue locking each section until you are finished.
6. After dreading the hair, sometimes the ends will be a little messy. Rub a little beeswax between your fingers and use them to twist the ends together and tuck in any stray hairs. You can do the same thing with Elmer's glue.

Practice all of these styling techniques until they become second-nature to you. Once you master these methods, you will be able to create an infinite number of hairstyles. In the next chapter, we will discuss how to put these techniques together in order to create different looks.

CHAPTER 10 Creating a Hairstyle

Figure 10-1 Beauty Thibodeau, Kara Meche, Tiffany Knight, and Amanda Ramirez model wig styles from different historical periods.

Now that you have mastered all of the styling techniques in Chapter 10, how do you put them together to create a hairstyle? Many people look at a picture of a complicated hairstyle and freak out. The style may seem impossible to achieve. Do not worry—you have all of the tools needed to put together any style you can dream up.

BREAK THE HAIRSTYLE DOWN INTO SECTIONS

Any job seems easier after you break it down into small, more manageable tasks. This is also true of wig styling.

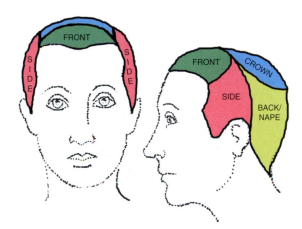

Figure 10-2 Break your hairstyle down into these sections.

Instead of looking at the hairstyle as one big blob, look at it as many pieces of a whole. Break all styles down into five sections (Figure 10-2):

- **Front**—This is the center section of hair above the forehead, in front of the ears in the center. This area is usually the width of the eyebrows.
- **Right and left sides**—This is the area on either side of the center front section. It starts over the ears and moves forward to the hairline.
- **Crown**—This is the area on the top of the head. It covers the head behind the ears on top to just below where the head begin to slope down to the neck.
- **Back/nape**—This is the remaining hair. This section covers all of the hair left below the crown section; the back of the head.

UNDERSTAND THE HAIRSTYLE

Once you start seeing the sections of the hairstyle, planning your attack should become easier. A way to refer to the method of breaking a style down into parts is by calling it the "Mr. Potato Head" theory of wig styling. Just as that toy has facial pieces that can be reconfigured in hundreds of ways to create many faces, the elements of styling (waves, curls, braids, smooth hair, rolls, and clusters) can arranged in ways to create an infinite number of styles. Look at the picture you are trying to recreate. What is the front doing—is it curly, Marcel-waved, or slicked back? Are the sides pinned off the face or rolled into sausage curls? Is the back hanging in loose curls? Are there braids wrapped around the crown of the head? Make sure you understand your hairstyle before you do any styling. Try to understand where all of the hair is coming from and going to. If the picture you are working from is a historical reference, consider what pieces of hair may have been the person's own hair and what pieces may have been added on for fashion. You may have to add other hairpieces to your wig in order to achieve the desired look. Also, in many reference pictures, it is impossible to see what is going on in the back. You can do research to determine what the style would likely look like. This can also be a place for creativity—you can decide exactly how the back of the style should look!

INTERPRETING RESEARCH

When planning out hairstyle, it is very important for you to be able to interpret your research accurately. You must train your eyes to analyze a picture and gain as much information as you can from it. There are two main kinds of research:

- **A primary resource**—information that is the original thing. For example, an actual wig from a historical period is a primary resource. A photograph of an actual hairstyle is also a primary resource (Figure 10-3).

Figure 10-3 An example of a primary resource is this photograph of Martha Ruskai's mother, father, aunt, and uncle, which was taken in 1942 at the time of their marriage.

- **A secondary resource**—an interpretation of a primary resource. For the purposes of wig research, this will usually mean an artistic representation, such as a painting, sketch, or sculpture or a hairstyle that was created from life of the way that the person looked at the time (Figure 10-4). Another way of defining primary resource is that it was created by an observer at "the moment in time."

Photographs of original portraits are also considered secondary resources. One must always be careful when looking at period art that has humans as subject matter. There are many examples of an artist painting an imaginary or fantasy image. Artists have always tried to flatter the person paying them!

- *A tertiary resource*—analyzes or interprets the information from a secondary source.

Examples of secondary sources for wig stylists are the wonderful line drawings done by Richard Corson in Fashions in Hair: The First Five Thousand Years; Georgine de Courtais in Women's Hats, Headdesses, and Hairstyles: With 453 Illustrations, Medieval to Modern; and by Ruth Turner Wilcox in The Mode in Hats and Headdress: A Historical Survey wit 198 Plates. These drawings were done by looking at historical portraits (a secondary resource).

Figure 10-4 An example of a secondary resource. Nicolas de Largilliere, *Portrait of a Man*, circa 1715, oil on canvas. Courtesy of the Blanton Museum of Art, the University of Texas at Austin, the Suida-Manning Collection. Photograph by Rick Hall.

Figure 10.5 A plate from The Mode in Hats and Headdress: A Historical Survey with 198 Plates by Ruth Turner Wilcox. This is a tertiary resource.

A movie, no matter how well done, cannot be considered a primary source for any time other than the year in which it was filmed. There are many films with historic subjects that have fabulous hairstyles. But these are interpreted by a contemporary director, designer and stylist and must be studied through that filter.

DRAW YOUR SETTING PATTERN

Now that you know what you are trying to do, put your plan down on paper. Use this blank form to sketch out the placement of all rollers, pincurls, braids, and so on.

Indicate what direction each roller should be rolled in and if any should be set over base or with drag on the hair. Make any notes that will help you as you work. Figure 10-7 is an example of a completed setting pattern.

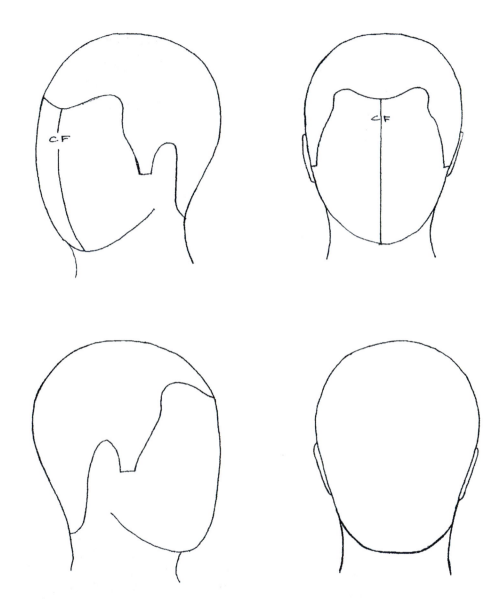

Figure 10-6 Copy this blank setting chart to use when planning out your wig styles.

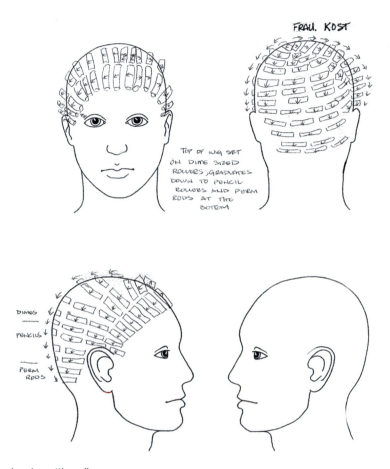

Figure 10-7 A sample wig-setting diagram.

SET YOUR WIG

Block your wig on a canvas block, get out the pins and rollers, and begin setting. Follow the pattern you have planned out and drawn, setting from the front hairline down the back of the head, ending with the hair at the nape of the neck. This will make sure the hair is evenly distributed in the rollers. (See the rest of this section for more setting and styling tips.) An important note—the material your wig is made of will determine the method you use to set it.

- **For human hair and animal hair wigs**—the curl is set in the hair by a combination of heat and drying. You must completely wet the hair as you set each piece. Using a styling product such as gel or setting lotion

will also help the curl to hold. When you finish setting the wig, use a spray bottle to completely wet the wig again before you put it into the wig dryer. (The first hair you set will already be partially dry by the time you finish setting all the hair.) Set the wig dryer on *high* for at least 60 minutes.

- **For synthetic wigs**—the curl is set in the hair by steam. You can dampen each section of hair as you set it (for control) but it does not have to be dripping wet. After you are finished rolling and pinning all of the hair, steam each roller, pincurl, and so on, with a steamer for at least 30 seconds. You will be able to see the hair move slightly as it meets the steam. Once you have steamed the wig, spray it with water and put it in the wig dryer on *low* for at least 60 minutes.

COMB OUT THE SET

Once the wig is completely dry, allow it to cool to room temperature. This will help lock the set into the hair. Your curls will loosen a bit if you take the set out while the hair is still warm. Test a section of hair before you begin styling. At the nape of the neck, unroll a roller—if the hair seems damp, roll it back up and stick it back in the wig dryer for another 30 minutes. When the wig is ready to be styled, begin taking out your rollers, pincurls, and so on from the nape of the neck up (Figure 10-8). This is the opposite direction from the one in which you set the wig. Unroll each roller.

Figure 10-8 Begin removing your rollers at the back nape of the wig.

Figure 10-9 Use your fingers to pull apart the curls.

TEASING AND STUFFING

You may find that you need to tease (or "backcomb") a wig in order for it to have the amount of volume you desire. Lightly teasing hair can also be a good way to fix roller breaks. To tease the hair, begin with a small section. Use your teasing/smoothing brush to comb the hair downwards toward the scalp while you continue to grip the section of hair (Figure 10-10).

Repeat the process until all of the hair in the section is packed down near the scalp. Spritz with hairspray, and then move to the next section. It is important to be spraying the hair constantly with hairspray as you work. If you only spray the outermost layer, the teased hair inside and underneath will collapse and not give you the look you want. Once you have finished teasing the hair, smooth the top section so the hairstyle looks neat. Use your teasing/smoothing

Start your styling at the front of the wig, because the face of your performer is what the audience should be looking at. It is much easier to conceal a shortage of hair or gaps in the wig in the back than it is at the front of the wig. Start by gently combing through the wig with a wide-toothed comb. This helps get rid of any roller breaks (gaps in the style caused by the set). I If you are trying to achieve the look of naturally curly hair, you can sometimes gently pull the curls apart with your fingers and bypass the comb entirely (Figure 10-9).

Next, begin smoothing the hair, braiding, curling the sections around your finger, rolling it into sausage rolls, or whatever else you need to do to achieve the style you want. Secure the hair as you go along with bobby pins. These will hold your hair securely in place. Your wig should always be able to withstand any action by a performer. When you are finished, take the wig block and give it a couple of firm shakes. If a section or cluster of curls comes loose, you know that you need to pin it more securely.

Figure 10-10 To tease the hair, hold a section taut and comb the hair towards the scalp with a teasing comb or brush.

brush to just lightly brush the top layer of hairs in the direction of the final style. Finish with aerosol hairspray.

If the hairstyle you are trying to achieve requires a huge amount of teasing to get the volume you want, it may make more sense to use a *rat* instead. A rat is any sort of hair pad or stuffing (Figure 10-11).

You can buy premade rats or make your own. You can make a rat by collecting loose bits of hair, forming it into a ball, and wrapping a hairnet around it several times. To use the rat, pull the hair away from the area you want the rat and bobby-pin the rat to your wig where you desire volume. Form X-shapes with your pins to firmly anchor the rat in place. Lightly tease the hair that is going to lie on top of the rat and smooth it over. Pin the hair over the rat so that it stays hidden. Finish with hairspray.

WIRE FRAMES

Some historical hairstyles are so large than mere teasing or stuffing will still not yield you the results that you want. In these cases, it may be better to build a wire frame to attach to your wig. You can then dress the hair over the frame and easily achieve a great deal of height or width. The frame will also allow your wig to be lightweight on your performer's head. Millinery wire (sturdy wire that is covered in cloth or paper) makes an excellent frame. Bend the millinery wire into the shape and size you want. Make you reinforce the inside of the wires to give the frame strength. Once you have blocked out your frame, connect the wires wherever they overlap by stitching them together with thread (Figure 10-12). Then wrap floral tape around each join.

Cover the frame with inexpensive netting in the similar color to your finished wig (Figures 10-13 and 10-14).

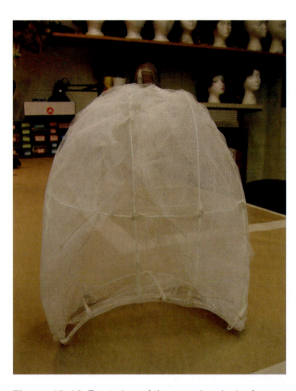

Figure 10-13 Front view of the completed wire frame covered in netting.

Figure 10-11 An example of a homemade hair rat.

Figure 10-12 Join the wires where they cross with stitching and floral tape.

Figure 10-14 Bottom view of the wired frame covered with netting.

After separating out the hair that will cover the frame and getting it out of the way, use a curved needle to stitch the frame on top of your wig (Figure 10-15).

Note that it may be helpful to set the wig in rollers first, allow it dry, remove the rollers, and *then* attach the frame. The frame may make your wig so large it won't fit into the wig dryer! Style the hair up onto the frame and secure it into the netting (Figures 10-16 and 10-17).

Finish and dress the wig.

Figure 10-15 Stitch the frame directly to your wig using a curved needle.

Figure 10-18 The finished and styled wig with a frame.

Figure 10-16 The hair has been set on rollers before the wire frame has been attached to the wig.

Figure 10-17 Styling the hair onto the frame.

STYLING MEN'S WIGS

You must be extra-careful when you are styling a wig that is going to be a contemporary men's style. If the wig is too curly or too voluminous, the performer will look as though he is wearing his grandmother's wig—not a good look for a leading man! Plan to style the hair with very little volume. An effective way to achieve this is to use finger waves and pin curls to add body and movement, but not excessive height.

Notice how T-pins have been used to hold the waves in place.

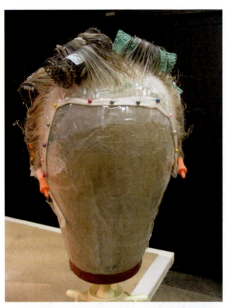

Figure 10-19 Michael Sullivan as Rogozhin in *The Idiot*, presented by the University of Texas. He is wearing a realistically styled short men's wig. Photograph by Amitava Sarkar.

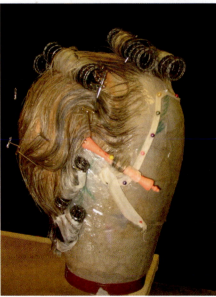

Figures 10-20 and 10-21 Front and side views of an example setting pattern for a men's wig.

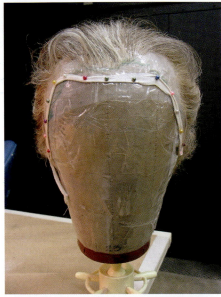

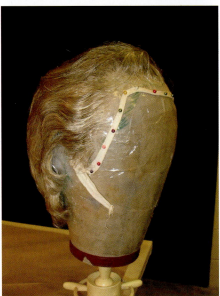

Figures 10-22 and 10-23 The set has been combed out and styled.

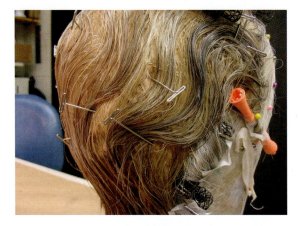

Figure 10-24 T-pins have been used to hold the waves in place. Let the wig sit with the T-pins in place overnight.

Setting lotion has been used to help hold the style in place. Tiny perm rods have been used behind the ears and at the nape to make those tiny curls or flips of hair that often show up as a man's haircut begins to grow out.

WIG SETTING AND STYLING TIPS

1. First and foremost, a wig is not a head of hair. No matter how beautifully the wig is made, it will need to be styled differently than if you were styling an actual person's hair. This must be factored into the final style—seeing the edge of the wig quickly gives away the fact that it is a wig. Consider both the hairline and the back edge of your wig. If your wig is not fully ventilated (and most are not), there will be a section where the hair is sewn on in strips or wefts. You will have to style the wig so that the gaps between strips are not seen. Also, keep in mind whether the wig is actually supposed to look like real hair or if it needs to look like a wig.

2. It is easier to style a wig in sections—never try to handle all of the hair at once. Even if you are pulling the hair back into a simple bun, the hair will lay smoother if you pull the back of the hair into a ponytail and then pull the front sections into the bun separately. Don't be afraid to use rubber bands on top of other rubber bands. (And if you are using rubber bands, don't try to pull them out of the hair—cut them out and use a new one if you need to redo the style.)

3. In order to look natural, the wig must hug the head someplace. When you cannot see the shape of the skull anywhere, the wig often looks very artificial. (An exception is teased 1960s styles—natural was not the desired look.) The style does not need to be tight all over—a small section styled close to the head will go a long way. Common places for the wig to hug the head are over the ears, at the nape of the neck, or right at the hairline.

4. On lace-front wigs, at least a small piece of hair should break the hairline onto the forehead or face

(Figure 10-25). This draws attention away from the wig lace and also looks more natural—people almost always have a little bit of hair hanging in their face. This is especially important on short men's wigs.

5. Don't try to make your style too perfect. People are rarely totally neat or perfect. If their hairstyle is too neat, it will draw attention to itself as a wig by contrast. This does not mean style your wig sloppily—it just means avoiding styling your wig too rigidly.

6. The audience does not want to see the effort that went into your hairstyle. It should not look tortured, lacquered, sprayed, tugged, and pinned within an inch of its life (even if this is actually true). Make sure you conceal all of your pins,

use the right color of pins, and avoid any obvious comb marks. The hairstyle should always look graceful.

7. Hairnets are your friend. One way to avoid the tortured look in a hairstyle is to use hairnets. Also—don't feel limited to using just one—different sections of the style may benefit from several small hairnets. When using hairnets, however, pin them in such a way that the hairnet cannot

be seen. This means to not only conceal the edges of the hairnet, but also to put some pins into the middle of the hairnet so we do not see a dome covering a style (Figure 10-26), but rather the shape of the style itself (Figure 10-27). Hairnets also keep a style looking smooth and staying together much longer; this is especially handy if you are working on a long run of a show with a lot of wigs.

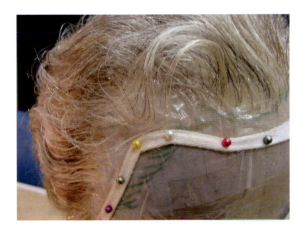

Figure 10-25 The hair in the front of the wigs dips down to break the exposed hairline.

Figure 10-26 An improperly pinned hairnet—it forms a dome around the style.

Figure 10-27 A properly pinned hairnet, following the shape of the hairstyle.

8. If the wig you are styling has to be worn with a hat, you must style it with the hat in mind. Try the wig and the hat together on the performer before you get to dress rehearsal so you can make any needed adjustments.

9. Make sure your finished style is reasonably balanced and not too heavy. Take this into consideration as you are working. The more bobby pins and hairpins a wig has in it, the heavier it will be on the performer. Wigs that are back heavy may tug at an actor's hair and be very uncomfortable to wear.

10. There are lots of new temporary styling products out. These can help you achieve some great, washable effects. Spray glitter, temporary colors, waxes, and pastes all have their place. Make sure to keep them out of the lace of your wig.

11. Consider the overall balance of wigs and natural hair on stage in a production. If everyone is wearing a wig except for one performer, the performer without a wig may stick out like a sore thumb. If only one or two characters are wearing wigs, then those wigs need to be styled very naturally so as not to stand out.

Obviously, there are exceptions to all of these rules. Make sure you choose to break the rules for a reason. The choice to do so can say a lot about the character or the world you are creating.

The world is full of people with messy hair, overly stiff hair, fried hair, ridiculous hair, suspiciously perfect hair, otherworldly hair, or plain and simple hair. Make use of your available tools to achieve the exact look you want.

FROM SET TO STYLE: EXAMPLES

To aid in you in developing your eye from a style from sketch to finished product, we have included a couple of examples of wigs from the beginning setting pattern through the end of the styling process. Please visit the companion website at http://booksite.focalpress.com/companion/Ruskai/wig/ for additional styles, photos, and step-by-step instructions.

EXAMPLE 1: COSETTE IN *LES MISERABLES*

Figure 10-28 Front view of Cosette's set.

Figure 10-31 Right side view of Cosette's set.

Figure 10-34 Back view of Cosette's finished style.

Figure 10-29 Left side view of Cosette's set.

Figure 10-32 Front view of Cosette's finished style.

Figure 10-35 Right side view of Cosette's finished style.

Figure 10-30 Back view of Cosette's set.

Figure 10-33 Left side view of Cosette's finished style.

Figure 10-36 The wig onstage in *Les Miserables* at the Pioneer Theatre Company. Trista Moldovan as Cosette and Gregg Goodbrod as Marius. Costume design by K.L. Alberts. Wigs by Amanda French.

EXAMPLE 2: 1930s HOLLYWOOD MOVIE-STAR LOOK

Figure 10-37 Research for a 1930s Hollywood hairstyle.

Figure 10-38 Front view of the wig set.

Figure 10-39 Top view of the wig set.

Figure 10-40 Left side view of the wig set.

Figure 10-41 Back view of the wig set.

Figure 10-42 Right side view of the wig set.

Figure 10-43 Anna Fugate models her finished style.

Figure 10-44 Back view of the finished style.

Figure 10-45 Left side view of the finished style.

CHAPTER 11 Choosing, Cutting, Coloring, and Perming the Hair

There are many types of "hair" available to make wigs. Sometimes the hair is available that looks, feels, and behaves exactly the way it needs to. Other times the hair needs work to look, move, and hold the style over a long run.

Mohair (Angora) is the finest of the hairs traditionally used in wig making. It is a wool, and—like its cousin used in clothing—is soft, fine, and fluffy. For this reason, it is often used in wigs for very young children; wispy, thin, balding wigs; and eyebrows for women and children.

Mohair has an uneven surface, is opaque, and does not hold a curl or wave. It takes most types of dye very well.

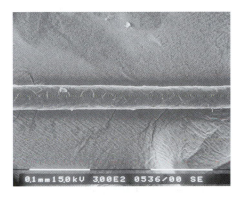

Figure 11-1 Mohair magnified 300 times.

Unprocessed human hair from people with genetic ties to northern Europe is among the thinnest of the human hairs. When healthy, the cuticle lies flat and the hair is somewhat shiny.

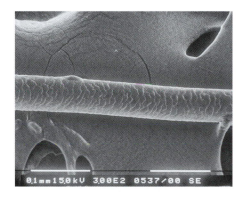

Figure 11-2 Unprocessed human hair from French-American, magnified 300 times.

Yak hair is thicker, stiffer, and coarser than any human hair. It lacks cuticle and so rarely tangles. It is also incredibly shiny. Yak will take most dyes quickly. Yak curls easily with water or heat. White yak does scorch if the irons are too hot.

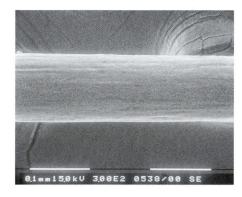

Figure 11-3 Yak hair magnified 300 times.

Horse mane and tail hair is much larger than yak. It will curl but resists bending even when wet. It is used

Figure 11-4 Horse hair magnified 300 times.

mostly for historic British legal wigs and for spiky-haired aliens. Horse takes most dyes very easily. It does have a cuticle and the health and care of the hair will determine shine or lack thereof.

Synthetic fibers are made by extruding plastic. The size of the fiber is determined by the size of the extruder.

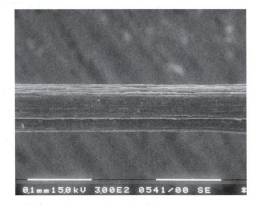

Figure 11-5 Fiber from normal "Elura-blend" wig magnified 300 times.

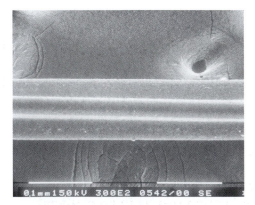

Figure 11-6 Fiber from very inexpensive bulk braids, sold at most wig stores for $0.99–$3.00, magnified 300 times.

The shine of the fiber is determined by the shape of the surface. Synthetics are solid acrylic or nylon. Most are heat-sensitive.

The genetic background of the human hair influences the strength, curl, and diameter of the individual hairs. It also influences the number of hairs that grow on the healthy head.

What we do to the hair also affects how it looks, moves, and feels. Genetic factors play a huge role. Hairs from most people of African descent are curly or kinky. This type of hair is usually quite thin and very fragile. Because of the fragility, it is rarely used in wig making.

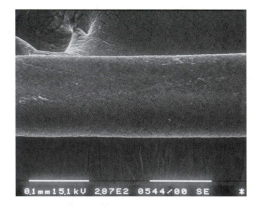

Figure 11-7 Healthy unprocessed Asian hair.

Hair from southeast Asia is usually strong and thicker than European or African hair. For wig making, the cuticle is stripped off, the color bleached out, and the hair is often given a chemical curl. If mishandled, the hair can change shape.

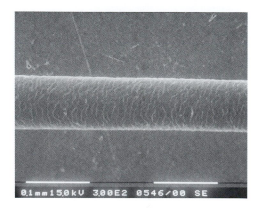

Figure 11-8 Asian hair that has been bleached and permed into irregularly curled hair; it has a warped shape, and the cuticle is mostly absent.

When human hair is bleached or permed, the cuticle becomes more visible and irregular.

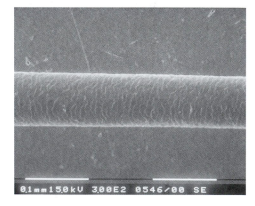

Figure 11-9 Bleached and colored Eastern European hair.

Most of the human hair sold for wigs is Asian hair that has had the cuticle completely removed by an aggressive bleaching process. By removing the

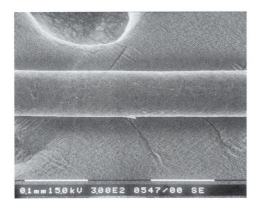

Figure 11-10 Cuticle-free processed Asian hair.

cuticle, the diameter of the hair is made smaller which more closely matches that of genetically European hair.

DYEING WIGS AND WIG FIBERS

All hair used in wigs and hairpieces can be dyed darker with both temporary and permanent color. Not all wig fibers can be lightened.

The color of any object is a mix of the pigments we learned about in basic grade-school color wheels. How we see it onstage is a combination of the color of the object and the color of the light.

UNIVERSAL HAIR COLOR SYSTEMS

There are two numerical hair color systems used to describe hair color. One, the *J&L color ring*, has been used by wigmakers and hair brokers for over a century. Many commercial wig companies still use this color system in their catalogs and websites. The second system is used by American cosmetologists to describe the hair color of people and hair dye. At first glance, the systems look like they might be the same, but this is not true. So when working with someone, make sure you are discussing the same color system! We recommend studying cosmetology to gain a complete understanding of hair dye and other chemical processes. The purpose of this chapter is to help you understand how and what is possible so that you can communicate with a professional colorist in the event that you need to use commercial dyes on your wigs or hairpieces.

AMERICAN COSMETOLOGY HAIR LEVEL SYSTEM

To this 12-number system are added color modifiers: Gold, Copper, Red, Violet, and Ash.

As you can see, both systems assign 1 to black and the number gets larger as the color gets lighter. But the systems match only for the lowest numbers and darkest browns; 1–black through 4–dark brown. After 4, the correlation falls apart. J&L Classic wig color 27–Strawberry Blonde matches up to approximately 9–Gold Neutral in the American Cosmetology system. The palest bleach blonde is 613 in the J&L Classic system and a 12 in the Cosmetology system.

Color 12 in the J&L Classic color system is closer to an 8 Neutral Ash in the Cosmetology system. This difference is further complicated by the fact that color swatch rings are only a guide and the real colors will vary with company and with dye batches. And color swatches change with exposure to light. The reality is that one simply has to learn both systems as different and not waste any time trying to "match" them up.

Fabric dyes can be used to color wig hair. These dyes open up a much wider range of colors to adjust wig hair color. These dyes are described in relationship to the standard color wheel.

TYPES OF HAIR COLOR PRODUCTS

Temporary color products simply coat the hair with something that can then be washed out. Permanent colors will bind to the hair through either a physical adhesive or a chemical process.

The two most commonly used temporary products are theatrical color sprays and brush-in products. These coat the hair shaft with a mixture of pigment suspended in a fast-evaporating solvent.

These generally add weight and stiffness to the hair. Excessive application results in an artificial, crunchy look. The best way to use these products is to apply them in layers and

Classic Color Chart (Also known as J&L color ring)

Blacks
1 - Black
1B - Off Black

Browns
2 - Darkest Brown
4 - Dark Brown
6 - Chestnut Brown
8 - Lt. Chestnut Brown
10 - Med Golden Brown
12 - Lt. Gld Reddish Brown
14 - Lt. Gld Brown
17 - Med Ash Brown
18 - Lt. Ash Brown

Reds
15 - Gld Reddish Blond
19 - Lt. Strawberry Blond
27 - Strawberry Blond
27A - Lt. Auburn
27C - Lt. Ginger
30 - Med Auburn
33 - Dk Auburn
118 - Wine Re
30 - Fox Red
131 - Burgundy Red

Blonds
16 - Honey Ash Blond
22 - Champagne Blond
24 - Lt. Gld Blond
24B - Lt. Butterscotch
25 - Golden Blond
26 - Med Gld Blond
144 - Yellow Gold
613 - Pale Blond
613A - White Blond

Whites & Platinums
60 - White
101 - Platinum
102 - Pearl Platinum

Gray Mixes
280 - Black + 5% Gray
281 - Dkst. Brwn + 5% Gray
34 - Chestnut Brwn+25% Gray
36 - Lt. Chestnut
      Brwn+25% Gray
38 - Lt. Gld Reddish Brwn+35%
44 - Dk. Brwn+50% Gray
48 - Lt. Chestnut
      Brwn+50% Gray
51 - Gray+25% Dkst. Brwn
56 - Gray+10% Chestnut Brwn
59 - Gray+5% Black
456 - Mix of 44-51-56

Frosted
16/22 - Honey Ash Blond +
         Champagne Blond
17/101 - Medium Ash Brown +
         Platinum
18/22 - Lt. Ash Brown +
         Champagne Blond
24/14 - Lt. Golden Blond +
         Lt. Golden Brown
24B/613 - Lt. Butterscotch +
         Pale Blond
27/30 - Strawberry Blond +
         Medium Auburn
27/33 - Strawberry Blond +
         Dark Auburn
27C/29 - Lt. Ginger + Cinnamon
8/27 - Lt. Chestnut Brown +
         Strawberry Blond

Highlights
8-H16 - Lt. Chestnut Brown +
         Honey Ash Blond
         Highlights
10-H16 - Med. Golden
         Brown + Honey
         Ash Blond
         Highlights
24-H613 - Lt. Golden
         Blond + Pale
         Blond Highlights
27-H613 - Strawberry
         Blond + Pale
         Blond
         Highlights
27C-H24B - Butterscotch

Tips
1BTPurple - Off Black
         tipped
         w/Purple
2-T130 - Darkest Brown
         tipped w/Fox Red
4-T144 - Dark Brown tipped
         w/Yellow Gold
4-T131 - Dark Brown tipped
         w/Burgundy Red
8-T613 - Lt. Chestnut
         Brown tipped
         w/Pale Blond
8-T26 - Lt. Chestnut Brown
         Root, tipped
         w/Med. Golden
         Blond
8-T124 - Lt. Chestnut Brown
         Root, tipped w/Lt.
         Golden Blond

12-T16 - Lt. Golden
         Reddish Brown
         Root, tipped
         w/Honey Ash

Blond
15-T613 - Golden Reddish
         Blond Root,
         tipped w/Pale
         Blond
17-T101 - Medium Ash Brown
         Root, tipped
         w/Platinum
18-T12 - Lt. Ash Brown Root,
         tipped w/Lt. Golden
         Reddish Brown
18-T22 - Light Ash Brown Root,
         tipped w/Champagne
         Blond
1B/130TP1B - Off Black + Fox
         Red Root, tipped
         w/Off Black
24B-BT27 - Lt. Butterscotch
         Root, w/Lt
         Butterscotch +
         Strawberry Blond
27-T613 - Strawberry Blond
         Root, tipped
         w/Pale Blond
30-T613 - Med. Auburn
         Root, tipped
         w/Pale Blond
31-T130 - Auburn Root,
         tipped with
         Fox Red
31-T27C - Auburn Root, tipped
         with Light Ginger

Figure 11-11 Classic color chart, courtesy Wig America.

American Cosmetology Color System	
1	black
2	very dark brown
3	dark brown
4	medium brown
5	light brown
6	dark blonde
7	medium blonde
8	light blonde
9	very light blonde
10	lightest blonde
11	super light blonde
12	ultra light blonde

Figure 11-12 Basic Cosmetology color system.

brush each layer after drying. Then style the hair. The gray and white coating colors are valuable when creating an eighteenth-century powdered look.

Another temporary product line that is very useful in the theater for adjusting hair color of a wig for a short run is Roux Fanciful Rinse. Fanciful is available at most beauty supply and drug stores. This is a liquid that adds a thin layer of fine pigment to the hair shaft. There is little binder to this type of rinse. This means that very little weight is added to the shaft of hair and the hair continues to move normally. However, the porosity of the hair directly affects how much change in color can be achieved. Most synthetic fibers are plastic and the color rinses just don't stick.

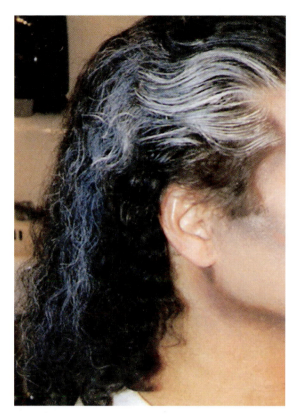

Figure 11-13 Ben Nye Hair White brushed into performer's hair and 3/4 wig.

Figure 11-14 Color products by Ben Nye Co.

To use a temporary color rinse on human or yak hair, apply the liquid directly from the bottle to damp or dry hair depending on the degree of change determined by the test sample. The tinted hair can then be set wet with rollers, drip-dried, or force-dried.

DYEING PROTEIN FIBERS

Human, yak, and mohair can be dyed permanently with a wide range of products, including color products meant for human hair as well as most fabric dyes. Human hair, yak, and mohair are all protein-based fibers and any color product meant for use on human hair or wool fabric will work well. Human hair can also be lightened, although this may result in damage to the hair and should be done only when absolutely necessary. Most hair used in wigs is already dyed and permanently waved and additional chemical process may result in excessive damage. Synthetic fibers are a bit trickier to dye. Standard human hair dyes will not affect synthetic hair. It is not possible to lighten synthetic fibers.

USING FABRIC DYES

Fabric dyes come in a wide range of brands and purposes. For more detailed information on the full range of fabric dyes and dye safety, see *Fabric Painting and Dyeing for the Theatre* by Deborah

Dryden (Portsmouth, NH: Heinemann Drama, 1993).

Always follow safety precautions provided by the MSDS from the manufacturer. This usually includes wearing rubber or vinyl gloves and a dust mask or using a dye box for mixing. Always use separate containers for dye and store away from all food containers to avoid accidental mix-ups.

Wear protective clothing and splash goggles and be sure to use caution when heating dye baths to avoid burns caused by splashing hot water or steam.

Union or household dyes are actually a mix of dyes meant to work on most fabrics. RIT and Tintex are both union dyes. In powdered form, union dyes are not good for the respiratory tract. If you can, use RIT in liquid form, because this will eliminate the need for a dye box. Union dyes work very well on human hair, yak, and mohair. Some synthetics will dye with union dyes.

Disperse dyes will dye many acetates, nylon, acrylic, and polyesters. Human, yak, and mohair also respond well to disperse-type dyes. Disperse dyes can be hazardous to the eyes and respiratory tract. Please follow all safety precautions.

Human, yak, and Mohair are protein fibers and dye very easily with just about any product ever tried. Union dyes (Tintex and RIT) work very well on yak and mohair. Any type of dye that is listed for use on wool will usually work quite well on yak and mohair. In many cases, color change can be achieved with room-temperature dye. Intense colors may require heating.

PREPARING HAIR BUNDLES FOR DYE

Tossing loose strands of any types of wig fiber into a pot of dye like you're cooking spaghetti is not recommended. Although this would give the most even color, the fibers will tangle into a birds nest and be totally useless after wards. When dye bulk or loose wig fibers, the strands must be sectioned in to small, pencil-sized bundles. Then the "root end" must be tightly bound to hold the strands together.

When placed in the dye bath, the bound portion will not dye. Buy hair 2 inches longer than you need to allow for cutting off the undyed portion at the root end.

It is safest to dye human, yak, and mohair at moderate temperatures. Excessive heat—beyond 200°F—can cause damage to the fibers as well as increase the risk of steam burns or hot water splash burns to the people. Most colors will fade with repeated washing. Although human hair can be dyed with fabric dyes, it is important to remember that fabric dyes should never be applied to hair that is attached to a human head! Use fabric dyes only on human hair that is already cut off.

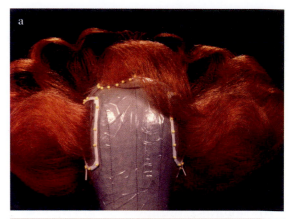

Figure 11-15 Yak hair dyed with a union dye. Wig, prosthetics, and makeup by Bradley M. Look, model Clayton Stang.

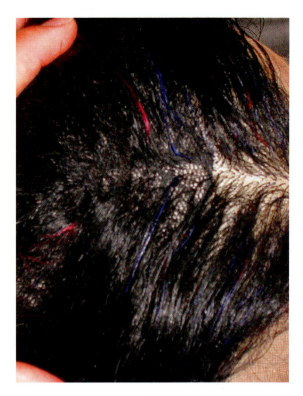

Figure 11-16 Royal blue and fuchsia hair added to black human-hair wig front.

DYEING SYNTHETIC FIBERS

Synthetic wigs and hairpieces are actually made from a range of fibers that include many different trademarked acrylic, modacrylic, polyester, and nylon blends. For this reason, a dye that works well on one wig or hairpiece may not work at all on something marked with the same name. In fact, fibers within the same wig may take color from the same dye bath very differently. Trial and error is really the name of the game with synthetic wig fibers. The best results will be achieved with union dyes like RIT or Tintex and with disperse-type dyes such as Aljo Acetate-Nylon. A few synthetic fibers may take color with basic dyes. Polyester dyes add color, but in most cases also ruin the hair. The addition of poly developer to polyester dyes creates a gummy synthetic fiber that is totally useless, as the smell is overwhelming, so this type of dye should be avoided.

Dyes that will dye acrylic and nylon require high temperatures—near boiling—to work. Synthetic fibers are very easily damaged by exposure to high heat. The goal is to find the lowest temperature and type of dye that gives the intensity of color with the least damage to the fiber. In some cases, a much stronger percentage of dye to weight of fiber than recommended by the manufacturer is needed to dye synthetic wig fibers. The addition of acetic acid may cause a subtle difference in color compared to samples dyed in a less acid bath. The addition of acetic acid to the dye baths has not made any difference to the depth of color or to the wash fastness of the color in any synthetic wig fibers tested by the authors to date. Because synthetic wig fibers are rapidly changing, test samples are a must.

Large double-boiler and dye vats are the best to use, because they protect the synthetic fiber from contact with the part of the pot where the heating element touches. In the absence of these types of pots, use the largest, deepest dye pot you can and create a system that keeps the synthetic fiber suspended in the water without touching the sides.

Figure 11-17 Box for safely mixing powdered dyes.

Figure 11-18 An enamel dye pot with steamer insert protects wigs from melting on the bottom of the pot.

1. Prewash the synthetic fibers to remove any oils or conditioners that might inhibit an even dye.
2. Keep the fibers in a warm wet bath while waiting.
3. Mix dye powder in a dye box while wearing gloves.
4. Add the desired amount of measured dye to a small amount of warm water and mix to an even paste.
5. Add dye to warm-water dye bath.
6. Add the synthetic fiber to the dye bath, making sure to stir the dye around and also to move the fibers around in such a way that encourages even dyeing. When dyeing a complete synthetic wig, lift the wig up through the dye bath with tongs to make sure that the dye is moving from root to tip. Avoid any movement that results in tangling the fibers.

When you will be using weft off of a hairpiece to make a wig, it is best to remove the weft from the hairpiece to allow the dye to reach the roots and tips evenly.

Heat the dye bath to boiling with care. Each combination of dye color and synthetic fiber will work at temperatures slightly below boiling. Because temperatures over 200° F significantly increase the risk of damage to the synthetic fibers, always raise the

Figure 11-19 (a) Original undyed swatches. Left to right: Kanekalon, 100-percent synthetic bulk braid, modacrylic, Toyokalon, modacrylic, keratin hair, yak. (b) Aljo Acetate-Nylon yellow. (c) Aljo Acetate-Nylon Red. (d) Aljo acetate-Nylon Emerald green. (e) Rit Dark Green.

temperature slowly. Once the desired color is reached, there is no reason to raise the dye bath temperature any higher.

Most dye manufacturers and theatrical dyer suggest leaving the fibers in the dye bath at the "optimal temperature" for 30 minutes. Test on most synthetic wig fibers show that the maximum intensity is achieved in 5–10 minutes after the magic temperature is reached. Wash fastness also seems to be the same at 10 minutes as at 30 minutes. When doing large batches, more than one wig at a time, the color was more even when left in the dye bath for 30 minutes.

7. Remove dyed wig or bundles and wash with shampoo and warm water. Continue to wash and rinse with lukewarm until the water runs clear. As long as body temperature rinse water has dye coloration, there is risk of the dye running when the person sweats.
8. Steam and brush to straighten out any odd kinks and curls created by the hot dye bath.

PERMING WIGS AND WIG FIBERS

If naturally curly hair isn't available, wig hair can be permed. Human and yak hair can be permanently (chemically waved) before or after the wig is constructed. It is easier to ventilate with straight hair and perm after the wig is completed. Perming after a wig is finished also provides the opportunity to completely control the direction of the curl and wave motion around the face. However, it is riskier to perm a finished wig. Because the chemical processes involved in permanent waving involve potentially harmful materials it is important to have a licensed experienced cosmetologist perform any chemical process on a wig, including permanently waving.

Perming the hair before the wig is constructed does provide a safety net—if the hair is too damaged, it doesn't have to be used.

Most human hair can safely be permanently waved. Hair that has been bleached and stripped of cuticle will damage very easily. Use products suggested for color treated hair and do more than one test sample before perming an entire wig. Yak will perm, but special attention needs to be paid to the timing. There is very little room for error between the hair taking the curl and totally disintegrating and turning into jelly.

Good results can be achieved with both acid and acid-balanced perms. One of the tricks to getting good perm results is an even, tight wrap on the rollers. This often requires extensive pinning of the weft or foundation to the block. Another tip for perming wigs is to remember that permanent waves assume a bit of body heat coming up from the scalp of a person. Endothermic perm solutions require the use of an outside heat source. A wig sitting on a block is room temperature, usually 30°F cooler than the perm was developed for.

Figure 11-20 UNCSA actors Joshua Morgan and Chris French as convicts in *Our Country's Good* in wigs made with permed hair. Wigs designed by Tera Willis, built and photographed by Raquel Bianchini.

Endothermic are usually acid waves and gentler on hair that has already been processed. For these reasons, endothermic perms often result in a better curl on a wig. To solve this pre-heat a wig dryer to 98°F and place the wig in the dryer once it is rolled and has solution added. Make sure the rolled wig has a plastic bag over it to keep it from drying out. Turn off the dryer after a few minutes to avoid over heating.

CUTTING WIGS

The cuts needed to create a given hairstyle on a wig are the same haircuts needed to create that hairstyle with the hair that grows out of the human head. The difference is in how to deal with the wig on the block as you cut to ensure that the hair cut will work when it is put on the human head.

Wigs that are completely hand-tied onto nonstretchy foundations can be cut just as you would cut hair on a human head.

Wigs that are hand-tied on a stretchy foundation can be cut just as you would cut hair on a human head, as long as the foundation is pinned securely every 2 inches.

Wigs that are made of weft need to be cut with extra care to ensure that the result is smooth. It is very easy to end up with choppy ends. Avoid blunt-cutting any weft wig. Wigs made from weft are best cut by "tipping," razor cuts, or with thinning shears.

All wigs should be cut on a block identical to the person's head shape with hair prep, so use a well-padded plastic tracing or choose a block with the right shape.

Pin the wigs all over the head at small regular intervals to ensure that the foundation is stable when cutting.

Figure 11-23 Hair pinned securely for cutting.

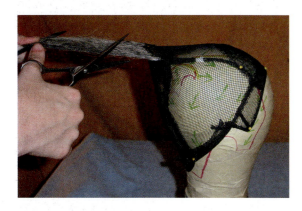

Figure 11-21 Caul net and other stretchy foundations will pull out of shape when the hair is pulled out for cutting.

Figure 11-22 By pinning weft and foundation at 2-inch intervals, the foundation will remain hugging the block and ensure a more accurate haircut.

Figure 11-24 Human-hair hand-tied wig with silk part. Built, cut, and styled by Isaac Grnya, UNCSA.

CHAPTER 12 Hair that Isn't Hair: Wigs Made from Other Materials

Figure 12-1 Nylon rope wigs made by Sarah Bahr for *The School for Scandal*, presented by the University of Minnesota-Duluth. Costume design by Bill Brewer.

Now that you have fronted, ventilated, and styled beautiful wigs, it is time for you to put aside that information and turn your attention to a very different kind of wig: a wig that is not made of hair.

Why, you ask, would someone want to do such a thing? Designing wigs that are made of alternative materials opens up a whole new realm of creative possibilities. Different materials allow you to achieve new and interesting looks, and, in some cases, even help you solve problems. For example, Allison Lowery was working on production of Stephen Sondheim's *Into the Woods.* In this musical, several different fairy tales are woven together to form one large story. Two of the characters are Rapunzel and the Witch who keeps her locked in the tower. In this production, the director wanted Rapunzel's hair to be both extremely bright yellow in color and to be able to actually be climbed by the Witch and the Prince.

After looking at different solutions, it was decided that bright-yellow safety

Figure 12-2 Amanda Chubb as Rapunzel in *Into the Woods*, presented by the University of North Carolina School of the Arts.

175

rope from the hardware store would be the ideal product to use. After it was unraveled, the rope had a lovely wavy texture and was strong enough to hold the weight of the actors playing the Witch and the Prince. (The actress's head and neck were not strong enough, however, so some of the "hair" was secretly anchored to the set.)

Different materials also lend themselves to some very stylized, magical, or otherworldly looks. If you wanted a creature to look as though they are part of a forest, what better way than to have them wear hair that is actually made of vines, plants, bark, or moss? If you desired a very artificial doll-like look, why not make the wig as artificial as possible, perhaps by making the hair of ribbons, satin, or paper? The possibilities are endless. In this chapter, we will touch on some basic techniques of making non-hair wigs. Let your imagination run free in order to expand these techniques and be inspired to make your own creations.

BASES AND FOUNDATIONS

Many materials that you may choose to use in a wig will need to have a stronger-than-usual base or foundation to support them. For lighter materials, you can use a typical wig foundation like those discussed in Chapter 6, but there are a couple of other techniques you can use to build a stronger base.

One of the bases that is commonly used is the buckram/felt base. To create this base, you will need a felt hood and buckram (both available from hat-making/millinery supply companies):

1. Take a plastic wrap tracing of the person you are creating the wig for and pad out a canvas or wood head block to the exact shape of the person's head.
2. Use an industrial steamer to thoroughly saturate your felt hood with steam. You will see tiny droplets of condensation form on the outside of your felt hood. Make sure to steam all areas of the hood—this will make the hood become soft and pliable. *Be careful when handling the hood—the steam makes the felt hood very hot!*
3. Have some push pins and elastic handy. Once the hood is fully steamed, remove it from the steamer. Pull the felt hood over the head block. Make sure you pull and tug on the felt hood until it is completely flat on top, with no bubbles, puckers, or creases. The felt hood should be snug against the top of the head block—no air should be trapped underneath. You will need to put a lot of your body weight into this—make sure the head block is on a secure wig clamp. Tie the elastic around the bottom of the felt. Use the elastic to flatten the shape. Use the push pins pinned into the elastic to secure the felt around

Figure 12-3 The felt hood has been pinned in place.

the bottom of the head block (Figure 12-3). Start by placing one at the bottom of the center front of the head. The second thumbtack you should place at the center back of the head. Continue working from side to side until you have pinned a flat shape onto the head block.
4. Cut a square of buckram larger than you think you will need. Before it is wet, buckram is a very stiff fabric, almost like cardboard. Once it is wet, it becomes a very soft, gluey material (Figure 12-4).

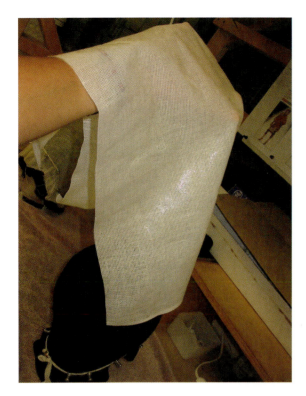

Figure 12-4 Buckram, after it has been thoroughly soaked with water.

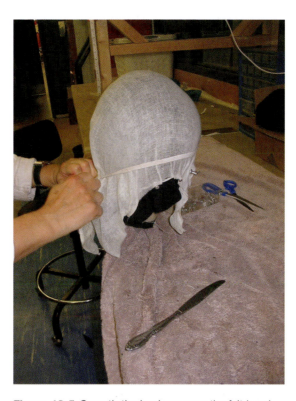

Figure 12-5 Smooth the buckram over the felt hood and secure with elastic.

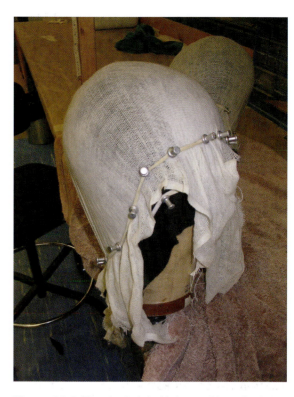

Figure 12-6 The elastic is held down with push pins.

Wet the square of buckram in warm water. Pull the buckram over the felt on the head form, using the bias direction for maximum stretch. Like you did with the felt hood, pull the buckram as tight as you can so that it lays smooth. Tie the elastic around the base very tightly (Figure 12-5). Smooth the buckram down under the elastic.

You may have to pleat the buckram in order for it to take the shape of the head form. Cut out the extra material in the pleat in order to eliminate some of the bulk of the finished base. Then smooth the remaining buckram down until it is as flat and smooth as possible. After the buckram is smoothed, pin the elastic in place with the push pins (Figure 12-6).

5. Allow the buckram and felt to dry. You can put the block into a wig dryer in order to speed up the drying process. Once the felt and buckram are dry, cut off any excess that is hanging past the tacks and elastic.

6. Slowly begin to work the felt and buckram off of the block. You will likely need to trim around where the face will be—just be sure to leave plenty of excess. Take your time—the base you have made will be narrower at the bottom than at the widest part of the head. Trim back the cap until you can get if off the block. It may also help to cut a slit up the center back; this also helps the wearer get into and out of this base easily.

7. Once you have the cap off of the block, baste the two layers together with heavyweight thread. Baste a line from center front to center back of the head; baste a second line going from ear to ear over the top.

8. Fit the person who is going to be wearing this cap (Figure 12-7). Use a pencil and sketch out where the cap needs to be trimmed in order to match up with their hairline. Again, work slowly—it always better to cut too little than to cut too much.

9. Once the cap fits the person perfectly, you can begin making your non-hair wig. The cap are able to be covered be sewing the fabric of your choice on the outside. Both the buckram and the felt are able to be sewn through—just be sure to use a sturdy needle.

FOSSHAPE™ BASES

Fosshape is another excellent material to use when making nontraditional wig bases. It is a soft, pliable fabric that responds to steam or dry heat. Once it has been treated with heat, it hardens to maintain the shape of the form it has been placed over. It can be trimmed into shape and can be painted. It is very lightweight and it remains breathable when it hardens, so it is very comfortable to wear.

1. There are two ways to begin your Fosshape base. You can either drape a square of Fosshape over a head block (Figure 12-8) or piece together a cap (Figures 12-9 and 12-10). If you piece together a cap, use a tight zigzag stitch on the machine to sew the pieces together. Trim your seams as closely as possible.

Figure 12-8 Draping a square of Fosshape over a block.

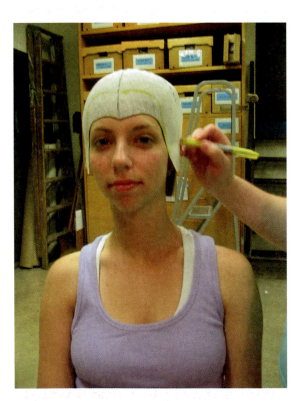

Figure 12-7 Fitting a buckram and felt cap on actress Molly Evensky.

Figure 12-9 The pieces of Fosshape before they are stitched together.

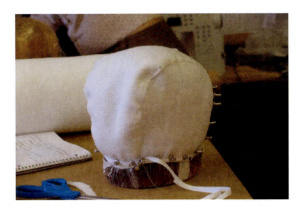

Figure 12-10 Stitch pieces of Fosshape together to form a skull cap.

2. Apply steam to the Fosshape (Figure 12-11). If you have seams in your cap, work the seams first, going from the top down to the bottom. You can also use a heat gun to apply the heat. Once you are done applying the heat, leave your base to cool and harden.

Figure 12-11 Steaming the Fosshape in place.

3. Once your base has cooled, this base is ready to be fit on your performer. Trim the hairline to the desired shape. You may find it helpful to wire the edge of the cap with millinery wire. This will allow the cap to be adjusted to closely fit the head.

Figure 12-12 A finished wig base made of Fosshape.

OTHER TYPES OF BASES

The buckram/felt base and Fosshape bases are just two examples of a base to go under your non-hair wig. Depending on the amount of support you need for your hair materials, you can choose one of several options:

- For a quick, lightweight base, simply cut the bill off a baseball cap. The adjustable baseball caps are better, because this will give you a wig base that is adjustable as well. Remember—a baseball cap usually leaves some of the sideburn area and the nape area exposed—be sure to consider this when using this type of base. This base is a little on the flimsy side.
- For a very sturdy, thick base, you can use a hard hat. The inside of a hard hat holds the shell away from the head and balances the weight very well. It is also possible to remove the innards of the hard hat and use them to construct your wig base if you do not wish to use the outer shell.
- For a base that will hold a very large or heavy wig, a bicycle helmet is a good choice. The multiple straps on the inside and under the chin will allow you to fasten the end product very securely on the wearer's head. All of the straps will also keep the wig stable on the performer's head if it is being worn during a lot of activity, such as dancing or stage fighting.
- Another lightweight base option is to sew a traditional wig foundation (see Chapter 6) using sturdier fabrics that can be found in your local fabric store. Crocheted net fabric, muslin, canvas, and flannel are options.
- The buckram/felt base can also be made using either just the felt or just the buckram. When making the base out of just felt, you will need to "size" the hood once it is dry. ("Sizing" refers to applying hat sizing, a starch/glue-like liquid, to the felt hood. The sizing dries hard, like shellac.) When using just a buckram cap, you will need to line the inside with a soft fabric like flannel; the buckram has rough edges and a scratchy texture.

Figure 12-13 Kara Meche creates a craft wig base out of felt. The pockets on the top of the cap will hold battery-powered strings of lights.

Figure 12-14 Kara Meche's finished wig. Model: Rachel Myhill. Photograph by Shannon Soule.

COVERING THE CAP

The first step after making the cap is to cover it with a fabric that is close in color to your final product. This will not only make your cap blend in with your product, but will also bind off the edges that you trimmed and add to the comfort of the wearer. Select an appropriate fabric and drape it over the cap. You may need to cut and pleat the material, just as you did with the buckram when you were making the base. Sew the pleats or darts in place. Next, stitch through the fabric, buckram, and felt all the way around the outer edge of the cap; do this a quarter of an inch from the edge. Once that is finished, trim away the excess fabric, leaving enough fabric to turn under smoothly. Sew the turned under edge on the inside of the cap. You can also paint your cap instead of covering it with fabric. Fosshape bases take paint especially well.

When are ready to decorate your cap, assemble your desired hair materials together. "Mock up" the wig before you begin attaching anything on a permanent basis. To do this, pin everything in place (be prepared to use a lot of pins!), then step back and take a look at it before you begin sewing, gluing, or otherwise attaching the materials. Always keep in mind real hair growth patterns when you are laying out your materials. Your wig will be more believable if it mimics what occurs on the head naturally. Once you are satisfied with the placement, begin to attach your materials. For any sort of fabric/ribbon/yarn/rope/anything in a long strip material, good old-fashioned sewing is usually the best way to affix them. Use a curved needle to do this, because it allows you to go in and out of the cap in one step. Just be sure not to sew the base to the block you are working on, if the block is canvas. Nothing is as frustrating as to think you are finished—only to find that you have to cut your wig free and start over. For materials like artificial flowers and plastics, a combination of sewing and gluing may work better. Be careful with hot glue—some hot glue products peel right off of whatever they are glued to once the glue has cooled. Specialty glues can also come in very handy when doing this type of work—there are glues made specifically for everything from fabric to Styrofoam to rhinestones to wood. Choose a glue product that matches your materials.

BUILDING A STRUCTURAL SUPPORT FRAME

If the material you are making your wig out of is very heavy, you will want as much of the wig to be hollow as possible—this will keep the weight down and make wearing the wig easier. If the wig is exceptionally wide or tall, you may also need to create some sort of frame to support the style. A frame can be built on any style of base or cap, especially the buckram/felt cap and the fabric cap. You will need several different grades (weights) of wire, pliers, wire cutters, floral tape, and inexpensive netting from your local fabric store:

1. Determine the shape you want your framework to be. Spend a little time measuring so that you will have a clear idea of the scale you wish to work in.

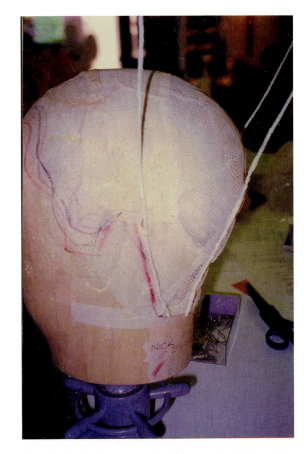

Figure 12-15 The cap is wired from behind the ears around the nape.

2. Wire the edge of the cap from the top of one ear to the top of the other ear down around the nape of the neck. Do this by laying the wire down along the edge of the cap and whip-stitching it on. Be sure you sew through all layers of the cap.

3. In order to get strong anchor points for your base, you will want to wire the cap in such a way that the weight of the hair materials is equally distributed. Wire the cap from ear to ear across the top of the head. Then wire the nape of the neck diagonally into the corners (Figure 12-15). You should also sew in a wire that ends at each sideburn area. As you work, be sure you cleanly bend the ends of the wires so that nothing is sticking out. It is very easy for a performer to become injured by a small piece of wire poking out. Bend the last inch of your wire over and clamp it tightly with your pliers. Cover the exposed ends with floral tape to hide any remaining sharp edges.

4. Once you have the cap wired, begin building your framework. Work in small sections until you reach your desired shape. Constantly think about how to make each section strong so that the frame does not collapse on itself. Add an occasional diagonal crosspiece of wire. Where each wire joins with the next, twist

Figure 12-16 Where the wires cross, stitch them together and then bind them together with floral tape.

the wires together, clamp tightly, and secure with floral tape (Figure 12-16).

5. After the framework is finished, cover the frame with inexpensive netting. This netting will fill in any empty areas as well as give you something to adhere your hair materials to. Choose a color that will blend in with or disappear behind your hair materials. When in doubt, a medium or dark gray is a good neutral color. Attach the netting by whip-stitching it to the wire framework (Figure 12-17).

Once the support structure is completed, you can stitch or glue your hair materials to the frame, and be well on your way to a finished product. (For more information on wire frames, see Chapter 10.)

Figure 12-17 A wire frame, before and after being covered with netting.

Figure 12-18 The finished wire frame is covered with marabou feathers to create the look of a powdered wig. Wig made by Allison Lowery.

COMBINING HAIR AND NON-HAIR MATERIALS

Sometimes you may wish to use both hair and non-hair materials together. The easiest way to do this is to select materials that can be sewn or ventilated into an existing wig. For examples, regular hair and yarn can be combined to form an unusual dreadlock look. Mylar or metallic threads can be ventilated in the same way as hair to create sparkling or shiny highlights in a wig. (The mylar thread is especially nice to combine with synthetic hair—it will

take the curl when the hair is steamed.) Other materials, such as rope, ribbons, or flowers can also be sewn into a wig to enhance its appearance.

Other times, you may wish to use a hair wig, but to have it appear stiff and rigid. This is especially useful if you are trying to make someone appear like a classical statue or a plastic doll with molded plastic hair. One simple way to achieve this is to style the wig using white glue. This glue dries clear and washes out (with patience!) once you are done with this particular style.

Be warned though—this styling is messy. Comb the glue through the hair and shape it the way you want. To achieve round curls or ringlets, you can roll the hair around a plastic curler. Allow the curl to dry and then remove the curler. Once the hair has dried, it will be very difficult to move, so be sure the hair is the way you want it to look when you stop working. You can also use a little white glue when you are styling a traditional wig, especially when you are creating spit curls à la Betty Boop (For an example, see Figure 12-19).

Figure 12-19 Jena Maenius in *Fefu and Her Friends*, presented by the University of Texas. Her spit curls have been styled with white glue. Costume design by Susan Branch Towne. Photograph by Mark Rutkowski.

Many materials can be used to form interesting and creative wigs. Always think of the comfort of the person wearing your creation—try and avoid any extremely heavy or scratchy materials. Beyond that, let your imagination roam free! Consider such materials as feathers, flowers, paper, curling ribbon, gift wrap, fabric, pipe cleaners, ethafoam tubing, toys, birds, artificial fruit, cotton balls, paper towel tubes, cardboard, tinsel, kitchen scrubbies, pom poms, beads, yarn, twine, raffia, coffee filters … inspirational materials are everywhere!

EXAMPLE OF THE STEP-BY-STEP PROCESS OF CREATING AN UNUSUALLY SHAPED WIG

As an example of the steps that one goes through to create an out-of-the–ordinary wig, we will describe the steps used to create the wig worn by the character of Bottom in *A Midsummer Night's Dream* after the character has been transformed into a donkey. (For this production at the University of Texas–Austin, Bottom was played by a female actor, LaTasha Stephens.)

1. The desired shape was mocked up in craft paper and other disposable materials:

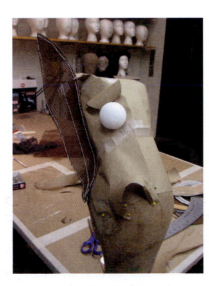

Figure 12-20 The shape has been roughed out in wire, craft paper, plastic canvas, and styrofoam.

2. After building a traditional wig foundation, we began adding the shaped pieces as determined by our mock-up. Here, plastic needlepoint canvas, heavy-gauge millinery wire, and nylon netting were used:

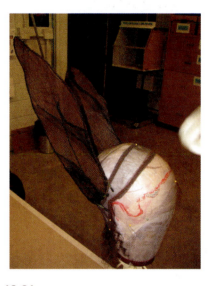

Figure 12-21

Figure 12-22 A close up view of how the ears were attached to the wig foundation.

3. Corset boning was used to add strength and support to the structure:

Figure 12-23

4. More nylon netting was used to cover the structure:

Figure 12-24

5. Wefting was added to the structure to form the donkey's mane:

Figure 12-25

6. The completed mane:

Figure 12-26

7. The ears were then covered by ventilated "pockets" that slipped over the ears like a glove. The eyes were made by wrapping Styrofoam balls with loose hair, spraying them, and then covering each of them with a hairnet. Sequins were added to accentuate the eyes.
8. The wig was then styled so that all of the pieces and parts went together.
9. The completed wig onstage.

Figure 12-27 LaTasha Stephens as Bottom in *A Midsummer Night's Dream*, presented by the University of Texas–Austin. Costume design by Jennifer Madison; wig construction by Allison Lowery. Photograph by Mark Rutkowski.

GALLERY OF NON-HAIR/ FANTASY WIGS

Figure 12-28 Ribbon wig constructed by Tammy Potts-Merritt at the University of North Carolina School of the Arts.

Figure 12-29 A raffia wig on a Fosshape base, constructed by Bill Brewer for *The Tempest*, produced by the British Resident International Theatre.

Figure 12-30 A wired ethafoam wig, made for *The Good Person of Szechuan* by Christina Grant. Presented by the University of North Carolina School of the Arts.

Figure 12-31 Felt and wire wigs made for *The Good Person of Szechuan*, presented by the University of North Carolina School of the Arts. Construction by Katie Ward.

Figure 12-32 Crayola® Model Magic™ wig with a felt and wig lace base. Constructed by Christina Grant for *Don Giovanni*, presented by University of North Carolina School of the Arts.

Figure 12-33 Nylon rope wigs created by Sarah Bahr for *The School for Scandal*, presented by the University of Minnesota–Duluth. Costume design by Bill Brewer.

Figure 12-36 Chamois foundation with Crayola® Model Magic™ for Commendatore statue in *Don Giovanni*, presented by the Atlanta Opera.

Figure 12-34 The cast of *The Very Persistent Gappers of Frip*, presented by the University of Texas, wearing wigs made of a variety of materials, including yarn, twine, horsehair, raffia, and wired piping. Costume design and photography by Candida K. Nichols.

Figure 12-35 Fosshape and hair-wefting wigs for *The Mikado*, presented by the UCF Conservatory Theatre. Design by Kristina Tollefson.

CHAPTER 13

How to Get a Show into Production

Figure 13-1 Kate deBuys as Titania in *A Midsummer Night's Dream*, presented by the University of Texas. Costume design by Jennifer Madison; photograph by Mark Rutkowski.

The ultimate goal of good wig and makeup design is helping to tell the story told by the script. If your design distracts from the story being told or does not fit into the world created by the playwright, director, and other designers, your design will not be a success. Knowing how to understand and analyze a play (or opera or movie) is vital to designing appropriate characters and having them live in a world that makes logical and aesthetic sense.

ANALYZING AND UNDERSTANDING THE PLAY

When approaching a play for the first time, it is often helpful to read it straight through in order to achieve some idea of the flow of the play and to allow yourself to form a genuine emotional response. After doing this, going back and rereading the play in order to break it down into very clear pieces is essential. Doing this breakdown helps lay out the important plot events and stage moments that are of critical importance. Once you see these events and moments clearly, you can make important design decisions that will help the director, actor, and the design team to visually draw attention to these moments.

FORMS OF DRAMA

One important thing to determine is the kind of play or movie you are designing—in other words, what genre your play falls into. Is it a comic opera? A Shakespearean tragedy? A contemporary, realistic film? An absurd fantasy? Knowing the genre is important, because certain genres are associated with built in expectations or theatrical conventions. For example, melodramas are expected to have a very obvious villain; most audience picture this villain twirling his dramatic mustache. You do not necessarily have to follow these traditions, but you do need to be aware of them. Not using these conventions should be a deliberate choice, not an unfortunate oversight on your part. Do your research! A list of dramatic forms all designers should be familiar with includes comedy, tragedy, tragicomedy, black comedy, farce, vaudeville, musical, melodrama, drawing room comedy, commedia del arte, opera buffa, Restoration comedy, fantasy, comedy of manners, Elizabethan drama, revenge tragedy, and many others.

BASIC PLOT STRUCTURE

Nearly all plays and movies follow a basic plot structure (This structure has been visually represented in Figure 13-2):

1. There is an *inciting incident*; this is an event that occurs before the beginning of the action we see on stage. This is the event that kicks things into gear; it is the reason the play is necessary. For example, in William Shakespeare's *Hamlet*, the inciting incident is the death of Hamlet's father. There can be more than one inciting incident.

2. Once the curtain goes up, the action is underway. The first thing that usually happens is *exposition*. Exposition is where the audience learns about the inciting incident as well as the given circumstances of the characters—what they want, how they relate to other characters, how they fit into the world of the play. For example, in *Hamlet*, we learn that Hamlet's father has died, his mother soon after his father's death has married his uncle, Hamlet has been called home from university to attend the funeral/wedding, and that there is a lot of intrigue going on in the court at Denmark. Exposition can continue throughout the play.

3. The action of the play really gets set into motion with the *point of attack*. This usually occurs when someone decides to actively pursue a goal. It

can come early or late in the play. To determine the point of attack, you have to find the event that motivates the protagonist to act. In *Hamlet*, the point of attack occurs when Hamlet decides to get revenge on his uncle Claudius for murdering Hamlet's father. Everything Hamlet does in the play after this point is leading toward Hamlet and Claudius's confrontation.

4. After the point of attack, the *complications and conflict* ensue. These are the events that change the course of the story and make the play last for longer than ten minutes. There can be any number of complications in a play; the action continues to rise, fall, and change direction. In *Hamlet*, the complications include Ophelia's madness and subsequent death, the accidental murder of Polonius, the double-dealing of Rosencrantz and Guildenstern, Hamlet's confused feelings about his mother, and the desire of Laertes to revenge himself on Hamlet.

5. The *climax* of a play is the highest, most exciting point of action in a play. It is arguably the single most important event of the plot. The climax answers the question that is asked at the point of attack. Will Hamlet revenge himself on Claudius? Yes—Hamlet kills Claudius.

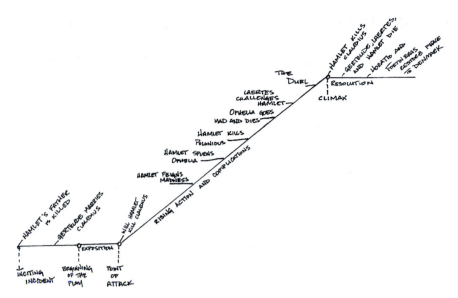

Figure 13-2 A diagram of the play structure of *Hamlet*.

Shakespeare's plays, which clearly state the act, scene, and line number.

Scene	Pg.	Scene's Starting Location
THERE'S A BOY IN THE GIRL'S BATHROOM BY LOUIS SACHAR		
I.1	2	Classroom
I.2	6	Bedroom
I.3	14	Hallway
I.4	36	Schoolyard
I.5	30	Bedroom
I.6	33	Carla's Office
I.7	37	Schoolyard
I.8	41	Schoolyard
I.9	43	Carla's Office
I.10	49	Neutral stage area
ACT II		
II.1	54	Carla's Office
II.2	59	Schoolyard
II.3	62	Bedroom
II.4	66	Hallway
II.5	71	Bedroom
II.6	76	Schoolyard
II.7	79	Boy's Bathroom
II.8	86	Hallway
II.9	91	Bedroom
II.10	92	Classroom
II.11	93	Carla's Office

Figure 13-3 A location/scene breakdown chart for *There's a Boy in the Girl's Bathroom* by Louis Sachar. Chart made by Jen Ash.

6. After the climax of the play, we are left with the *resolution*. This where all of the loose ends are tied up. It ends the action of the play. Sometimes there is an implied continuation of the action, but after the resolution is where the audience stops watching and goes home. In *Hamlet*, Gertrude drinks the poisoned drink, Hamlet stabs Claudius, Hamlet and Laertes die from poisoned stab wounds, and Horatio restores order to the court of Denmark.

SCENE BREAKDOWNS

In order both to understand a play and to physically produce and run a show, you need to break it down into pieces. These breakdowns make it clear where the action of each scene is taking place, when they change locations, what the weather is like, what time of day it is, who is in what scene, and exactly how much time you have to quick-change an actor into a new costume and wig. By nature of the way they are written, film scripts are already broken into scenes and locations for you. Plays, musicals, and operas, on the other hand, can be broken down and organized in several different ways:

1. **Location/scene changes as mentioned in the script.** It is always nice when the structure of the play lays a logical breakdown out for you. These scenes are usually separated by a change in location or time of day. Good example of this are

2. **Scenes/musical numbers.** This type of breakdown can be done for both operas and musicals. The structure is broken down into dialogue and/or recitatives (in a musical, the dialogue is usually spoken; in an opera, the recitative is almost always sung);

songs or arias (sung by one person); and songs performed by more than one person (duets, trios, quartets, right up through full choral/ensemble numbers).

3. **French scenes.** A French scene chart consists of every entrance and exit of

a character. To clarify, a scene begins whenever a character enters or exits, no matter how short of a time they might be onstage or how small the character's part is. French scenes move directly into each other without pause.

ASSASSINS BREAKDOWN							
SCENE #	1	2	3	4	5	6	7
SONG	Everybody's Got the Right	Ballad of Booth	How I Saved Roosevelt	Gun Song	Ballad of Czolgosz	Unworthy of Your Love	Ballad of Guiteau
CHARACTER							
Proprietor	x						
Leon Czolgosz	x			x	x		
John Hinckley	x					x	
Charles Guiteau	x			x			x
Giuseppe Zangara	x		x				
Sam Byck	x						
Squeaky Fromme	x					x	
Sara Jane Moore	x			x			
John Wilkes Booth	x	x		x			
Balladeer		x			x		x
Lee Harvey Oswald							
Ensemble		David Herold	5 bystanders, photographer		fairgoers, attendant, Pres McKinley		hangman, crowd

Figure 13-4 A scene/musical number breakdown chart for *Assassins* by Stephen Sondheim.

WAY OF THE WORLD—SCENE BREAKDOWN									
ACT 1	CHOCOLATE HOUSE								
SCENE	1	2	3	4	5	6	7	8	9
PAGE NUMBER	2	5	6	7	7	8	10	11	11
Mirabell	x	x	x		x	x		x	x
Fainall	x		x		x	x		x	x
Witwoud						x		x	x
Petulant									x
Mrs. Fainall									
Mrs. Marwood									
Millamont									
Mincing									
Foible									
Waitwell									
Sir Wilfull									
Betty	x		x	x			x		x

Figure 13-5 A French scene chart for *The Way of the World* by William Congreve.

Figure 13-6 A sample makeup and wig rendering for Lydia in *Pride and Prejudice*. Rendering by Ariana Schwartz.

ORGANIZING YOUR SHOW NOTEBOOK

As a designer, you should keep all of your information readily at hand in your show notebook, often referred to as the show bible. Having all of this information well organized will ensure that you do not forget anything and can easily look up the answer to any questions the rest of the production team may have. The information may be arranged in any order that seems right to you, but here is what information should always be included:

1. Contact sheets and information— include names, email addresses, and multiple phone numbers for the cast, crew, and design team.
2. The production calendar—make sure to include all relevant deadlines for all departments. (Sometimes there will be projects on which multiple departments will need to coordinate. Knowing everyone's deadlines will make this process easier.)
3. The script and scene breakdowns.
4. Measurements sheets of all of your performers—your measurement sheet should include all head measurements, hair color matches, length of the performer's hair, and texture of the performer's hair.
5. The costume renderings.
6. Your hair and makeup renderings.
7. Research, notes from the director— include pictures from the time period of the script you are working on, paintings, sculptures, inspirational magazine ads, photographs of people from the period, clothing catalogs from the time period—anything that might aid your design.
8. Budget information.
9. Plan of attack—make a complete list of all items you will need in order to produce and run your show. Make a list of where each of these items is coming from—what items will be built, pulled from stock, rented from

an outside company, or altered from existing pieces. Don't forget to include things like hair pins, rollers, hairstyling products, blocking pins, hairbrushes, Styrofoam heads, and so on.

10. Show crew information—make a chart of who changes wigs when, where, in how much times. All information about each performer should be included here, even if they wear only one wig and keep it on throughout the entire show. This is especially important for performers who will be playing multiple roles. A crew member should be able to look at this chart and know, for example, that at the top of scene 3, in the stage left wings, Susie Actor will need help changing from her curly blond wig into her ragged peasant wig and that she has six minutes to do it.

11. Pictures of all of the finished styled wigs, setting patterns, and any how-to instructions—take a front, back, left side, and right side picture of each wig in your production. Do this for both the set of the wig and for the finished product. This will allow you to redo the wig multiple times while maintaining a consistent finished look.

12. List of resources—include any information about products that you are likely to run out of, various people you can contact if there is an emergency, and other places to get needed supplies.

A good, thorough show notebook is a valuable asset. Think of this book as the "I got hit by a bus" book—if

something happens to the designer, there should be all the information that a crew would need to get the show onstage without them.

CHARACTER DESIGN

How does a designer create a look for a character? Characters and their needs, desires, circumstances, quirks, and eccentricities are what make for lively stage action. Character interaction is the source of conflict in most plays; when characters want different things, they are going to struggle until one of them prevails. As a wig and makeup designer, you must know your characters. If the characters are clearly portrayed, the audience will have a clear insight about who each person is. This will make it easier to understand the play. Bold character statements can also be great fun in their own right—think of the characters designed by Bob Mackie for Carol Burnett on *The Carol Burnett Show* or about the wacky characters all played by Mike Myers in the Austin Powers movies. You knew who those characters were before they ever opened their mouths to speak. Many of these characters walked onstage or on screen and had an instant impact because of the bold visual choices an audience could readily identify with.

Several factors should contribute to a character's look:

1. **Given circumstances.** These are the concrete things you are actually told about a character in the script. These

may include age, physical appearance, social status, marital status, environment, occupation, mannerisms, and speech patterns. These things are either stated in the stage directions or are said about one character by another character.

2. **Character types.** Traditional character types all serve clear functions in the script. Knowing different character types will help a designer place the character in the world. Some common character types necessary to most plays:
   - **Protagonist.** Also known as the leading man or the leading lady. This character must be pursuing a goal. A play can have more than one protagonist. They do not have to achieve their goal, but they have to pursue it.
   - **Antagonist.** The person who is blocking the protagonist's way to their goal. Sometimes this person is the villain; sometimes the antagonist's role is not that clear-cut.
   - **Confidant.** A friend to the protagonist. It is this character's job to hear (and through the confidant, the audience also hears) the protagonist's thoughts. The confidant often gets to advise the protagonist. The audience usually needs to like the protagonist; this character should be relatable and familiar to the audience.
   - **Foil.** Usually a minor character that sets off a quality in the protagonist by being the opposite quality. For example, in Shakespeare's *Twelfth Night*, Orsino and Olivia (disguised as Cesario) are

more attractive to Olivia as suitors because of the sheer ridiculousness of Sir Andrew Aguecheek, who serves as their comic foil.

- **Raisonneur.** The voice of reason. They are the moderators and peacemakers; they are also often the characters who express the playwright's own point of view. They bring the sides together and tie up all of the loose ends. In Shakespeare's *Romeo and Juliet*, the Prince is the raisonneur.
- **Utilitarian characters.** People with a job to do. They deliver messages, drive the carriages, and bring the principal characters their dinner.

3. Historical time period—all historical periods have their own fashions in clothing and hairstyles. All designers should have a thorough knowledge of costume history, art history, and hair history. Once a designer is familiar with the given period in which they are designing, they can make appropriate choices for their characters. Who would have the most elegant, chic hairstyle that is the height of fashion? Who would not care what their hair looks like? Whose hair would be terribly overdone? It is important to realize the many options available within a time period—the characters can look appropriate without looking like clones on each other.

In the above, Charles Dana Gibson has rendered a group of women, in one place and time, whose personalities can be determined at a glance by their

Figure 13-7 *When Women Are Jurors*, by Charles Dana Gibson. Note that although the women have very different looks, they all fit into the same historical period.

fashion and hair choices. Knowing the relationships between your set of characters will help you make these choices.

4. **Audience expectation.** All audiences, whether they realize it or not, come to the theatre with certain expectations about what they are going to see. If the designer's choices are so far away from what the audience expects, the design will not have as much impact as it could. For example, standards of beauty are constantly changing. If you go back and look at films from the 1930s and 1940s, the women always reflect that

era's aesthetic, even the film is supposed to represent an earlier time. Another example is the film version of Cleopatra that was made in the 1960s starring Elizabeth Taylor. Although the film is set in ancient Egypt, there is still a certain 1960s feeling and look to the hair and makeup choices. We cannot help but be influenced by the standards of beauty of the time we live in.

GROUP RELATIONSHIPS

Once you understand each individual character, you need to turn your attention to how the characters work together as a group. Group dynamics move the plot forward. Drawing out these relationships on paper makes them easier to see.

We use two different methods to examine character relationships: the cluster method (Figure 13-8) and the line graph method (Figure 13-9). For the cluster method, we write each characters name around the edge of the page and draw lines to connect them to each other. Use different colors to

Figure 13-9 An example of the line graph method of group character analysis for *Hamlet*.

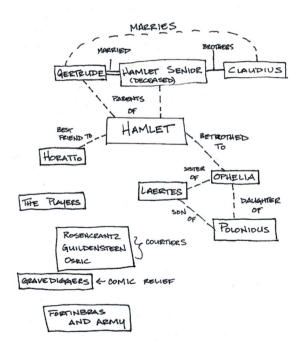

Figure 13-8 An example of the cluster method of analyzing character relationships for William Shakespeare's *Hamlet*.

indicate different relationships—who is married to whom, who is in love with whom, who hates whom, who is related to whom, and so on.

For the line graph method, we draw a straight line and place basic qualities (old/young, ugly/beautiful, rich/poor, silly/dignified, comic/tragic, and so on) and place each character on a line to show their place within those basic concepts.

It seems like a simple concept, but it may surprise you how doing this forces you to think about the characters in depth and make decisions for them. If Helen of Troy isn't the most beautiful woman on stage, the story of the Trojan War starts to fall apart.

DESIGNING AN OVERALL LOOK FOR A PRODUCTION

Where does the inspiration come from that leads to an overall design concept for a production? It can come from anywhere. Any design must begin with the script. Learn all you can from what the playwright or screenwriter gives you. As you read a script, jot down any ideas that come to mind—don't limit yourself to what seems logical. Some plays will require a straightforward, realistic design, and that is a perfectly valid choice. But other shows (and directors and design teams) will lend themselves to choices that will not be so obvious at first.

Figure 13-10 Matrex Kilgore and Ashley Hayes as Grotto and Gretta Good in *Still Life with Iris*, presented by the University of Texas. These characters were specifically designed to have a cold, hard, metallic look. Costume design by Ariana Schwartz; photograph by Mark Rutkowski.

After reading the play, the next step is research. No show ever had too much research. Thoroughly examine the historical period that has been chosen for the show. (If the period has been made up or does not matter—in the future, on the moon, under the sea—research what you can, such as the moon or the sea.) Look for images that inspire you that do not necessarily have anything to do with the time period. A designer should always be picking up inspirational images and keeping them in a file. Organize your images into categories that will allow you to find them quickly when necessary.

Next, you should have a meeting with the costume designer. Exchange ideas and see what they are thinking about the design of the show. Talk about how the wigs can enhance the overall look. Show your research to the costume designer, and look at theirs. You should inspire each other.

It is then time to start putting ideas on paper. Brainstorm with words ("what if Titania's hair looked like cotton candy with twinkling pink lights?"), and then move on to pictures. Quick thumbnail sketches allow you to experiment with different ideas and work out any potential problems ahead of time. An efficient way to do this is to make

yourself a form with a head shape already drawn out and copied multiple times that you can quickly start drawing on top of. You should meet with the costume designer again at this point and compare ideas.

Once you have a solid set of ideas, it is time to meet with the director and other designers. Having lots of sketches and reference pictures for everyone to look at is much better than trying to describe ideas with nothing to refer to. The collaborative work that happens at these meetings can be wonderful—a picture of yours may inspire another designer, and their ideas in turn may inspire you in a different direction. First and foremost, theatre, television, film, fashion, and advertising are collaborative art forms. Working together to tell a story in a way that it has never been told is why we keep working.

After meeting with the design team and finalizing your choices, do finished renderings of your characters. Once that is done, the budgeting and building can begin!

BUDGETING FOR A PRODUCTION

When the time comes to budget for your production, it is helpful to set your priorities. After determining what your ideal vision for the show is, you must determine what is possible. (You should do this before presenting your ideas to the director—you do not want the director to fall in love with a look you cannot actually achieve!) Before you begin working on your budget, you must know how long you have to put the show together and how long the show will be running. Knowing this will help you figure out how much any potential labor or rental will cost.

Take into account what labor you have available, what wig stock you have access to, and what supplies the company or theatre keeps in stock. Then make a list of everything you need—include everything. Factor in wigs, hair, laces and nets, pins, thread, Styrofoam heads, canvas wig blocks, wig caps, hairpins, hair spray, hairnets, spirit gum, spirit gum remover, hair accessories (flowers, jewelry, ribbons), and anything else that you could possibly need. If you are working with an established company, it is likely that many of these items will already be on hand.

If the company does not have a wig stock, find out if they have a relationship with a wig rental company. If they do not, you will need to make such a relationship. It is a good idea for any wig designer or wig master to develop relationships with a couple of wig rental houses. Some of these companies will also send the wigs prestyled—this can be helpful if you are doing a large show with a small wig crew or if you have a

short amount of time to mount the production.

Make a chart of every wig, hairpiece, and facial hairpiece that you will need. For each of these items, make several columns—pull from stock, build, buy, and rent. Determine where every piece is coming from. Things you can pull from stock obviously do not cost you anything from your budget, so you will want to pull as many items as you possibly can. Examine your stock carefully—things that may not appear appropriate at first glance may be easily adjusted (adding weft in the back for length, cutting a layer of bangs in, and so on) so that they work for your production.

When you have determined what you need to buy, disperse your budget appropriately. You will want to spend more money on the wigs for your principals since the audience will spend more time looking at them. Do not forget to allow money for expendables such as pins, spirit gum, and spirit gum remover. Leaving a depleted shop when you finish a job will make you less likely to be hired again.

Make an expense chart. There are a lot of computer programs available to help you keep track of all of your expenditures—make use of them. Different companies will want you to handle money in different ways. Some have company credit cards, some will want you to do the purchasing and reimburse you, and some will want you

to use petty cash and purchase orders. Make sure that you know ahead of time how the company you are working for operates. Enter every purchase into your expense chart so that you know how much budget you have left at all times. Keep an envelope or pouch with all of your receipts. Make sure that the receipts have adequate information in case you have to make returns.

At the end of the production, settle your receipts with the company. It is a good idea to save a little money in your budget for things like cleaning or repairs that may come up at the end of a show.

You must be realistic when it comes to the budget of your production. Before accepting a job, you must find out how much they are expecting and how much money you have to do it. Look at the needs of the show. Some companies dream big, but do not have the funds, space, or labor that those dreams would require. If it is not possible to do the job with the available funding, say so. Do not take a job, no matter how appealing it seems, if you will not be able to deliver the final product.

WIG JOBS AND HOW TO GET THEM

How do you get these wig jobs in the first place? There are a lot of different specialties in the wig field. Once you know all of the options, you can pick the niche that fits your skills best. As it is a field that requires very specialized skills, there are not tons of people trained to perform these jobs. If you have the skills, many opportunities will be open to you.

Some examples of different kind of wig and hair jobs:

- **Wig designer.** Wig designers for theatre, opera, dance, film, and television make the artistic decisions for a given production. They determine what the hair will look like, what the hair accessories will be, and make any other aesthetic decisions related to the hair. They usually work closely with the costume designer. Sometimes wig designers are also in charge of realizing the design; sometimes there is a separate crew who does that.
- **Wig master/mistress.** These people are the people who make the design a reality. They are in charge of building, buying, styling, altering, and taking care of the wigs for a production. Sometimes a company will hire a wig master just to run a show; they are then in charge of maintaining the hairstyles and putting the wig on the performers. In other companies, the term "wig master" is synonymous with "wig designer."
- **Wig run crew.** The people who put the wigs on the actors during a performance. At many theatres, this person is also a member of the wardrobe crew.
- **Key hair.** The person on a film who is responsible for styling the hair and maintaining the continuity of these hairstyles. Sometimes this position applies only to the women's hair; the men's hair and facial hair may fall under

the makeup department. This position also sometimes requires putting wigs on the performers.
- **Wig salon employee.** Many wig salons employee someone who specializes in fitting, styling, and restyling wigs for customers. This job may also require assisting customers in choosing what wig will work best for their needs.
- **Wigs for hair-loss patients.** This person will specialize in working with patients with hair loss due to chemotherapy, alopecia, trichotillomania, or chemical damage. These patients may need full wigs, hairpieces, extensions, or some combination of all the above. As hair-loss patients may have extra sensitive scalps, special consideration will need to be taken with the comfort of their wigs.
- **Hair puncher.** A person who punches hair directly into heads or bodies made of silicone, latex, or other material. This is position is usually found on film and television productions. Fake heads, bodies, or animals may be needed when using the real thing is not possible. Animals may need to talk, heads may need to explode, and bodies may need to be autopsied for a crime drama.
- **Wigs for everyday.** Lace-front wigs are enjoying a surge in popularity. Many celebrities (such as Tyra Banks and Beyonce) often wear wigs on a daily basis. These wigs are high-quality, lace-front, ventilated wigs. Wearing wigs allows a celebrity or model to quickly and easily change their look without suffering the wear and tear on their natural hair.

Other potential places to find wig and hairpiece jobs include historical re-enactors, drag queens, anime characters, cosplay, Renaissance fairs, and Halloween costume supply shops. There are so many ways to apply hair work—find your niche!

Once you have found your specialty, you need a job! There are many ways to get your name out there and sources to aid you in finding a job:

- For theatrical, dance, and opera work, there are publications and websites dedicated to advertising jobs. *ArtSearch* is a publication that lists these jobs for many theatres and opera companies. They also have listings for touring jobs. You must pay a yearly fee to access these listings. They are part of Theatre Communications Group (www.tcg.org). Other websites include www.playbill.com and www.backstagejobs.com, and there are many others. Search online to find the best ones for the area where you live.
- Major job websites may have listings for wig and hair jobs. Check listings under salons, beauty, or general employment.
- Craigslist.com can be a great resource for your city, especially for freelance artists. They list many one-time jobs under "gigs." These gigs are a great way to build contacts in your community.
- If you are a member of a theatrical or film union, there will often be call sheets available to you listing what jobs are available for a given period of time.
- Most states have a film commission. Contact the film commission (most have

websites) and ask about their job postings.

- Make business cards with your contact information and specialty and take them to appropriate places. You may leave some at community bulletin boards, wig salons, cancer centers—anywhere you might find potential clients. Always be sure to ask if you can leave your card first.
- Contact theatres or other places and volunteer your services. This can be a good way to get your name out there, especially if you have moved to a new town.

As time goes by, if your work is good, word usually gets out about you and jobs may start finding you. It is important to be proactive when you are establishing yourself, however; waiting for jobs to come to you might leave you unemployed. Word of mouth is probably the number one way to find employment in the wig industry. Be nice to everyone and always do your job in a professional and pleasant manner. People will always talk—don't give them anything bad to say about you!

CHARGING FOR YOUR WORK

Once you have a job, you have to figure out how much to charge. This can be extremely confusing for people just starting out in wig work. There are a couple of ways to determine how much your work is worth:

1. Do your research—look on the Internet at sites for wig companies and see how much they are charging for their products. An average of these prices will give you an idea what the going rate is for things. Different areas of the country will likely have different rates—what you sell a custom wig for in New York City will be more expensive than what you are able to sell it for in a small midwestern town.
2. Charge by the hour—sometimes, charging by the hour is the best way to approach payment. This is especially true if it is an unusual project that is nothing like anything else you have done before. Guess how long it will take, so that you can at least give a company an estimate. If you begin work and it seems like you greatly underestimated the time involved, contact the company immediately. They may wish to find a different solution to this problem or have you continue with the wig project as planned, but they need to be notified. A word of caution—charging by the hour can backfire if you are very slow. A company should not have to pay for your lack of speed. In this case, it may be better to determine a fee ahead of time.
3. Charge by supplies—one formula that can be used to price a project is to determine how much the supplies for a project will cost and then double that number to find your labor charge. For example, if the supplies for a project cost $100, then the labor will cost $200, bringing the total of the project to $300.
4. Charge by stock usefulness—this method is used when you have a wig stock that is rented out to customers. The first few times you rent out a stock item, it is in prime condition and will cost the renter more. You will need to charge an appropriate price to pay for the supplies and labor that it took to make the wig. As the wig gets used over and over again, it will begin to show some wear and tear. You will then charge less each time you rent out the wig.

Wig jobs require attention to detail, consistent work, speed, a pleasant demeanor, sensitivity to insecurities, and lots of organization. Use the tools in this chapter to build a reputation as a wig person who can be counted on to put a show onstage or do any wig job at hand. Use the skills in the rest of this book to build a reputation for excellent high-quality work.

CHAPTER 14 Care and Maintenance of Wigs

Figure 14-1 Backstage between shows of the Broadway production of *West Side Story*. Wig designer: Mark Adam Rampmeyer.

Opening night has passed, the first day of shooting has come and gone, and all decisions have been made. What next? Because every audience deserves to see as good a show as opening night (including the beautiful wigs), you must care for and maintain the wigs you have created. And once your production has wrapped, you should clean and store your wigs for future use or reshoots.

CLEANING WIG LACES

Before you leave any production at the end of the night, you should make sure that the lace for your wigs and facial hair pieces are clean:

1. After removing the pieces from your performer, place your wig on a block.
2. Go to a well-ventilated area. Put on chemical-resistant gloves and a properly fitted respirator.
3. Gather together your cleaning supplies. You will need a glass bowl,

Figure 14-2 Gather together your lace-cleaning supplies.

201

a towel (you will probably want to keep a couple of towels that are used only for cleaning lace pieces), a wooden-handled toothbrush or stencil brush with natural bristles, and either 99-percent rubbing alcohol or acetone.

4. Pour a small amount of the alcohol or acetone into the bowl. Do not pour a lot, because it evaporates very quickly and you will end up wasting it.

5. Slide the towel under the edge of the lace where the spirit gum residue is (Figure 14-3).
6. Dip your brush into the alcohol or acetone. Once the brush is wet, push the bristles into the wig lace from the outside, going in towards the towel (Figure 14-4). Always work from the right side of the wig in, because you are pushing the glue residue off of the lace and onto the towel.

Do not scrub at the lace with the brush. The remover works by dissolving the glue, so you will have to be a little patient. Work the remover into the glue by gently pressing the bristles into the holes of the lace, and then wiggling the brush around. Scrubbing the spirit gum off of the lace will eventually weaken the lace and make it more prone to tearing and fraying. Dip your brush into the bowl and add more remover as necessary.

7. Continue moving the towel to the areas where there is spirit gum residue until all of it has been removed.

Sometimes there will still be makeup on the lace even after you have cleaned off the spirit gum residue. If there is, take an alcohol prep pad (sold in the first-aid aisle of any drugstore) and run it along the underside of your wig. This will take off any makeup that has been left behind. You may also find that the wig is damp with sweat after the performer has worn it. If so, gently place the wig on its back (with the inside of the wig face up) and let it air out a bit. If it is truly soaked, you may even need to dry it with a hair dryer. Don't leave it to sit on the head all night while it is damp—it may not dry in time for the next performance. If the wig gets smelly from the sweat, mist the inside with alcohol (mint-scented alcohol is especially good for this). Once the wig is clean, replace it on the head you having been using for storage. Many companies store their wigs on Styrofoam heads once they are being

Figure 14-3 Place the towel underneath the wig lace.

Figure 14-4 Push the spirit gum residue from the wig to the towel.

Figure 14-5 A wig being stored on a Styrofoam head.

used in a production. Styrofoam heads are much cheaper, and most companies can't afford a canvas block for each wig to live on during the production.

Make sure when you put the wig back on the head that the lace is not tucked under and that there are no ringlets or wads of hair accidentally caught up underneath the wig. Remember—a wig always wakes up the way it went to sleep! You do not want to come in the next day and find that your wig is creased or has a ringlet that has gone flat because it was smashed under the wig.

CLEANING FACIAL HAIR

1. Put on your chemical-resistant gloves and respirator and move to a well-ventilated area. Gather your supplies together.
2. Place the facial hairpiece hair-side-up on a towel.
3. Dip your brush into the remover and push the bristles into the holes of lace. Wiggle the brush around and let the remover dissolve the glue. Push the spirit gum residue onto the towel. It is especially important to clean facial hair with the right side up. If you cleaned it with the lace side up, the dissolved spirit gum residue would run down into the hair and cause the facial hair to become stiff when it dries.

If you do have a piece of facial hair that has become caked with spirit gum (spirit gum residue will often turn whitish in color over time), you can try to rescue it by soaking the entire piece in the alcohol or acetone. Take it out of the bowl periodically and use the brush to remove layers of spirit gum. Once all of the spirit gum residue is gone, wash the facial hair gently with shampoo to make sure all remaining gunk is gone. You will then need to restyle the facial hair, but it should still be usable.

Figure 14-6 Spirit gum residue left on a mustache. The residue has tuned a whitish color.

Figure 14-7 Use the brush to clean the facial hair right side up.

TOUCHING UP A WIG

You will need to touch up your wigs constantly to keep them looking fresh. Wigs can be mussed by strenuous stage action, wearing hats, quick costume changes, and many other things. For films, it is very important to keep up the continuity of the wig look. Some touch-up tips for you:

1. Make sure that the lace is clean.
2. Always block your wig with blocking pins and blocking tape on a canvas head block before you begin touch-ups.
3. Use your teasing/smoothing brush to smooth any flyaway hairs (Figure 14-8). Lightly spray hairspray on the wig before you run the brush over the wig to help the flyaway hairs stay smoothed down.

Make sure that as you are doing this you are only skimming the brush along the surface of the hair. You do not want to dig the bristles down into the hairstyle—this will only further destroy the hairstyle instead of making it neater.

4. Do not keep adding hairspray to your wig! After a few coats of hairspray have been sprayed on the wig, it is going to stop working. Rather, the layers of hairspray will begin to build up on each other and start to weight the wig down. Instead of using hairspray, light mist the section you are touching up with rubbing alcohol in a spray bottle. The alcohol will reactivate the hairspray that is already there long enough for you to smooth the hair. When it dries, it will hold like fresh hairspray again.
5. Revive any hanging curls by brushing them around your finger (Figure 14-9).
6. Make sure that if you are storing the wig on a shelf or cart where the length can hang down that you put a hairnet around any hanging curls. If left to hang overnight, sometimes the weight of the hair will pull out any ringlets or curls.
7. If the wig has become truly trashed, you may need to take sections of the hair down, brush through them, and put them back up. If you do this, make sure you take the section down carefully and remember how you did it. Also try to disturb the rest of the style as little as possible. Careful use of hairnets, as discussed in Chapter 10, will help a wig stay looking nice for a longer amount of time.
8. Make sure if your wig is being worn with a hat that your performer knows how to put on the hat properly. Ideally, you will pin the hat on for them and take it off for them, but these things may need to happen onstage as part of the performer's blocking. Hats will disturb a wig style least if they are put on from front to back, and taken off from front to back. Never lift a hat off of the back of the head forward towards the front, because this is most likely to mess up the hairstyle. (If you are working on a musical and taking a hat off from back to front is part of the choreography, there isn't much you can do! Be prepared to meet the actor in the wings to check their wig after the dance number if this is the case.)

Figure 14-8 Using a teasing brush to smooth flyaway hairs.

Figure 14-9 Use a teasing brush to brush curls around your finger to make them neat again.

Figure 14-10 An example of a wig being worn with a hat. Smaranda Ciceu as Nastasya in *The Idiot*, presented by the University of Texas. Photograph by Amitava Sarkar.

9. Periodically brush and rebraid any braids that may be part of your hairstyle.

10. If the wig has a lot of long hanging hair as part of the style, detangle it by combing it with a wide-toothed comb. Pay special attention to the hair at the nape of the neck, as this often becomes very snarled while the wig is being worn. You may also have to brush some of the curls around your finger. If the desired look is not ringlets, gently pull the

curls apart after you have brushed them around your finger.

11. Eventually, the wig will be in such bad shape that you need to wash the wig and start over. Keep an eye on all of your wigs so that you can plan out when to redo each wig and not have to rush your styling.

WASHING WIGS

Some performer's unions may have specific rules about how often a wig must be washed. For example, the Actor's Equity union requires that a wig be washed every 14 performances. No matter what the rules say, you can use

Figure 14-11 An example of hairstyling records kept for a wig style.

your good judgment to determine when it is time for a wig to be washed. If it is smelly (spraying the inside with alcohol will only take you so far) or the curls won't bounce back, it is time for a wash and reset. Because you will be completely redoing the wig, it is important for you to have made notes of your entire process. You should have front, side, and back pictures of both the setting pattern and the finished style on file.

Whether you are washing the wig to be reset for more performances or you are washing the wig to put away when the production is over, you will follow the same washing instructions.

WASHING THE WIG OFF THE BLOCK

1. Block the wig on a canvas block and remove all hair accessories, styling pins, and rubber bands. (If the rubber bands are covered hair elastics, remove them from the wig by untwisting them. If they are actual rubber bands, cut them out of the wig—it is not worth the trouble of trying to untangle them from the wig.

2. Brush out the wig so that it is completely free of tangles.

3. Remove the wig from the block and take it to the sink. Fill a clean plastic washtub with lukewarm water. Making sure that you are not holding the wig by the lace, dip the wig into the tub (Figure 14-12).

Figure 14-12 Dip the wig in a washtub using a smooth sideways motion.

Figure 14-13 Add the shampoo.

Use a smooth side-to-side motion to dip the wig—do not just plop the wig in the tub and swirl it around. This will lead to tangling.

4. Place a small amount of shampoo on the top/front area of the wig (Figure 14-13).

Add a little water to make the shampoo lather up. Work the shampoo down the length of the wig with smooth downward strokes. Never scrub the shampoo into the hair with both hands tousling the hair.

5. Dip the wig through the washtub several times to rinse out the shampoo (Figure 14-14).

Figure 14-14 Rinse the wig in the washtub.

You may need to put fresh clean water into the tub after you have dipped the wig through a few times. If the wig needs further rinsing, support the wig with your hand from the inside and use a hose attachment for the faucet to rinse the wig out with a bit more force.

6. Apply conditioner to the wig the same way you applied the shampoo. Work it down the wig with smooth strokes.
7. Rinse the conditioner out of the wig in the same way that you rinsed out the shampoo.
8. When the wig is thoroughly free from all shampoo and conditioner, lay it out on a towel. Roll the wig into the towel (Figure 14-15) and gently squeeze out the excess water (Figure 14-16).
9. Remove the damp wig from the towel and block it back onto the canvas block. Spritz the wig with detangling spray. Section the bottom nape area of the wig out and pin the

rest of the hair out of your way with duckbill clips (Figure 14-17).

Begin combing through the wig with a wide-toothed comb, starting at the ends of the hair. Work your way up to the roots. Once the first section is comb free of tangles, start on the next section up on the head. It is very important that you take your time and get the tangles out of the wig gently. Tugging on both the foundation materials and the hair when they are wet can stretch them out of shape.

10. Always make sure that you are combing the hair off of the face unless the wig has bangs (comb those forward). It will be easier to set if the production is continuing or it will be easier to fit for the next production if the wig is going to be put away.
11. If the wig is human or animal hair, you can put it directly into the wig dryer for one hour. If the wig is synthetic, you will need to steam it straight before you dry. Your style

Figure 14-15 Roll the clean wig in a towel.

Figure 14-16 Squeeze out the excess water using a downward motion with your hand.

Figure 14-17 Divide the wig into sections before you begin to untangle it.

will always turn out better if you do the set on straight hair with no bends or kinks.

WASHING THE WIG ON THE BLOCK

A deep sink with a clamp attached makes washing long wigs much easier (Figures 14-18 and 14-19).

12. Cover the block with a plastic bag or plastic wrap (Figure 14-20). If you are using a bag, knot it at the bottom to make it tight the bottom of the canvas block. If the bag has printing on it

(such as a store logo), turn the bag inside out so that the printing does not rub off onto the inside of the wig.

13. Block the wig. Remove all hair accessories, styling pins, and rubber bands. Brush out the hair until it is completely free from tangles.

14. Take the wig on the block over to the sink. Use a hose attachment for the faucet and wet the wig with lukewarm water (Figure 14-21).

15. Place a small amount of shampoo on the top and front of the wig. Add a little water and work the shampoo

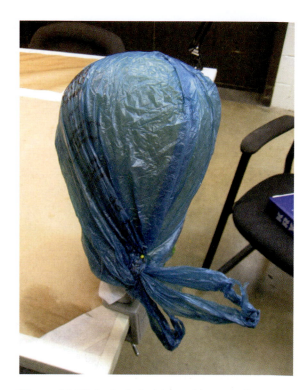

Figure 14-20 A plastic bag is used to cover the canvas block.

Figure 14-18 Standard plastic wig clamp bolted to a stainless-steel sink at UNCSA Wig Studios.

Figure 14-19 Freestanding floor clamp that adjusts to fit a salon shampoo sink.

Figure 14-21 A hose attachment for the faucet will help direct the water to wet the wig.

Figure 14-22 Pull the shampoo through the hair with your hands—do not work the hair in a circular motion.

Figure 14-23 Use a towel to blot the excess water out of the wig.

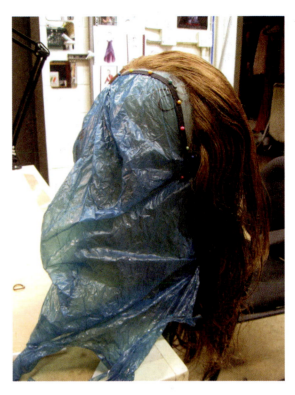

Figure 14-24 The wig is now steamed straight and ready to be dried. Note that the bag covering the block has been untied at the bottom.

into a lather. Using smooth downward strokes, pull the shampoo through the wig to the ends of the hair (Figure 14-22).

16. Rinse the hair with the hose attachment. Add conditioner to the top of the wig and work it through the hair in the same way you did the shampoo. Rinse the hair again until all of the conditioner is out of the wig.

17. If the wig has a lot of hairspray (or other styling product) buildup, use baking soda to remove it. Make a paste by adding a small amount of water to the baking soda. Massage the paste into the areas with the product buildup. The baking soda will act as an abrasive and buff away the hairspray residue. Thoroughly rinse the baking soda

paste out of the wig (this may take a little time). After rinsing out the baking soda, proceed to shampooing the wig.

18. Once the wig is clean, use a towel to blot out the excess water (Figure 14-23). Do not tousle the hair in an attempt to dry it.

19. Return to your workspace and put the wig block on a wig clamp. Section out the bottom of the hair and begin detangling it. Comb all of the tangles out of the hair, working from the nape up of the wig up to the front hairline.

20. If the wig is human hair, put it in the wig dryer for an hour. If the wig is synthetic hair, steam it completely straight before putting it into the wig dryer. Before putting the wig in the dryer, untie the knot that you made in the plastic bag (Figure 14-24). This

will allow air to get to the canvas block and prevent any mildew from forming because of moisture that may have seeped into the block.

STORING YOUR WIGS

Once your wigs are clean, they are ready to be stored until their next use. Proper storage will help prolong the wig's usefulness. Store your wigs in a place that is protected from moisture, dust, and sunlight. Prepare your wigs for storage in the same way every time:

1. Once the wig is dry, brush through the hair to remove any tangles or stiffness. Make sure the hair is brushed off of the face. Being able to see all of the hairline during a fitting is extremely important.
2. If the hair is long enough to braid, go ahead and braid it. The braid will help prevent the hair from tangling while it is being stored.
3. Remove the wig from the canvas block. Tuck the braid (if there is one) into the inside of the wig base. Fold the wig in half like a taco. You can store each wig in its own plastic bag, box, or cubby hole. The amount of room you have for storage will

dictate what you choose. Slide the wig into the bag, box, or cubby hole (Figure 14-25). The wig is now stored until you need it again.

STORAGE SYSTEMS

Every wig shop has a different system for storing and organizing their wigs. Some shops store their wigs in plastic bags that are organized into boxes.

Some shops use a system of boxes with cubby holes where each slot holds a wig. Some shops store wigs that are styled on head blocks.

No matter what system you choose, you should have some organizational method that will allow you (or your assistants) to find a wig you need quickly. Most wig shops organize their wigs by hair color, at the very least. Your system can be as detailed as you are willing to make it—you can also organize by the length of the hair, the type of hair (human, animal, or synthetic), and whether the wig is a hard-front wig or a lace-front wig.

It will also prove valuable to keep records of what each wig has been used for. Keep a card file or a computer chart for each wig, noting all of the details

Figure 14-26 Example of a wig storage system (the University of Texas).

Figure 14-25 A wig that has been readied for storage.

Figure 14-27 Example of a facial hair storage system (Pioneer Theatre Company).

about it. Include when the wig was made; whether it is a lace-front or hard-front wig; whether it is synthetic, human, or animal hair; the colors of hair used (use the numbers from the hair color ring to make sure this is precise); the length of the hair; and any particular notes about the style (for example, that the wig has bangs or is cut into a mullet). Every time the wig is used, add who wore it and in what show. If you often work with the same performers, having these notes will be a huge advantage. You can either pull a wig that you have that you already know fits them, or you can use the wig to make a pattern for a new one without having to call your performer in for a fitting.

We hope this book has given you many answers to wig questions that you may have had. We have tried to cover every aspect of the wig making and styling business, from first being hired for the job through executing every step to create your vision for the hair. We hope we have given you new ideas about what is possible with wigs and inspired you to strike out with your own creations. We wish you the best of luck in the world of wigs!

Figure 14-28 An example of an index card record of a wig's prior use and construction details.

Subject Index

Page numbers in *italics* refer to photographs or illustrations. Page numbers in **boldface** refer to glossary definitions.

A

ACE bandages, for short hair, 122
acid and acid-balanced perms, 173
across nape, measuring, 37
acrylic fibers, dyeing, 171. *See also* dyeing wigs
    and wig fibers; synthetic hair
adhesives
    applying wigs with, 124
    removing after performance, 127
African hair, 166
afro, **1**
air ventilation in work area, 13
alligator clips. *See* duckbill clips
alopecia, **1**
alternative materials for wigs, 175–186
    combining with hair, 182–183
    covering the cap, 180
    examples, 183–184, *183–186*
    foundations, 176–179
    structural support frames, 180–181, *182*
Amazon pins, **1**, 11, *11*
American Cosmetology color system, 167, 169
anchor points
    important locations for, 119, *119*
    structural support frames, 181
angora (mohair), **1**, 24, 165, *165*
    combining with non-hair materials, 182–183
    dyeing, 169, 170. *See also* dyeing wigs and wig
        fibers
animal hair wigs, setting, 155
antagonists, 194
applying facial hairpieces, 61–62
applying wigs. *See* wig application

B

back, designing hairstyles for, 151
back lace, **8**, 21, *21*
back of ear to back of ear, measuring, 39
backcombing, **1**
balanced designs, 162
balding wigs, 105–107, *106–107*
baldness, about, 105
base, wig. *See* foundations
baseball cap, as base, 179
baths, for dyeing hair, 170–172
beards and goatees, 56–58
    applying, 61–62
    cutting and styling, 58–60
    growth patterns, *56*
    removing, 62
    textures for, 47, 49–52, 60
beehive, **1**
bias (fabric), 23
bicycle helmets, as base, 179
blenders, 79–81
blending. *See* color blending
blocking a wig, **1**, 15–16, *16*
blocking pins, **2**, *14*, 14
blocking tape, **2**, 14
blocks. *See* head forms/blocks
blunt cut, **2**
boardwork, **2**
bob, **2**

ArtSearch publication, 199
Asian hair, 166, *166–167*
audience expectation, 195

bobbinette, 21, *22*, 23
bobby pins, 11, *11*
    conditioner and, 121
    for pincurls, 137
boxing wigs for storage, 210–211
bracing threads, 90, *90–91*
braiding hair, 4, 120, *120–121*
braids (wig style), 146–149
    dreadlocks, **3**, 149–150
breakdowns, scene, 191–193
bridal tulle, for short hair, 122
bridge (nose) to hairline, measuring, 38
bridge (nose) to receding point, measuring, 38
brushes, *10*, 10
brush-in color products, 167
bubbles in lace, removing, 57
buckram/felt bases, 176–179
budgeting for production, 197–198
burning hair, 129–130
business cards, 200

C

C-shaped waves. *See* pincurls
caps. *See* foundations
care and maintenance of wigs, 201–211
cascade, **2**
caul nets, **2**, *21*, 21
    circumference-band foundation with, 89–93,
        91–96
character design, 194–195
    group relationships, 195–196
charging for work, 200
checkerboard ventilation pattern, 29, *30*

chignon, **2**
chin blocks, *2*, **2**
    pin patterns to, 49
chin tuft, **2**
circumference of head, 36
circumference-band foundations
    about, 88, *88*, 89
    building, 89–93, *90–96*
    parts, crown swirls, and cowlicks, 103, *103–104*
circumstances, character (in play), 194
clamps, **8**, *13*, 13, *208*
classic color chart, 168
cleaning
    facial hair, 203
    wig laces, **2**, 201–203
climax (in play), 190
clippies, **2**, 11, *11*
    for pincurls, 137, *137*
clips. *See* hairpins and clips
cluster method of group character analysis,
        196, *196*
coif foundations, *88*, 88
color (natural hair), about, 115
color blending, 31, *31*
color matching, 39
    custom weft, 115–118
    mustache and beard hair, 54–55
color sprays, 167
coloring. *See* dyeing wigs and wig fibers
comb clips, 12, 121, *121, 122*
combs, 10, *10*
complications and conflict (in plays), 190
conditioner, 15, 207, 209
    bobby pins and, 121
confidants, 194
copying hairline with plastic tracing. *See* plastic-
        wrap head tracings
cornrows, **2**
corsage pins, 14, *14*
    with roller setting, 139
Cosmetology color system, 169

costume designer, working with, 197
cowlicks, adding to foundations, 103
Craigslist.com, 199
crepe wool, **2**
crepeing hair, **2**
    facial hairpieces, 50–52
crepeing sticks, 15
    with facial hairpieces, *50*, 50–52
crimped hair. *See* wavy hair (wig style)
crimping irons, 138
cross grain (fabric), 23
cross stitch, 17, *17*
crown, designing hairstyles for, 151
crown swirls, adding to foundations, 103,
        103–104
curlers. *See* rollers and curlers
curling. *See* rollers and curlers
curly hair (wig style), 139–146. *See also*
        wavy hair
    perming, 172–173
cuticle-free hair, 166–167, *167*
cutting wigs, 173–174
    facial hairpieces, 58–60

D

darkening hair. *See* dyeing wigs and wig fibers
daylight, hair color and, 116
deep fronts, 64–65, 78
density patterns. *See* growth patterns
design team, working with, 197
designing hairstyles. *See* hairstyles, designing
detangling wigs, 205
direction, ventilating, 30, *30*
    lace-front wigs and, 70–72, *72, 73*
disperse dyes, 170, 171
double knotting, 27–28
double-boiler vats, for dyeing, 171
dragged from base (roller setting), *139*, 139–140
drama, forms of, 190
drawing cards, **3**, *3*, 9, 27, *31*
drawing setting pattern, 154, *155*

dreadlocks, **3**, 149–150
dryers. *See* wig dryers
drying for straight hair, 130
duckbill clips, **3**, 11, *11*
dye vats, 171
dyeing wigs and wig fibers, 167–172
dyes, 115–116, 167, 169–172

E

ear to ear, measuring, 36, *36*, 37, *37*, 39
ear to nape, measuring, 38, *38*
edges, net lace, 102
Elura-blend hair, *166*
end papers, **3**, 14
era of play, 195
everyday wigs, 199
expense charts, 198
exposition, 190
extensions, **4**. *See also* falls
eyebrows, 53–54, 61
    applying, 61
    cutting and styling, 58–60
    removing, 62
    textures for, 47, 49–52, 60

F

fabric dyes, 80, 116, 167, 169–170
facial hairpieces, 47–62
    adding texture to, 49–52
    applying, 61–62
    beards and goatees, 56–58
    cleaning, 201
    creating patterns for, 47–49
    cutting and styling, 58–60
    eyebrows, 53–54, 61
    mustaches, 54–55
    removing, 62
    sideburns, 55–56
    textures for, 47, 49–52, 60
falls, **3**, 111–113, *111–113*
    wig application, 125–126

felt bases. *See* buckram/felt bases
film commissions, 199
film lace, 21, *21*
finding jobs, 198–200
finger shields, **3**, *9*, 9
finger waves, **3**
    creating, 132–134
first piece, *88*
fishtail braids. *See* herringbone braids
five hairs, two of three holes (pattern), *30*, 30
flat iron, **3**
flat-ironing for straight hair, 130–131
foils, 194–195
fontange, **3**
forms. *See* head forms/blocks
forward of base (roller setting), 139, *139*
Fosshape bases, 178–179, *186*
foundation laces, 21
foundations, **3**, *3*, 176
    alternative materials for, 176–179
    balding wigs, 105–107, *106–107*
    circumference-band foundations, *88*, 88,
        89–93, *90–96*
    coif foundations, 88, *88*
    covering with alternative materials, 180
    fringes, 107–108, *108*
    nape-piece foundations, *88*, 88–89, 96–97,
        98–99
    one-piece foundations, *88*, 88–89, 100–101,
        102
    parts, crown swirls, and cowlicks, 103, *103–104*
    types of, 88, *88*
four hairs, two of three holes (pattern),
    30, *30*
framework for alternative-material wigs, 181
French braids, *147*, 148
French scenes, 192, *193*
fringes, 107–108, *108*
front, designing hairstyles for, 151
front to nape, measuring, 36, *36*, 39
frontal bone, **4**

fronting lace, **4**, 20–21, 72, 78, *78–79*, 97. *See also*
    lace-front wigs
    building, 68–69
    deep fronts, 64–65, 78
    direction, hair growth and, 70–72
    mini fronts, 79
    nape lace, 81–83, *82–83*
    quick fronts, 63, *63–65*, 74–75
    silk blenders, 79–81
    standard fronts, 64, *65*, 75–76, *77*
    stretching, 72, *73*
full-bottom wigs, 115
    piecing together wigs for, 83, *83–84*

G

galloon, **4**, *4*, *22*, 22
geisha styling, 69
genetic background of human hair, 166
glue
    for alternative objects, 180
    cleaning wigs and, 201–203
    for facial hairpieces, 61–62
    removing after performance, 126–127
goatees, defined, **4**. *See also* beards and goatees
grain, lace, *23*, 23
Grateau, Marcel, 5, 134
graying temple pieces. *See* temple pieces
group relationships in plays, 195–196
growth patterns, **4**
    beards and goatees, *48*
    eyebrows, *53*
    fronting lace direction and, 70–73
    mustaches, *55*
    sideburns, *56*

H

hackle, **4**, *4*
hair color (natural), about, 115
hair color (natural), matching. *See* color matching
hair color systems, 167
hair density, 29–30

hair extensions, **4**
hair from non-hair materials, 175–188
    combining with hair, 182–183
    covering the cap, 180
    examples, 183–184, *183–186*
    foundations, 176–179
    structural support frames, 180–181, *182*
hair growth. *See* growth patterns
hair pins, 11, *11*
hair preparation for wig application, 119–123
hair puncher, 199
hair rats, **6**, 157
hair selection, 165–167
hair types, 23–24
hair color. *See* J&L Classic color system; American
    Cosmetology color system
haircutting shears, **4**, 10
hairline
    about, 65, *65–68*, 68
    changing, 68
    distance to nose bridge, measuring, 38
    male pattern baldness, 105–107, *106*
    setting and styling tips, 160–162
    tracing with plastic wrap. *See* tracing with
        plastic wrap
    truing, 69–70
hair-loss patients, wigs for, 199
hairnets, 161, *161*
hairpieces, **4**
    custom weft, 115–118
    falls, 111–113, *111–113*, 125–126
    full-bottom wigs, 83–85, 115
    pull-throughs, 110–111, *111*
    switches, **6**, 113–114
    temple pieces, *88*, 110
    toupees, **7**, 109, *110*
hairpins and clips, **8**, 11–12, *11–12*, 14, 14. *See*
    also specific kind of pin
    clippies, **2**, 11, *11*, 137
    for pincurls, 137
    removing after performance, 126–127

hairstyles, designing, 151–164
  drawing setting pattern, 154, 155
  examples, 162, *163–164*
  geisha styling, 69
  for men, 159–160
  research on, 152–154
  setting and styling tips, 160–162
  setting wig, 155
  teasing and stuffing, 156–157
  understanding the style, 152
  using wire frames, 157–158
hairstyles, implementing. *See* styling
hand sewing
  basic stitches, 17
  with invisible thread, 32–33, *32–33*
  needles for. *See* sewing needles
handling wigs, 15–17
hank of hair, **4**
hard hat, as base, 179
hard-front wigs, **4**, 15–16
  wig application, 125–126
hatmaker's coif foundations, 88, *88*
hats, as base, 179
hats, wig design and, 161, 204, *205*
head forms/blocks, 13, *13*
  padding out with plastic tracing, 44–45
  transferring head measurements to, 39–41, *40*
  washing wigs on, 205–209
head measurements, 35–45
  padding block with tracing, 44–45
  plastic-wrap tracings. *See* tracing with plastic
    wrap
  taking accurately, *35*, 35–39
  transferring to block, 39–41
helmets, as base, 179
herringbone braids, 149, *149*
historical time period of play, 195
hooks. *See* ventilating needles
horizontal circumference of head, 36
horse hair, **4**, *165*, 165–166

hour, charging by, 200
household dyes, 170
human hair, **4**, 23–24, 165, *165–167*, 166
  combining with non-hair materials,
    182–183
  dyeing, 169, 170. *See also* dyeing wigs and wig
    fibers
  perming, 172–173
  setting wigs of, 155–156
  styling and, 129. *See also* styling

I

inciting incident, 190
interpreting hairstyle research, 152–154
invisible thread, **4**, 9, 32–33, *32–33*

J

J&L Classic color system, 167
jobs
  charging for, 200
  finding, 198–200

K

Kabuki-inspired lion wigs, 114–115
key hair, 199
knots, untying, 30–31
knotting. *See* wig knotting
knotting positions, *28*, 28–29

L

lace. *See* wig laces
lace-front wigs, **4–5**, 16–17, 63–85
  building fronts, 68–69
  changing hairlines, 68
  deep fronts, 64–65, 78
  as everyday wigs, 199
  lace direction and hair growth, 70–73
  mini fronts, 79
  nape lace, 81–83
  piecing together wigs, 83–85

quick fronts, 63, *63–65*, 74–75
setting and styling tips, 160–162
silk blenders, 79–81
standard fronts, 64, *65*, 75–76, *77*
truing hairline, 69–70
types of, 63–65
understanding hairlines, 65–68
wig application, 123–125
ladder-back falls, 112, *112*
large wooden brush, 10, *10*
left side, designing hairstyles for, 151
lifting picks (teasing picks), 10, *10*
lightening hair. *See* dyeing wigs and wig fibers
lighting, hair color and, 116
lighting in work area, 12–13
line graph method of group character
    analysis, 196
lion wigs, *114*, 114–115
loading ventilating needles, 20, *20*
location changes in play, 191
long hair, applying wigs over, 119–121

M

magnetic pin cushions, 14
maintenance of wigs, 201–211
makeup, removing, 202
male pattern baldness, 105–107, *106*
Marcel irons, **5**, *5*, *59*, *60*, *134*, 135, *135*
  with facial hairpieces, 58–60
Marcel ovens, **5**, 59, *59*, 134
Marcel waves, **5**
  creating, 134–136
measurements. *See* head measurements
medical adhesive, **5**
Medusa set, 145–146
men, designing wigs for, 159–160
millinery wire, 10, *17*, 157
mini fronts, 79
mixed hair, 27
mohair (angora), **1**, 24, 165, *165*

combining with non-hair materials, 182–183
dyeing, 169, 170. *See also* dyeing wigs and wig fibers
mohawk, **5**
money, making, 198
monofilament ribbon, 22, *22*
monofilament top, **5**
mullet, **5**
musical numbers breakdown, 192
mustaches, 54–55
    applying, 61
    cutting and styling, 58–60
    removing, 62
    textures for, 47, 49–52, 60

N

nape, designing hairstyles for, 151
nape lace, 81–83
    removing after performance, 127
nape pieces, 88, *88*
nape pins. *See* hairpins and clips
nape to ear, measuring, 38
nape to front, measuring, 36
nape wispies, 81
nape-piece foundations
    about, *88,* 88–89,
    for balding wigs, 105–107
    building, 96–97, *98–99*
    parts, crown swirls, and cowlicks, 103, *103–104*
natural hair color, about, 115
natural hair color, matching. *See* color matching
natural-looking wigs
    need for, 87
    setting and styling tips, 160
nature lace, **5**
needle-nosed pliers, 9, 9–10
needles. *See* sewing needles; ventilating needles (hooks)
    net lace, **5**, 21, *21*, 87, *88*
    seams and edges, 103

new wigs, creating. *See* wigs, building from scratch
nose bridge to hairline, measuring, 38
nose bridge to receding point, measuring, 38
notebook for show production, 193–194
nylon fibers, dyeing, 171. *See also* dyeing wigs and wig fibers; synthetic hair
nylon net, for short hair, 122

O

occipital bone, **5**
off base (roller setting), 139–140
on base (roller setting), 139
one-piece foundations
    about, *88,* 88–89,
    adding hair, 102
    building, 100–102, *100–102*
    parts, crown swirls, and cowlicks, 103, *104–105*
organizing wigs for storage, 210–211
overall look, creating, 196–197

P

padding out blocks with plastic tracings, 44–45
paintings as hairstyle resources, 153
parietal bones, **5**
partial wigs. *See* hairpieces
parts, adding to foundations, 103, *103–104*
postiche, **6**
patterns, ventilating, 29–30
perfection, avoiding, 161
performance. *See* production considerations
performer's hair
    color matching. *See* color matching
    facial hair, 48
periwig, **5**
permanent color products, 167
perming. *See* rollers and curlers
perming wigs and wig fibers, 172–173
peruke, **5**

picks for lifting/teasing, 10, *10*
piecing together wigs, 83–85
pigtails. *See* switches
pincurls, **5**
    applying wigs over long hair, 119–120
    creating, 136–138
    important locations for, 119, *119*
pins. *See* hairpins and clips
plait. *See* braids (wig style)
plastic-wrap head tracings. *See* tracing with plastic wrap
play. *See* production considerations
pliers, for tool kit, 9, *9*
plot structure, 190–191
point of attack, 190
polyester dyes, 171
pompadour, **5**
ponytails. *See* switches
preparation for wig application, 119–123
preparing wigs for storage, 209–210
primary resource (research) on hairstyle, 152
production considerations, 189–200
    budgeting, 197–198
    character design, 194–195
    charging for work, 200
    finding jobs, 198–200
    group relationships, 195–196
    organizing show notebook, 193–194
    overall look for production, 196–197
    understanding the play, 189–193
protagonists, 194
protein hair. *See* human hair; mohair (angora); yak hair
pulling on wigs (how to), 123–125
pull-throughs, 110, *111*
putting on wigs, 119–127
    hair preparation, 119–123
    hard-front wigs and falls, 125–126
    lace-front wigs, 123–125
    quick changes, 127

Q

queue, **6**
quick fronts, 63, *63–65*, 74–75
quick wig changes, 127

R

raisonneur, 195
rats, **6**, 157
rat-tail combs, 10, *10*
receding point to nose bridge, measuring, 38
receipts for purchases, 198
relationships among characters, 195–196
removing facial hairpieces, 62
removing wigs after performance, 126–127
research on hairstyles, 152–154
research on play, 189–193, 197
resolution (in play), 191
resources (research) on hairstyle, 152–154
reverse French braids, *147*, 148
reversing, 123
right side, designing hairstyles for, 151
right-side-out construction, 89
ringlets, **6**, 142–143
RIT dyes, 170, 171
roller breaks, 142
roller pins, 11, *11*
rollers and curlers, 12, *12*, 136, 139–146
    Marcel irons, **5**, *5*, 58–60, *59*, *60*, *134*,
          134–135
    perming facial hairpieces, 49–50
    setting for ringlets, 142–143
    setting for straight hair, 130–131
    spiral rolling techniques, 143–144
    for straightening hair, 130–131
    styling facial hairpieces, 58–61
    taking out rollers, 142, 143, 155
roots, **6**
rope braids, *147*, 148–149
Roux Fanciful Rinse, 169
rubber bands, 121

S

safety equipment, 13
sausage curls. *See* ringlets
scene breakdowns, 191–193
scene location changes in play, 191
scenes, identifying, 192
scissors (for tool kit), 9. *See also* shears
seams, net lace, 103
second piece, *52*
secondary resource (research) on hairstyle, 153
selecting hair for wigs, 165–167
set with drag (roller setting), 139–140
setting diagrams, *154–155*
setting lotion, 15, 60
setting pattern, drawing, 154–155, *159*
setting wigs, 155
sewing. *See* hand sewing
sewing needles, 9
shag, **6**
shampoo, 15
shears
    haircutting shears, **4**, 10
    thinning shears, **6**, *6*
short hair, applying wigs over, 121–123
show notebook, organizing, 193–194
sideburn pieces
    applying, 61
    creating, 55–56
    cutting and styling, 58–60
    removing, 62
    textures for, 47, 49–52, 60
sideburns (of performer)
    growth patterns, *56*
    marking on block, 40
    taking head measurements, 37, 38, 40
    width of, measuring, 37
silk blenders, 79–81
silk gauze, 22, *22*
silk ribbon. *See* galloon
single hair, every hole (pattern), *29*, 29

sketches, creating, 197
skin-top wig, **6**
smoothing brushes, 10, *10*, 156
    to touch up wig, 204
speed of wig making, 87
spiral rolling techniques, 143–144
    Medusa set, 145–146
    sprocket set, 143–144, *144*
spirit gum, **6**, 61–62
    applying wigs with, 124
    cleaning wigs and, 202
    removing after performance, 127
sports wrap, for short hair, 122
spray bottles, 15
sprays, color, 167
sprocket set, 143–144, *144*
S-shaped waves. *See* pincurls
standard braid, 147
standard fronts, 64, *65*, 75–76, *77*
stays, 22–23, *23*
steamers, 14, *14*, 131
steaming a wig, **6**
    for straight hair, *131*, 131–132
    for wavy hair, 134
stem switches, 113
stitches, basic, 17
stock usefulness, charging by, 200
stock wig, **6**
storing wigs, 209–211
straight hair (wig style), 130–132
straight pins, 14, *14*
stretching, *81*, 88
stretching fronting lace, 72, *73*
structural support frames, 180–181, *182*
stuffing plastic-wrap tracings, 44–45
styling, 129–150
    braids, 146–149
    creating styles. *See* hairstyles, designing
    curly hair, 139–146
    dreadlocks, **3**, 149–150
    elements of hairstyles, 129

facial hairpieces, 58–60
    straight hair, 130–132
    wavy hair, 132–139
    wig material concerns, 129–130
styling products, 15, 155, 162
Styrofoam heads, 202–203
super lace, 6, 20
supplies, charging by, 200
support frames for alternative-material wigs,
        180–182
swatches, 172
switches, 6, 113–115
    Kabuki-inspired lion wigs, 114–115
symmetrical hairlines, creating, 69–70
synthetic hair, 6, 24, 166
    combining with non-hair materials,
        182–183
    dyeing, 169, 171–172. See also dyeing wigs
        and wig fibers
    setting wigs of, 155
    styling and, 129–130. See also styling

T

T-pins, with roller setting, 139
tap dancing, 127
tape tracing. See tracing with plastic wrap
teasing brushes, 10, 10, 156
    to touch up wig, 204
teasing pick (lifting pick), 10, 10
teasing wigs, 156
Telesis adhesive
    applying wigs with, 124
    removing after performance, 127
temple pieces, 70, 84, 110
temple to sideburn, measuring, 38
temple to temple, measuring, 36, 37
temporary color products, 167
tendril, 6
tertiary resource (research) on hairstyle,
        153–154
textures for facial hairpieces, 47, 49–52, 60

thimble, for tool kit, 10
thinning shears, 6, 6
thread
    invisible, 4, 9, 32–33, 32–33
    for tool kit, 9
three hairs, checkerboard pattern, 29, 30
3/4 wig, 1
three-stem switches, 114
time period of play, 193
Tintex dyes, 170, 171
tips, 6
tonsure, 6
tool kits
    for wig making, 8–10, 9
    for wig styling, 10
touching up wigs, 204–205
toupee clips, 7, 12, 12, 112, 121, 122
toupee tape, 7
toupees, 7, 109, 110
    pull-throughs, 110, 111
tracing with plastic wrap, 41–45
    building fronts, 68–69
    for facial hairpieces, 47–49
    for hairpieces, 109
    padding out head block, 44–45
    truing hairline, 69–70
tracking expenditures, 198
tracks, 6
trichotillomania, 7
truing patterns, 49, 69
T-shaped pins, 11, 11
tweezers, untying knots with, 30–31, 31
two hairs, checkerboard pattern, 29, 30

U

union dyes, 170, 171
universal hair color systems, 167
unprocessed human hair, 165. See also human
        hair
untying knots, 30–31
utilitarian characters, 195

V

vegetable nets, 7, 21, 21
    circumference-band foundation with, 89–93,
        92–95
Velcro rollers, 12
ventilating, 7, 19–33
    basic technique, 24–31
    color blending, 31, 31
    needles and holders for, 19–20, 20
    sewing with invisible thread, 32–33,
        32–33
    wig lace, 20–23
ventilating direction, 30
    lace-front wigs and, 70–72, 74, 76
ventilating needle holders, 9, 9, 19–20
ventilating needles (hooks), 7, 9, 19–20, 19
    loading, 20, 20
    proper position for, 24, 24
    types of hair, 23–24
    untying knots with, 30–31, 30–31
ventilating patterns, 29–30
ventilating positions, 28–29, 28
ventilation in work area, 13
virgin hair, 7

W

washing wigs, 205–209
water spray bottles, 15
water waves, 3
    creating, 132–134
waving iron, 7, 138
wavy hair (wig style), 132–139
    Marcel waves, 5, 134–136
    pincurls, 136–138
    water waves, 3, 132–134
websites for finding work, 199
weft, 7, 7
    custom, 115–118
    cutting wigs and, 173–174
    dyeing and, 172

wefting, **7**
    nape lace, 81
wefting sticks, 15
wetting for straight hair, 130
whip stitch, 17, *17*
wide-toothed combs and brushes, 10, *10*
width of sideburn, measuring, 37
wig application, 119–127
    hair preparation, 119–123
    hard-front wigs and falls, 125–126
    lace-front wigs, 123–125
    quick changes, 127
wig bags, **7**, *7*
wig block, **8**
wig caps, **8**, 120, *121*
wig care and maintenance, 201–211
    cleaning, 201–203
    storage, 210–211
    touching up, 204–205
    washing, 205–210
wig clamps, **8**, 13, *13*
wig designers, 199
wig dryers, **8**, 14, *14*
wig foundations. *See* foundations
wig handling, 15–17

wig knotting
    basic technique, 24–31
    sewing with invisible thread, 32–33, *32–33*
    untying knots, 30–31
wig laces, *17*, 20–23, 87
    bubbles in, removing, 57
    cleaning, 201–203
    fronting. *See* lace-front wigs
wig making tool kit, 8–10, *9*
wig masters/mistresses, 199
wig pins. *See* hairpins and clips
wig points, *8*, **8**
wig prep, **8**
wig removal after performance, 126–127
wig run crew, 199
wig salon employees, 199
wig silk, 79–81
wig stays, **8**
wig stock, 198, 200
wig storage systems, 210–211
wig styling. *See* styling
wig work area. *See* work area
wiglets, *8*, **8**
wigs, building from scratch, 87–108

balding wigs, 105–107, *106–107*
circumference-band foundations, 88, *88*, 89–93, *90–96*
coif foundations, 88, *88*
fringes, 107–108, *108*
nape-piece foundations, *88*, 88–89, 96–97, *98–99*
one-piece foundations, *88*, 88–89, 100–101, *102*
parts, crown swirls, and cowlicks, 103, *103–104*
wigs, partial. *See* hairpieces
wigs, piecing together, 83–85
wigs for hair-loss patients, 199
wire frames, 157–158
Wonder Lace. *See* back lace
work area, 12–15, *13*
    ventilating positions, 28–29
work table, 12
    ventilating positions, 28–29

Y

yak hair, **8**, 24, 165, *165*
    combining with non-hair materials, 182–183
    dyeing, 169–170, *170. See also* dyeing wigs and wig fibers
    perming, 172–173